Almost Englishmen

Almost Englishmen
Baghdadi Jews in British Burma

Ruth Fredman Cernea

LEXINGTON BOOKS

A division of
ROWMAN & LITTLEFIELD PUBLISHERS, INC.
Lanham • Boulder • New York • Toronto • Plymouth, UK

LEXINGTON BOOKS

A division of Rowman & Littlefield Publishers, Inc.
A wholly owned subsidiary of The Rowman & Littlefield Publishing Group, Inc.
4501 Forbes Boulevard, Suite 200
Lanham, MD 20706

Estover Road
Plymouth PL6 7PY
United Kingdom

Copyright © 2007 by Lexington Books

All rights reserved. No part of this publication may be reproduced, stored in a retrieval system, or transmitted in any form or by any means, electronic, mechanical, photocopying, recording, or otherwise, without the prior permission of the publisher.

British Library Cataloguing in Publication Information Available

Library of Congress Cataloging-in-Publication Data
Cernea, Ruth Fredman.
  Almost Englishmen : Baghdadi Jews in British Burma / Ruth Fredman Cernea.
    p. cm.
  Includes bibliographical references and index.
  ISBN-13: 978-0-7391-1646-3 (cloth : alk. paper)
  ISBN-10: 0-7391-1646-0 (cloth : alk. paper)
  ISBN-13: 978-0-7391-1647-0 (pbk. : alk. paper)
  ISBN-10: 0-7391-1647-9 (pbk. : alk. paper)
  1. Jews—Burma—History. 2. Jews, Iraqi—Burma. 3. Burma—Ethnic relations.
I. Title.
  DS135.B87C47 2007
  305.892'40591—dc22   2006024353

Printed in the United States of America

Dedicated to

Zachary, Alexander, Natalie, Jane, Eve,
Dylan, Evan, Sarah, Rebecca, Elana

Contents

Acknowledgments		ix
Letter from Ellis Sofaer		xiii
Introduction: The Baghdadi Diaspora		xv
1	Adventurers and Entrepreneurs	1
2	Beautiful Burmese Days	21
3	Three Cheers for the King and the British Empire	37
4	The Comforts of Home	51
5	Bene Israel vs. Baghdadis: The Court Case	71
6	Desperate Passage to India: The War in Burma	79
7	Return to Burma	99
8	Burma and Israel	121
9	Embers	127
Appendix A	Proceedings of the High Court of Judicature, Rangoon, 1935–1936	139
Appendix B	Detailed List of Families to Be Evacuated from Burma to Israel, 1949	145
Appendix C	Additional List of Potential Emigrants to Israel, 1949	149

Appendix D	Jewish Community of Burma, 1959	151
Appendix E	Jewish People and Their Descendents in Burma, circa 1986.	159
Bibliography		161
Index		167
About the Author		175

Acknowledgments

Facts are framework; it is memory that gives substance and texture to documents and transforms them into experience. It is always an anthropologist's dream to find individuals who are generous with and accurate in their recollections; a great bonus is also to encounter people whose memories are sensitive to historical data and whose intellect shines through in their beautifully written words. Much of the material record of Jewish life in Burma was lost in the devastation of World War II, and therefore it is only with the help of such extraordinary persons that the social history of the period can be told.

Such a rare "find" par excellence was Ellis Sofaer, who kindly shared with me the memoirs written for his grandchildren. The memoirs were written in London, long after he had left Rangoon, and after a happy and successful family and professional life. Ellis Sofaer's reflections inform many parts of this book, his insights and images conjuring up the atmosphere as well as the attitude of early twentieth century Rangoon. In commenting on some of my initial interpretations, Mr. Sofaer also contributed even more directly to the text. His niece Ruth Sofaer recommended these memoirs to me and put me in touch with him, and I cannot thank Ruth sufficiently for this, nor for her friendship, her abundant enthusiasm for this project, her knowledge, and for her generous, unending assistance.

Similarly, the pristine memories and written accounts of Solly Saul, Saul Ezra Saul, Margaret Raphael Glicksohn, Yascha Malkhoo, and Abraham Shalom Judah were invaluable to this effort. They took time to recall and write, and provided "primary" documents that gave life to the dry dates. Shaul Abraham not only sent numerous pages and documents from his home in Sydney, but also sent my queries to relatives and friends in London and elsewhere in Australia. I also thank Geoff Saul for sharing his excellent family history.

In Burma, it was my great fortune to get to know Moses Samuels, his wife Nellie, and their children, Dinah, Kuzna and Sammy. Moses Samuels could not have been more gracious and helpful both in conversation and by giving me full access to the synagogue archives. In his every action, he demonstrates his love and respect for his father and his loyalty to Baghdadi tradition—a loyalty that motivates him to devote considerable time and personal resources to maintaining the synagogue and the cemetery, to caring for the few Jews still remaining in Burma, and to welcoming the stream of visitors from abroad. And, that has allowed him to send his beloved son Sammy so far away, to Israel and America, to equip him to assume this responsibility. I share Moses's pride in Sammy's outstanding accomplishments at Yeshiva University and, like his family, am confident of Sammy's ability to continue his father's and his grandfather's work in sustaining the legacy of the Jews of Burma. Thank you also to Moses's brother Jack Samuels, whose recollections have been very important to the research, and to their Burmese Buddhist friend, U Aung Kwye, who served as my very valuable guide and source of information in Rangoon.

I am deeply indebted to Nathan Katz, whose own fine scholarship about the Jews of India has been an inspiration. Nathan's thoughtful suggestions about the manuscript as well as his early encouragement to pursue this research are greatly appreciated.

With great fear of omitting some of the numerous people who helped along the way, I thank the many other individuals scattered around the world who contributed to the construction of this collective memory of Jewish life in Burma. Many graciously opened the doors of their homes as well as their hearts to reminisce with me. The joy of doing this type of research is meeting with such delightful people and entering into their lives. In the United States, I gathered the insights of Ezra Solomon, Seemah Betz, her brothers Solly and Charlie Saul, and her granddaughter Evelyn Dean, Morris Battat, Esther Joseph, Flora Joseph Shamash, Sally Joseph, Maurice Shamash, Joseph Sassoon, Judah and Flora Sassoon, David and Mozelle Sofaer, Ruth Sofaer, Luisa Benson Craig, Saw Benson, and Dawn Swift. Lauren Fredman Huot thoughtfully reviewed the manuscript, and Shan Princess Ying Sita contributed her wise but sad commentary on recent events in Myanmar. Thank you also to Sam Daniel, Judith Freidenberg, Roberta Cohen, Yoma Ullman, Yoheved and Sonny Karlin; and to Dorothy Smith, Jacob Rader Marcus Center, American Jewish Archives, and Misha Mitsel, Archivist, American Jewish Joint Distribution Committee.

In Australia, I have greatly appreciated the hospitality and reflections of Fortune and Saul Ezra Saul, Edna and Alan Solomon, and Esther and Charles Solomon, as well as the recollections of Shaul Abraham, Jack Cohen, Freda

Acknowledgments

Jacob Isaacs, Ezekiel Jacob, Renee Cohen Moses, Dinah Samuels, Mrs. K. Samuels, and Edwin Azariah Samuel. Thoughts flowed from the United Kingdom, where I met relocated Jews from Burma, many in person, others through correspondence. Thank you to Albert Judah, Joseph Ezra Menasseh, Scott Aaron, Helen Abraham, Ezekiel Aaron, Meda Aaron, Seemah Abraham Ezekiel, Ramah Agasie, Rachel Margaret Burgess, Manfred Brod, Ezekiel Isaac Cohen, Jacob Moses Cohen, Seemah David, Helen Einy, David Hay Saul Einy, Flora Judah Jacob, Flora Moses Jacob, Percy S. Gourgey, Sol Gubbay, Nancy Hayeem, Rachel Joseph, Ruby Moses, E. M. Saleh, and Joseph Samuels. Charles Tucker, Archivist of the London Beth Din, and Charlotte Shaw, of the London Metropolitan Archives, were invaluable in providing access to the correspondence between London and Rangoon.

Mornings with David Nahoum in his famous bakery in New Market, Calcutta, as well as "pilgrimages" to Calcutta's synagogues and Girls' School, evoked the counterpart to Jewish life in Burma. Flora Judah Jacob's brother Abraham Judah sent recollections from Germany, Ellis Joseph offered another perspective from Calcutta, and Rose Van Camp wrote from Belgium. And, in addition to Margaret Raphael Glicksohn, my irreplaceable correspondent from Kfar Sava, Israel's contribution to the collective memory came via Sarah Sassoon Raphaeli, Shimon Aaron, Shmuel Yosef, and Willy Lindwer. Thank you also to Judy Shotten, Fred Lazin, and Ray Boxman, who occasionally served as my rather overqualified research assistants.

Last, first, and always, I thank my husband Michael, for his caring, invaluable encouragement and support throughout the many years of this research, as well as that of all my family—Jonathan, Judy, Andrew, Kerry, Lauren, Greg, Andrei, Lauren, Dana, Eric, and their many delightful children—who came to believe that the story of Burma's Jews was an inextricable part of my own life.

ELLIS SOFAER
CROYDON, SURREY
U.K.

5 October 1992

Dear Ruth,

I have as yet to thank you for the photocopy you sent me of the school performance of the Mikado. It caused a great stir in the family, and my children and grandchildren were especially excited to see me as I was in the dim past. As for myself, I was put into a philosophical mood, and mused over the thought that one's past has a way of catching up on one, undeterred by the lapse of three-quarters of a century and a circumnavigation of the globe!

Kindest Regards,

Ellis

Introduction

The Baghdadi Diaspora

Like points in a silken cobweb, the Baghdadi Jewish diaspora once spread throughout Southeast Asia, from Bombay to Shanghai. Woven into the web were distant, but never isolated, communities in Singapore, Calcutta, Rangoon, Karachi, Dacca, Penang, Hong Kong, Yokahama, and Surabaya, and in many small towns throughout the countryside. The threads of the cobweb were far from fragile; they were active communication lines that belied and defied the physical distances and wove these dots on the map into a coherent community. Along these lines flowed trade, information, religious emissaries from Baghdad or Jerusalem, and marriage partners, all enabled by a common language, a common world view, and adherence to a proud traditional religious belief and structure. Intricate social relationships and common daily practices negated space; ritual adherence negated time by introducing the eternal into transitory days.

To understand the Baghdadi experience in its full light, then, it is necessary to see beyond the numbers: they were not three thousand in Bombay, thirty-five hundred in Calcutta, twenty-one hundred in Burma, or one thousand in Shanghai and Singapore, but a highly integrated totality of upwards of thirteen thousand Jews.[1] This richly textured community maintained its vitality and integrity while living in a vast sea of Chinese, Indians, Burmese or Malays, and interacting with Bene Israel and Cochini Jews from India, as well as with a multiplicity of other ethnic groups, tribes and nationalities who were also seeking their fortune in Southeast Asia.

In Burma, Jews found a wide-open land of opportunity for commercial enterprise, especially once the British extended their empire in India east to Burma in the latter half of the nineteenth century. Rangoon, across the Bay of Bengal from Calcutta, was a small, satellite city of that great metropolis, but of a different character—more provincial, Buddhist rather than Hindu in context, quieter. As Calcutta remained the reference for Rangoon's Jews, so Rangoon itself became the center of a mini-diaspora of Baghdadi Jews living throughout the countryside, in Mandalay, Yenangyaung, Toungoo, Bassein, Moulmein, Pegu, Akyab, and similar small towns. Today one might wonder at the courage of a religiously traditional Jewish family to settle in a small town in Upper Burma, in the delta of the Irrawaddy River, or on the Andaman Sea, apparently alone and apart from other Jews. Yet such were the spiritual and communal ties among Baghdadi Jews that though physically separated, they were never apart. Until this extended community was devastated by World War II, they maintained their religious traditions, customs, values, and social boundaries without the benefit of modern communications for more than a century. The particular experience of Jews in Burma is a microcosm of Baghdadi experience everywhere throughout Southeast Asia.

The story of the Baghdadi community's florescence and decline, and of its attempt to preserve the past while accommodating to the present and preparing for the future, is also indicative of the experience of many dispersed communities and presents the same questions. It is easy to recognize "community" when social institutions and patterns of social interaction are intact and people meet face to face, when a collection of people appears to share an ethos and world view, a common purpose, a common history and apparent destiny. But when and how does "community" disappear, disintegrate, and through partial and idealized memories become a virtual construct rather than a valid concept? At what point do the symbolic forms that sum up reality lose their coercive power? When and how, in other words, do key symbols such as the Torah and communal rituals such as the Passover Seder lose their power to define the essential truths of existence and the right, the only, code of social interaction? And how are these compelling truths replaced by equally compelling symbols that constitute a new form of seeing and acting in the world?

It is interesting to ponder the role of collective memory in preserving community throughout the generations. In the early years, collective memory of life in the Middle East was the "glue" that bound the dispersed people. But memory, like "community," is always in flux: based in the individual, shared and reworked through public institutions, utterances, and actions, it refines, reassembles and redefines reality to fit the current context and needs, to construct a story that is satisfying and validating to the teller. How, in conversation or in research, does one retrieve the past through individual narratives? What happens when the context is changed, when people disperse across the globe, when individualized experience enters the mix? Is collective memory of life in Burma many years later still a valid concept when presented by people in Los Angeles, Sydney or London?

With great insight, James Barrie mused that "God gave us memory that we might have roses in December."[2] So it is with most memories recalled by former residents of Burma. Days were happy and beautiful. Yes, Burma did offer a lovely landscape, hospitable people and a comfortable life, but it is also true that recollections rarely mention the less pleasant side of life: health and sanitation conditions, family arguments, business misfortunes, or criminal behavior. And documents which are, after all, written memories also exclude as much as they include. The ample birth records of the community don't reveal deliberate omissions; court records of arguments among synagogue trustees only hint at motivations or personalities of the petitioners. One way of looking at the role of the researcher may be to reconstruct collective memory from all these fragments, to fill in the blanks as faithfully as possible, and to recreate a collective memory that would otherwise be forever lost.

THE BAGHDADIS

In constructing this dispersed but cohesive community along economic, religious, familial and linguistic lines, the Jews who came to Southeast Asia were replicating patterns of diaspora interaction set years before throughout the Ottoman Empire. Although they are known collectively as "Baghdadis," and the majority did depart from Baghdad or Basra, in fact their numbers included many with ancestry not from ancient Babylonia but from Spain. Impelled by the persecutions of Jews which began in 1391, Jews from Sepharad—Spain—sought haven throughout the Mediterranean basin; especially after 1564, they found a welcome home in the Ottoman Empire, which at that time included today's Iraq as well as Turkey, Syria, Palestine, Egypt, and the Balkans. Jews were valued by the militant Ottoman Turks for their economic and professional skills. Jews carried another advantage to the Turkish Empire: unlike the Greek population who might seek protection from Christian powers, the Jews had no foreign protectors and therefore promised to be loyal subjects. These Judeo-Spanish speaking Jews maintained dense economic, religious and familial networks whether in Monastir or Salonica, Istanbul or Aleppo, prospering in the early years especially because of the economic benefit derived from the extensive ties of trust afforded by their religious and family networks. The integration of the exiles from Spain into the trading networks and settlements of the Middle East can be traced through names such as Sasson (Sassoon) and Gubbay, which were once common in Spain and centuries later in India and Burma.

Such networks naturally led to Baghdad, which continued as a center of trade long after it was no longer a terminus on the Silk Road, the caravan routes to China. Jews had been in the region since the exile to Babylonia following the fall of the First Temple in Jerusalem in 586 B.C.E., and it was from Baghdad that the ancestors of the Jews of Kaifeng, China, most likely departed. For more than two thousand years, a vibrant Jewish community life existed in what is now Iraq. Baghdadi Jews were the heirs to and custodians of a proud Jewish heritage: the most influential Talmud, the Babylonian Talmud, was compiled in the third to fifth centuries in the religious academies of Sura and Pumbedita (present-day Fallujah), and it was to these academies that Jews throughout Europe, North Africa and the Middle East wrote for advice on religious and practical matters. The written decisions sent back to these communities, called *responsa*, guided Jewish life throughout the world for some seventeen hundred years. Pride may indeed be an essential element in the distillation that is collective memory, and is a potent force in preserving a community. Such pride was evidenced in the loyalty to tradition of the first Baghdadi settlers throughout Southeast Asia. Why, after all, keep a memory that debases or disgraces the collectivity, and why discard—consciously— memories that are ennobling? And yet, through neglect or in pursuit of other goals, such as acquiring another ennobling history, this can happen. In Burma it did. But others remembered: a casual inquiry concerning Baghdadi history, for instance, elicited this response:

> May I observe that we Jews of Baghdadi origin in India and the Far East trace our ancestry to the 2500-year-old Babylonian Jewish community who maintained an unbroken sojourn for that period in Babylon (the site of which is, incidentally, about 50 miles from Baghdad) . . . We take pride in our historical background first referred to in Psalm 137: "There by the waters of Babylon we hanged up our harps and wept at the remembrance of Zion . . ."; then the return under Zerubbabel and Yeshua the High Priest following the Cyrus Declaration, in 538 BCE; Ezra and Nehemia about 80 years later; Hillel the Great born in Babylon; the evolution of the Babylonian Talmud which was a tremendous contribution to Jewish religion and literature; the period of the Gaonates of Sura, Pumbedita and Nehardea; the independent Kingdom of Mehoza under Mar Zutra II in the 5th century C.E.; the office of the Exilarch; the great Gaons like Saadia and Rav Amram who first set out the basis of the Orthodox prayer book, till the 11th century C.E.; the period of the Hahamim under Ottoman Turkish rule for four centuries till 1918—the defeat of Turkey in the First World War; and the modern period when Iraq was under British Mandatory rule after it was created by Britain, till 1932; Rashid Ali the pro-Nazi collaborator in 1941 when many Jews were killed in his abortive coup, till the State of Israel and the atrocious public hangings of Jews in Baghdad in 1969 to bring down the curtain on 2500 years of this glorious history.[3]

During the Ottoman Empire, Baghdad's importance as center of trade continued and reached all parts of the Middle East. Jews had settled in the major cities of the Empire and along its outposts, honing their mercantile skills and establishing long-distance family and trade connections. Aspects of Jewish culture served them well in these endeavors. The prohibition against intermarriage meant that communities were often linked through extensive kinship ties, and trust. A trader could travel great distances and be assured of hospitality at journey's end. And their common languages—Judeo-Arabic, Judeo-Persian, and Hebrew—provided them with "secret languages" with which to conduct business, just as the Ladino script served the Sephardic traders of the Balkans and Yiddish the Jews of Eastern and Central Europe. The Baghdadis were, therefore, well poised to take advantage of the economic opportunities offered by the British Raj during the nineteenth and first half of the twentieth centuries.

Despite their relative comfort and prosperity, the Jews of Baghdad—as other minority communities—were always dependent upon the good will of the Ottoman rulers, and this varied according to the vicissitudes of time and personalities. In the early part of the nineteenth century, the persecutions of the ruler Daud Pasha, the forced conversion of the Jews of Meshed in 1839, and the advent of the plague threatened the Baghdadi Jewish community and made it urgent for many to find a safer haven. British-ruled India was an attractive destination because of its open economic and religious climate and its heterogeneous society. Iraqi Jews moved south, to paraphrase the Irish saying, with a bitter wind at their back, to the port cities of the Indian subcontinent. They found themselves but a small drop in the churning social waters of these and other southeast Asian cities: many other groups were also enticed by the economic promise of British India, and the cities were made up of innumerable religious and national groups—Hindus, Muslims, Buddhists, Parsees, Sikhs, Animists, Armenians, Chinese, Nepalese, Afghans, and others—each with its own values, religious practices, taboos, world view, social norms and language. Within this complex mix, the Baghdadis as a group were relatively invisible, and that invisibility afforded them protection as well as the opportunity to create their own social world. The Baghdadis, themselves a collection of Jews from many parts of the Middle East, arrived in Southeast Asia with their traditions intact and maintained their way of life no matter where they settled.

In a relatively short time after arriving in India, the Baghdadis in Bombay and Calcutta commanded trading networks throughout Southeast Asia, trading in opium,[4] rice, teak, tobacco, jute, saltpeter, textiles, and precious stones, or acting as owners, middlemen, and exporters of cotton goods and other commodities to the Far East and to England. In Shanghai and in Singapore, as in Bombay and Calcutta, they invested in great holdings of real estate, built beautiful homes, and vacationed with the British in the cool hill stations, traveling from Calcutta to Maniphur or Darjeeling in the foothills of the Himalayas, from Rangoon to Maymyo or Kalaw, or from Bombay to Poona.

Other Baghdadis excelled in a variety of smaller businesses, such as supplying the ships that stopped in the ports or as purveyors of fine goods to the British. They sold groceries, pharmaceuticals or liquor, owned ice factories or artesian wells, or worked as opticians, customs officials, or as clerks in the businesses of their wealthier compatriots. Families such as the Ezras and Gubbays in Calcutta, the Sassoons in Bombay and Shanghai, the Meyers in Singapore, and the Kadoories in Hong Kong and Shanghai used their great wealth to build synagogues, schools, and other Jewish communal institutions, and also became important philanthropists for the welfare and enhancement of their adopted cities.

DAVID SASSOON

The first threads of the silken web were spun about 1830 with the arrival in Bombay of David Sassoon from Baghdad. A few Jews from the Middle East had already made forays into Southeast Asia prior to this, but David Sassoon's entrepreneurial energy and devotion to Baghdadi religious tradition set the pace and standard for other Baghdadi Jews. While certainly wealthier and more influential than the average Baghdadi, still he exemplifies the spirit and qualities that motivated the Baghdadis.

David Sassoon was born in Baghdad in 1792, a member of a prominent family that was well-known in international trade and that had long held the position of chief treasurer to the governor of Baghdad. But times were changing, and persecution by Daud Pasha forced him to flee the country. When he arrived in Bombay in 1832, British and Parsee merchants dominated the import-export business. He began by exporting textiles to Persia, Baghdad, and the Gulf states and importing goods that could be resold to England. Then he began to buy the wharfs, offering dock space and storage space to small merchants arriving from Afghanistan or Russia. In return, he had the first choice of the exotic goods they brought. He also anticipated the growth of Bombay, and his real estate holdings contributed greatly to his wealth. His success was due of course to his great intelligence and foresight but also to his ability to speak Arabic, his knowledge of the conditions within the countries he was dealing with, his willingness to take risks with traders shunned by the more established firms, and his absolute trustworthiness. He was also helped by his large family, which included eight sons. The Sassoons have been called "the Rothchilds of the East" for, like the Rothchilds in Europe, he sent his many sons to other commercial centers to become his trusted agents abroad.

While there were often Baghdadi traders in place before the Sassoons arrived, their investment and the connection to the Sassoons' extensive trading network stimulated commercial and communal growth wherever they landed. Singapore provides a case in point. Prior to the arrival of the Sassoons in 1840, Singapore was a swampy fishing village, with about nine Baghdadi traders. Soon after the Sassoons arrived, a small synagogue for forty people was built. On April 4, 1878, the Maghain Aboth synagogue was consecrated, with Torah scrolls brought from Baghdad, to serve the growing population. Similarly, the Sassoons' need for teak for their docks brought them to Burma, where in 1853 they may have provided money for Rangoon's first small synagogue. As in Singapore, by the latter part of the century, a larger synagogue was needed to accommodate the growing population.

In the early 1840s also, the Sassoons extended their network to China, spurred on by the favorable prospects for trade in textiles and opium. Recognizing Shanghai's vast potential as a market for metals, wool, and cotton goods, and the city's favorable location as a gateway for the spice trade, David's second son Elias made Shanghai his base of operations in 1850. Within five years, the Sassoons consolidated their hold along the China coast, and extended the family's trading empire to Japan, opening branches in Yokohama and Nagasaki. The Shanghai Sassoons were joined in their success in the import and export trade by the Kadoori family and Silas Hardoon, as well as by a stream of Baghdadi clerks and their families, ultimately swelling the small but influential community to about one thousand. As in other ports, the Baghdadis invested in real estate, manufacturing and public utilities, and became the most active commercial and industrial group in Shanghai. In 1867, Elias Sassoon separated himself from the family business and started an independent Sassoon company in Shanghai. E. D. Sassoon and Co, as the new firm was called, continued through Elias' descendents until the Communist takeover after World War II.

Philanthropy

As the Baghdadi wealth grew, so did their philanthropy. The list of David Sassoon's gifts to Bombay is very long: he built schools, museums, hospitals, orphanages, libraries, and many other civic institutions, in addition to great wharfs and factories. In founding these businesses and institutions, David Sassoon greatly accelerated Bombay's growth as a modern industrial city. He remained an Orthodox Jew, and he stopped work daily for prayer and study. In 1861, he built the Magen David Synagogue in Byculla, followed in 1863 by the Ohel David Synagogue in Poona, which was to become his burial site upon his death a year later. He was instrumental in the publication of a newspaper in Judeo-Arabic and supported scholars and scholarly publications. His son Albert (Abdullah) followed his example, not only establishing the first large textile mill in Bombay but also maintaining a school, the David Sassoon Benevolent Institution, other buildings, supporting newspapers and university scholarships, and becoming active in civic institutions and as an advisor to the British on their relations with Russia. For his service and loyalty to Britain, Albert was honored with the Order of the Star of India and the Order of the Lion and the Sun. In 1872, he was knighted for his role in advancing the British Empire. The new Sir Albert celebrated the event by giving an elaborate ball at his estate, San Souci, to welcome the new Viceroy to India, Lord Northbrook. More than a thousand guests, including every member of Bombay's elite, danced throughout the night at the grand home of David Sassoon's son.

COMMUNAL RESPONSIBILITY

This pattern of communal responsibility, both to Jews and to the wider society in which they lived, was replicated in other locations where Baghdadis resided. The Ezras were great benefactors to the city of Calcutta. The first synagogue, Beth El, was built in 1831. In 1884, Calcutta Jewry was wealthy enough to build the largest Jewish house of worship in the Far East, the Maghen David Synagogue, which was constructed within a few years of the new, larger synagogues in Singapore and Rangoon. Calcutta's Baghdadi community also contributed to the civic landscape, as did several benefactors in Rangoon.

The success of families such as the Sassoons, Ezras, Gubbays, Abrahams, and Kadooris enticed many other, often poor immigrants from Baghdad, Aleppo and other points in the Middle East. These new arrivals benefited from the benevolent and educational institutions set up by the Sassoons and others. Ezekiel Musleah, who was raised in Calcutta and became the rabbi there for twelve years, suggests a darker side to this great giving by the wealthy. Institutions, from charity organizations to synagogue structures, were benevolent but exclusionary: the line between rich and poor was clearly articulated; the rich controlled all decisions in the synagogues—which was, after all, the center of community interaction. In the early years there was no schooling for the poorer and less commercially able immigrants from Iraq, so the poor stayed poor and dependent while the rich grew richer and more distant.

A SYSTEM ORDAINED FOR MANY, BUT NOT SOME

David Sassoon's story, while unusual in its outstanding success, is indicative of many aspects of the Baghdadi experience, especially in the nineteenth and early twentieth centuries. Like other first generation Baghdadis, David Sassoon wore Arabic dress to the end of his life, setting himself visually as well as mentally apart from the populations among whom he lived. Like other Baghdadis, he spoke Arabic, Judeo-Arabic and Hebrew, and had limited knowledge of the local language, other than what he needed for trade. When the Baghdadis felt it necessary to excel in another language, it was not Hindustani or Burmese they acquired but English, and their children attended schools whose curriculum was based on the English model. As time went on, their dress, manners and culture increasingly approximated that of the English.

David Sassoon became a naturalized, and very loyal, British subject in 1853, signing his naturalization certificate in Hebrew. All students in the Sassoon schools sang "God Save the Queen" in English, Hebrew and Arabic, and a flagpole bearing the Union Jack signaled David Sassoon's headquarters.[5] David Sassoon's loyalty to Britain was probably far more than political expediency; it certainly was an expression of gratitude for the substantial opportunities and protections the British administration had offered to a Jew fleeing persecution. Ultimately all but one of David Sassoon's sons moved to England. His third son, S. D. (Farha), had gone to London in 1858 to anchor the Sassoon trading empire in England, and most of his brothers followed as they became more and more attracted by and comfortable with British ways and British culture. In Britain, the Sassoon family achieved outstanding social and political, as well as economic, success, socializing with British royalty and political leaders, as well as with international figures such as the Shah of Persia, and intermarrying with their counterparts, the Rothchilds.

The social success of the Sassoons in Bombay and London illustrates a paradox within the British class system, which was displayed throughout the empire by pageants, honors, buildings and dress. David Cannadine points out that the seemingly immutable, timeless, "ordained" British class system that ordered social relationships was based on the hierarchy of classes of people, not of individuals. Therefore, outstanding individuals such as the Sassoons, or Indian rajahs, or African tribal chieftains, could achieve a social equality unattainable by members of the class to which they belonged—Jews, ordinary Indians, Africans.[6] This way of construing the world had significant impact on the aspirations of the Baghdadis who came to Burma, as well as other parts of the empire. Despite the individual attainments of the Sassoon family, for the majority of Baghdadis, theirs was an international but closed world: in caste-conscious India and class-conscious British India and Burma, the light-skinned Baghdadis were seemingly of a higher status than the darker-skinned, native Bene Israel but always beneath the British, whose schools they attended and whose citizenship they sought.

AN EVOLVING NETWORK OF TRUST

At the same time the Baghdadis were seeking to become socially and politically British, they were united across the miles by tradition, language, world view and marriage. Marriage within the fold was an essential value. Tradition and heritage sustained the society, and especially in these diaspora conditions, no breach in this sustaining wall could be allowed. So it remained until the twentieth century, and even then defections were rare. Brides were often sent from Iraq or sought in other Baghdadi communities. Intermarriage with the Indian Jewish populations—the darker-skinned, Marathi-speaking Bene Israel of the Bombay area or the Cochinis of the southern Malabar coast—while permitted, was discouraged. As can be expected, marriage to anyone other than a Jew would result in shunning by the community. The result of this adherence to religious tradition was an international network of trust, forged by kinship, language and social and economic interdependence that stretched across the vast distances of Southeast Asia.

How this support network operated in practice can be seen in the life of Sir Manasseh Meyer, the great benefactor of Singapore Jewry. Born in Baghdad in 1846, he received his primary education in Calcutta. At the age of fifteen, he came to Singapore and attended a Roman Catholic school. Three years later, he returned to Calcutta to learn bookkeeping, and then at twenty-one opened a small business in Rangoon. Six years later, he returned to Singapore to establish an import-export business, with a monopoly on the opium trade, and became the largest trader with India. He also acquired great wealth through real estate holdings, and was the prime mover behind the building of Singapore's two great synagogues, especially the Chesed El Synagogue, in 1905. He was knighted in 1906 for his contributions to the development of Singapore.

Burma's Jews had similar extended relationships, if not the great wealth of a Sassoon or Meyer. In their own context, there were gradations of financial success, with the accompanying grand homes and influence within the community, as well as internecine arguments and social tensions. But there were also great joys and a sense of security derived from strong religious traditions and intricate family interrelationships. And the Burmese themselves were gentle "hosts," the English cool but comfortable embodiments of political ideas as well as good customers, the city was cosmopolitan, and the land was lovely. It was a full life in many respects, one that all but came to an end with the cataclysm that was World War II.

No one knows better how days unfolded than the people who lived them. First person testimony—when it is articulate and perceptive—enriches and brings immediacy to the text. It also evokes a mood, a spirit that helps us apprehend the meaning and texture as well as the progression of everyday lives. To this end, many of the Jews of Burma will speak for themselves.

NOTES

1. These rounded figures are best guesstimates, based on a number of informal reports. The World Jewish Congress reported that in 1939, 2150 Jews were in Burma. *The Jewish Communities of the World*, ed. Roberta Cohen, 60. The figure for Calcutta comes from David Nahoum in Calcutta today, who argues that the community only reached five thousand during World War II with the influx of refugees from Burma. This would accord with the figure given by Rabbi Ezekiel Musleah, who says that Calcutta's Jewry was never more "than 5000 souls." According to Musleah, the total number of Jews in India itself was once some thirty thousand, but the vast majority of these were Bene Israel, in the Bombay area, and Jews of Cochin. *On the Banks of the Ganga*, 1955:14, 11.

2. Quoted in Elkins, Rabbi Dov Peretz, *Moments of Transcendence* (N.J.: Aronson), 1992, 185.

3. Percy S. Gourgey, Letter, February 10, 1989. Ironically, many years later, Psalm 137 was used to describe the feelings of Iraqi Jews displaced to Israel. Rachel Lazin recalls: 'I remembered how, during our early years in Israel—living in an abandoned Arab house near the banks of the Yarkon River, without running water or electricity—my parents had longed for the comfortable lives they had left behind in Iraq. You know the Biblical poem about the exiled Jews sitting by the rivers of Babylon and weeping when they remembered Zion" she elaborates, quoting the opening lines of Psalm 137. "Well, when we were growing up in Tel Aviv in the 1950s, we experienced exactly the opposite: our parents weeping with longing when they remembered Baghdad." *The Jerusalem Report*, May 19, 2003, 14.

4. Opium was a legal substance until 1910.

5. Stanley Jackson, *The Sassoons*, 35.

6. David Cannadine, *Ornamentalism*, 8–9.

Chapter One

Adventurers and Entrepreneurs

It would be easy to miss Musmeah Yeshua, the grand and all-but-silent synagogue in the heart of Rangoon. It stands behind high white walls, on a narrow street filled with vendors of betel nuts, bananas, books, paint, and homeopathic medicines. From the busy street corner one catches a glimpse of the Sule Pagoda, reputed to be twenty-five hundred years old, an important center of Buddhist worship in this deeply religious land. A few blocks away is the Strand Hotel, where dignitaries, royalty and writers stayed when the British ruled the country in the late nineteenth and early twentieth centuries. Balconied buildings line the roads, ever confronting the incessant press of nature in hot, humid Burma.

But if you turn from the sights of the streets, and raise your eyes, you will see above the white walls an archway decorated with a seven-branched blue candelabra and the name of the synagogue in large blue letters. Surprisingly well maintained amid the graying buildings that line the street, the synagogue stands as a testimony to the proud community that constructed it in the late nineteenth century, and to the devotion of the few remaining Jews of Burma, who hold it in trust for an uncertain future.

Once the focus of a vibrant Jewish community life in this outpost of the British Empire, Musmeah Yeshua (Heb: "Brings forth salvation") has witnessed the florescence and decline of Jewish and British fortunes in Burma, and has endured global war and local rebellions, Japanese occupation and Burmese national ascendancy. Despite the dramatic political flux, Buddhist Burma has been, for the most part, a tolerant home for the Jews for more than one hundred and fifty years.

The Jews of Burma have always been but one very small minority among the many religions and nationalities that have comprised Burma's diverse population. Like the other minorities in British Burma, Jews had always to negotiate the dynamic between traditional values and lifestyle and an enticing, though alien, political and social environment. Refuge, economic opportunity and freedom of religion came at a price then, as now.

TO THE FAR REACHES OF THE BRITISH EMPIRE

When the first Jewish settlers left their homes in Baghdad to seek their fortune some three thousand miles[1] to the southeast, Burma was relatively unknown. True, stories had come back to the Middle East from relatives in India describing the fortunate conditions under British rule, where Jews were finding their place among an extraordinary variety of peoples drawn from all over Southeast Asia and the Middle East. Burma, however, was quite different from India: the majority of the population was uniformly Buddhist, free from the caste divisions and religious diversity that characterized the predominantly Hindu Indian society. It was primarily an agricultural land of rice fields and teak forests, hill tribes and sultry cities, fine natural ports, Buddhist monasteries and golden pagodas, sweet fruit and tropical flowers. Its kingdom was based far up the Irrawaddy River in Mandalay. Rangoon in the early nineteenth century was still a dusty work-in-progress, its enhancement by the British envisioned but not yet realized. As the British Raj spread eastward from India, this beautiful land offered excellent economic opportunities and was not uncomfortably distant from relatives in Calcutta just across the Bay of Bengal.

The British were tempted by the abundant teak forests, rich agriculture, precious stones, and good ports, as well as the potential of Burma as a market for British goods. It also offered superb outdoor activities, such as hunting wild game and fishing in clear streams.[2] But action to acquire Burma was ultimately prompted by defensive concerns for the Empire as well as by rivalry with France's colonial presence to the east. The French in Indo-China had designs on Upper Burma which, if successful, might affect British interests in East Bengal and Assam. Sovereignty over the border areas between British India and Burma were also being contested by the Burmese. A Burmese army had even crossed into British India in pursuit of rebels. While this army posed no real threat to the British, it did provide a pretext for action. The Burmese were no match for the well-equipped British, and the country was conquered during a purposeful series of three wars. After the first Anglo-Burmese War in 1826, the British East India Company extended its hold to the maritime provinces of Arakan, on the Bay of Bengal, Tenasserim, on the Andaman Sea, and the Rangoon area. Lower Burma, including Pegu

Province and the city of Rangoon, fell to the British following the second Anglo-Burmese War in 1852; and the third Anglo-Burmese War in 1885 brought Upper Burma into British hands with the fall of the Burmese kingdom in Mandalay. Queen Victoria's birthday present on January 1, 1886, was the announcement of the annexation of Upper Burma.[3] British interests in Burma were codified in a dual system of rule, through the military and through the overseas representatives of powerful European businesses.

The British conquest of Burma had important implications for populations, such as the Jews of the Middle East, who were seeking a better life. British annexation meant Burma's integration into a global economic and political framework. Trade, not cultural domination, was the primary motivation for the expansion of the Empire, and good administration was necessary to assure this goal: as Niall Ferguson points out, "... the British Empire acted as an agency for imposing free markets, the rule of law, investor protection and relatively incorrupt government on roughly a quarter of the world."[4] Peoples within the Empire could practice their religions and continue their customs as long as they did not interfere with the economic and administrative functions of the Empire.[5] The imposition of an international system of law, combined with religious freedom, in turn encouraged a worldwide movement of peoples to and within the British Empire.

As an adjunct to its economic goals, Britain aggressively developed systems of international communication. "By 1880 there were altogether 97,568 miles of cable across the world's oceans, linking Britain to India, Canada, Africa, and Australia."[6] While such improvements in communication were designed to facilitate commerce, they also made it possible for individuals in Calcutta, Rangoon and Mandalay to be integrated into a worldwide culture through the timely exchange of news and other information. For the Baghdadi Jews, resident as they were in many parts of Southeast Asia, it meant that community—as a derivative of communication—could be easily maintained.

ARRIVAL IN BURMA

The first Jew in Burma was not Baghdadi but probably a Bene Israel, Solomon Gabirol, who served as a commissar in the army of King Alaungpaya (1752–1760).[7] In the early part of the nineteenth century two Europeans, Solomon Reinman from Galicia and a Mr. Goldberg from Romania came to Upper Burma as suppliers to the British army and to trade in teak and bamboo. Solomon Reinman arrived in Burma about 1840, made and lost a fortune, and after a period in Rangoon settled in Cochin where he married and lived for some twenty-five years. After returning to Europe, he wrote an account of his travels, *Masot Shelomo* (*Travels of Shlomo in the Lands of India, Burma, and China*), in Hebrew. The book, which was published after his death in Vienna in 1884, contains the first Hebrew record of Burma.[8] Calcutta's Baghdadi Jewish opium merchants arrived, but did not settle, during the early years of the nineteenth century when Rangoon was part of the opium trade route that linked Singapore, Shanghai, Manila and other ports in Southeast Asia.

The Baghdadis, whether from Baghdad or Basra, Syria, Egypt or other areas in the Middle East, came as extended family, settling down, marrying, building businesses and establishing essential communal institutions—the cemetery, the *mikveh* (ritual bath), the synagogue. They utilized their family connections abroad to become middlemen traders, importing fine foods and other goods desired by the British and others in the international community or trading in more mundane materials—crockery, textiles, whatever was needed—throughout the Burmese countryside. They also serviced the ships that docked in the busy Rangoon harbor. Some entered the civil service as government officials and customs officers; others worked as clerks in Baghdadi stores on Mogul or Dalhousie Streets. A few served in the Military Police guarding the frontiers.[9] Even as they became more comfortable in Burma, the Burma Jewish community was an intrinsic part of the broader Baghdadi world that existed throughout Southeast Asia. The ties were historical, emotional, religious, linguistic, and economic as well as familial, and this conceptual world, this Baghdadi world view, was one they inhabited no matter where they lived. Rangoon or Mandalay might be their mailing address, but their "home" could not be so easily defined or confined. Ellis Sofaer, who was born into a Baghdadi family in Rangoon early in the twentieth century, writes: "It was quite common in the early part of the nineteenth century for Jewish families in the Near East to be sprawled over the different Turkish dependencies like an outstretched net, and yet to remain cohesive. The separate branches chose their centers of activity not from sentiment, but for the trade opportunities they discerned in the territory of their choice; and it is certain that the same attitude motivated the Jews who drifted to India at the time."[10]

Indian Jews—the Bene Israel and a few Cochinis—came to Burma in smaller numbers. Literate in English, most remained in Rangoon as clerks and managers for the British and for the Baghdadis who, in the early days especially, could not read or write English well enough for the needs of their trade. Other Bene Israel moved north to Mandalay to become railway workers.

The earliest Baghdadi settlement in Burma may be that of Azariah Samuel, who arrived in 1841 in the port of Akyab (now Sittwe) on the Bay of Bengal in the British-held province of Arakan.[11] Akyab offered excellent commercial opportunities: since the British had taken over the area fifteen years before, rice and timber exports had greatly increased, and the city was similarly increasing in size and importance. One drawback for a Jewish settler, however, was that the surrounding Arakan Yoma Mountains made communication with the rest of Burma, including the eventual Jewish community, very difficult. But Samuel came prepared to continue his Jewish lifestyle even without a Baghdadi community in Akyab, then or ever. Traveling with him on his journey from Bushire on the Persian Gulf was his *shochet*, his ritual slaughterer, to assure a supply of fresh kosher meat while he established himself as a merchant. By 1884 he was dealing in wine and general supplies at Well and Silver Streets. The business prospered as did his family, which came to include five children, one of whom, Ezekiel, is buried in the small Jewish cemetery in Akyab. Another son, Samuel Hyam Samuel, who was born in 1883, had several occupations: he was a wine and general merchant, a cinema proprietor, photographer, optician and boat owner. He was also trained as a *shochet* by the *shochet* who accompanied his father from Bushire many years before. As the only Jewish family in Akyab, the Samuel family celebrated religious events together or with the Jewish relatives across the Bay in Calcutta. In 1931, ninety years after Azariah Samuel came to Akyab, his descendents left together for Calcutta; from there they settled in London and Sydney.

About the same time as Azariah Samuel settled in Akyab—in 1840 or even earlier—two brothers, Judah and Abraham Raphael Ezekiel, traveled from Baghdad to the royal city of Yadanabon,[12] the "City of Gems"—the present-day Mandalay—in Upper Burma.[13] For a time, they worked in the Court of King Mindon as accountants or bookkeepers.[14] The merchants Aaron Jacob Elias Aaron, born about 1840, and his son, David Hai Aaron, born in 1868, also settled in this royal city. David Hai Aaron eventually had shops in Mandalay, Rangoon, Akyab and Moulmain.

When King Mindon's ruthless son Thibaw ascended the throne in 1878, the Ezekiel brothers left Upper Burma. After a severe argument, Abraham dropped the last name Ezekiel to disassociate himself from Judah, and from then on used the name Abraham Raphael. Judah settled in Rangoon and Abraham in Bassein, a port in the rich, rice-producing delta of the Irrawaddy River. So began the long history of the Raphael family in Bassein.

Despite these difficult beginnings, a small Jewish community flourished in Mandalay until the coming of World War II. Mordecai Saul, one of the first Jewish settlers to remain in Mandalay, traveled from Baghdad to Rangoon with his father, Saul Reuben Hakham Rabbi Sassoon, in about 1878. Marriage appears to be the immediate purpose of his travel to Rangoon, for a marriage had already been arranged with his second cousin, fourteen-year-old Seemah Ezekiel Ezra Sassoon. Her family had fled Baghdad after Seemah's older sister Sulka (Sally) was abducted, legend says, by an Arab sheik; as romantic as this may sound, the abduction was probably a kidnapping for ransom and seems to have ended with Sally's death. Soon after the marriage, the Sauls traveled to Yadanabon to try to set up a business. When Mordecai Saul arrived in the royal city, it was already the home of numerous merchant groups—Chinese, Armenians, Persians, Indians, Europeans—who occupied different occupational niches and whose trade was facilitated through distinct international networks. About half of the population was Muslim. The Burmese sought to tie the merchants to the court, to integrate and control them, and to encourage them to settle in Yadanabon and even to adopt local dress. On the king's prerogative, some private traders became "high merchants" (*thuhtes*) and were offered particular commercial opportunities.[15] This may have been the fortune of Mordecai Saul. He was able to attain an audience at the court of King Thibaw, and as a good will gesture presented Queen Supayalat with two bottles of fine French perfume. She was delighted with the gift: she immediately turned the bottles upside down, spilling the expensive perfumes on the tiled palace floor, and dedicated the pretty new flower holders to the golden Buddha on palace grounds. King Thibaw also liked the elegant vases. The Sauls returned to Baghdad to procure more "vases" and for a few years, in a shop on palace grounds, Mordecai Saul sold bottles of fine perfume to be poured out.

This charming memory of his grandfather by Saul Ezra Saul belies the savagery that accompanied the reign of King Thibaw. It's daunting to think of the courage of the first peddlers in Mandalay and to reflect on the urgency that drove them from Baghdad to a lawless city, where royal ritualized slaughters of hundreds of people were common, where armed robbers roamed the city, and where pigs filled the streets and wandered among the glorious monasteries and around the opulent palace.[16] "Mandalay in 1880 was not a safe place for a white man. Apart from a handful of people sheltering in the poorly fortified British residence, only three Europeans dared to wander the streets: a fiery Baptist missionary, a retired major 'of weak intellect,' and Scott (British adventurer Sir George Scott)."[17] It was into this environment that Mordecai Saul, and the Ezekiel brothers before him, came to seek their fortunes.

After the British took over, and despite a stifling summer climate, Mandalay appeared pleasant and picturesque to casual visitors of the 1890s, who commented on Mandalay's heterogeneous, exotically dressed populations: Hindu Marwarees from Gujarat, in India; Muslim Moguls from Persia, "who dress exactly like the pictures that are drawn of Bible scenes and characters," with their turbans and long, loose outer garments; Hindu Cheeties, keen businessmen from Madras, with the "appearance of mere savages," with their naked, almost black skin; Kathays from Manipur; Ponnas or Brahmins from Manipur, with their distinctive dress; the Suratees; and Jews: "A cosmopolitan place would be incomplete without some Jews. We have them in Mandalay of various nationalities, European and Oriental, and they seem to be all shopkeepers. One firm hails from Baghdad, very near the dwelling-place of our first parents, and speak a vernacular which they call Hebrew."[18] Another traveler "spent many happy, but expensive, hours wandering about the silk bazaar, buying from the fascinating little ladies, and watching the constant and ever-changing panorama of the brilliantly coloured crowd. Every nationality appeared to invest the bazaar: Shans with their great flopping hats and ugly uncouth faces, Chinamen of course, Jews, all mixed with the endless stream of lovely Burmese, who were by far the most interesting of the community."[19]

South of Rangoon, in the port city of Moulmein on the Andaman Sea, a Jewish merchant, a Mr. Jacob, had set up shop by 1864. A traveler to Moulmein in 1871 describes the setting into which these first Moulmein Jews ventured: " . . . we dropped anchor abreast of the business quarter of the town, with but a half-dozen small vessels in sight. The town does not appear to advantage from the river, almost hidden as it is by immense groves of the cocoa-nut and betel-nut palm, banana, papaya, bamboo, and other tropical plants. The population, comprising Burmese, Chinese, Parsees, Armenians, Klings, Jews, and Cingalese, is about 10,000; the European residents may number less than a hundred."[20] Moulmein was an important center for the export of teak logs, which were cut from the forests on the banks of the Salween River. As such, the city offered excellent economic opportunities and, indeed, Abraham ben Aharon (Aaron) Cohen was very financially successful there. He made substantial charitable contributions to the core Jewish community in Rangoon and to Baghdadi communities elsewhere before moving to Calcutta in 1887. His six sons and six daughters continued their father's tradition of philanthropy, becoming great benefactors to the Rangoon community as well as to other charities. His eldest son, Jacob Meir, became one of the leaders of the Rangoon community. Other members of the Aaron family remained in Moulmein.

RANGOON

Most Baghdadis came to the rapidly developing city of Rangoon, which was well situated as a protected port on the Rangoon River, a tributary of the mighty Irrawaddy River. Because the Irrawaddy is navigable for nine hundred miles, the port of Rangoon is in a strategic location for trade from the interior as well as for international trade. The port's commercial potential was well-appreciated by the British, the Baghdadis, and scores of similarly minded minorities who flooded the region once British administration was in place. A visitor to Rangoon in 1846 casually noted the presence of Jews in Rangoon, remarking that "if Christians, Jews, and Turks will but select for their picnic time those days not devoted to Burmese festivities," they would find the riverbanks less crowded.[21]

The British lost little time in enacting a plan for the city. By the end of 1853, they had allotted and received payment for town sites in what was to become the residential and commercial heart of the city, in the blocks between Strand and Merchant Streets and near Sule Pagoda Road. They created this town center by filling in the marshland around the Sule Pagoda, and by constructing imposing, multi-storied, British-style brick administrative buildings nearby. The non-Burmese character of the city they envisioned is apparent not only in the imperial style of the buildings but also in the early land allocations. Free sites for religious groups were allotted to Hindus, Armenians, Muslims, Baptists, Chinese, and Jews. The synagogue was to be built between 25th and 26th Streets, south of the broad avenue, Dalhousie Street, and not far from the Sule Pagoda. Land for a cemetery was also allotted at that time, as were rights to a building at 66/70 31st Street containing eight apartments. In 1857 the first synagogue, of wood, was built and the first Torah scrolls brought from Baghdad. Like the other religious buildings, it was to be free of taxation.

Land allocation for religious institutions was in keeping with Britain's endorsement of religious freedom, for imperial as well as commercial reasons. As Donald Smith points out, "The British policy of religious neutrality was clearly stated in the eighteenth century and reflected in the commercial-imperial interests of the British East India Company.... [They believed that] interference in religion would produce neither good business relations nor loyal subjects."[22] Britain's civil administration kept a hand in the administration of the synagogue, and a Scheme that governed the number of synagogue trustees, the timing of elections, and similar matters remained in force throughout British rule. Changes in the Scheme had to be appealed to the British authorities.

In 1861, Burma's first newspaper, the British colonial *Rangoon Gazette*, began publishing news from all over the world, shortening the distance between London's world of ideas, commerce and fashion and the remote outpost on the Andaman Sea, and helping to create a society that saw itself as merely Britain displaced, Britain with a hot and muggy climate, Britain with tigers and elephants. Also in 1861, one of the first Jewish businesses in Rangoon, E. Solomon and Sons, was established as a water supply company; the company provided the British navy with water from their artesian wells on the riverbank, as well as with ice and aerated soda.

During the latter half of the nineteenth century, several missionary schools were established in Burma, events which were to have educational consequences for the Jewish population. In 1862, the Anglican Diocesan School was founded on Pagoda Road, under the auspices of the Society for the Promotion of Christian Knowledge. Two years later, the Society for the Propagation of the Gospel founded St. John's College. In January 1868, St. Paul's School was opened near the Sule Pagoda, not far from the area of densest Jewish settlement; the most popular school of its time, St. Paul's, Rangoon, included many Jews in its student body. Similar schools followed, offering British-style education and political training to European and Anglo-Indian students. In *Burma Through Alien Eyes*, Helen Trager offers an amusing insight into the role the missionary schools played in supporting and justifying the British Empire. She quotes this teaching: "And ever since the English governed the country the tigers do not seem so ferocious as they were when the Burmans governed it. Then the tigers would catch people traveling through the jungle in the daytime. They (tigers, now) fear the English because they are upright and worship the true God."[23]

The Jews apparently were a step above the Burmans, but never the Christian (British) equal, or so it would seem from this observation by an American missionary of the day: "The Roman, the Greek, the Jew, the Egyptian, was far less of a brute, than the savage or semi-civilized object of *our* philanthropy...." Both Jews and Pagans '*were trained to think*' but the people among whom current missionaries must work present a much more difficult challenge: "With them the human intellect has for ages been at a stand. Without valuable books, without foreign commerce, without distant conquest, without the strife of theology, without political freedom, without public spirit—what is left for them but listlessness, ignorance, and pride? Such of them as attempt study, learn only falsehood and folly; so that the more they learn, the less they know."[24] The problem, it would seem, is that without being British or, in this case, American—enjoying commerce, conquest, books, and the strife of theology, the Burmans were doomed.

Other institutions set up by the British were not so easily available to others. The most elite, the Pegu Club, on Prome Road, was established in 1882; the Burma Club, on Merchant Street, in 1885; and Rangoon's Gymkhana Club on Halpin Road, in 1877 and extended in 1903–1904. The Gymkhana Club, which stared across Halpin Road at several Jewish homes, sat on ten acres of land, with two lakes, a ballroom, a bowling alley, and fields for cricket, football, and hockey. Military bands played at the club three times a week, dances were regularly held for the club's more than a thousand members, and elegant social functions took place regularly. Throughout the Raj, the purposefully impressive English architecture of the clubs declared their importance and their policies:

> The clubs were islands of Britishness in the great Indian sea, to which the imperialist might withdraw whenever they felt a personal, social or ritual need: for a drink at the bar, that is, for a stag dinner, for a dance, a horse show, a wedding reception or a game of bridge. Though they were seldom distinguished buildings, the architectural symbolism of the grander clubs was at least frank—Come In! it cried to suitable sorts of Briton, Keep Out! it hissed to everyone else. Visually their tone was generally dictated by their setting, which was above all prohibitive—daunting gateways, stern name-plates, sentry-boxes for deterrent watchmen, long drives to make the intruder feel uncomfortable, terraces from which he might feel he was being stared at by superior officers. It took nerve to gatecrash a really upstage Anglo-Indian club, and this sense of impeccable exclusivity impressed itself upon everyone.[25]

These bastions of exclusivity were to be emblems of all that the Baghdadis strived for socially but that would ever be denied them. Like children reaching for a soap bubble, the Baghdadis reached for total acceptance by the British—an elusive goal that conditioned their experience in Burma and even beyond.

Rangoon's commercial promise drew immigrants from all over the world, and the city grew rapidly. Indians, Europeans, Chinese and Armenians soon dominated the Burmese populations within city limits. The British preferred English-speaking Indians as dock workers, agricultural labor, house servants, and in other capacities, and encouraged huge migrations of Indians, including Tamil Chettier moneylenders, into the Rangoon area.[26] Dutch, French and German firms also established businesses in Burma, with corresponding private clubs to cater to their nationals.

The trading networks throughout Southeast Asia that the Jews were establishing mirrored similar networks created by Indian and Chinese entrepreneurs, whose business relationships also flowed along community lines. Jacob Isaac Cohen made the journey from Hamburg, Germany, in 1888, adding Yiddish and German to the mélange of languages being spoken by Rangoon's Jews (his grandson Jacob Moses Cohen recalls speaking Arabic, Burmese, Hindi, Urdu and Bengali, as well as English). Jacob Cohen was joined by other Ashkenazim who, through marriage and custom, were absorbed into the dominant Baghdadi community. In 1872, Rangoon's population was 98,138, including 83 Jews; 1881, the total population was 134,176, with 172 Jews; ten years later it stood at 180,324, including 219 Jews; and by 1901, the population had reached 248,060, with 508 Jews listed by the census.[27] The British acknowledged the increasing importance of the city by making it their colonial capital in Burma in 1885. In 1896, a grand statue of Queen Victoria was placed at the central crossroads of Fytche Square.

Jews were guaranteed a seat on the Municipal Council of Rangoon when it was newly constituted on June 23, 1883. Burmese representatives held five seats, and the European, American, Eurasian, Jewish and Parsi electorate each had one representative. There was one representative for the Chinese community; two for the Hindu, two for the Muslim, as well as a few delegates chosen by other means. The Municipal Council faced numerous problems, above all that of public health and sanitation. Smallpox, plague, cholera, dysentery, malaria and typhoid were endemic, with corresponding mortality rates.[28] The *Rangoon Gazette* of these years chronicles the number of deaths from day to day, from place to place, as well as the daily total of rats killed. The Council struggled to get enough ambulances and considered trash removal an emergency. Construction of the Rangoon General Hospital began. At the same time, chickens were being slaughtered in the streets to ward off diseases. The *Rangoon Gazette* reported that Burmese in Prome were certain that the plague was caused by the Nats, nature "spirits" of the powerful folk religion, as punishment by superhuman agencies.[29] Similarly, amid social notes from Paris and London, and news of the fall of Port Arthur, were headlines such as "Killed by a Demon."[30]

As energetic as these efforts were to transform Rangoon into an extension of England, the city still presented itself as a different place altogether. "A study in greys, browns, and greens, toned down with dust," is how a traveler to Rangoon in the latter half of the nineteenth century described the city.

> The town does not look inviting. The buildings have a substantial solvent air, but the general effect is glaring baldness. It improves on closer acquaintance. The better streets throughout are wide and clean; guiltless of sidewalks but shaded on either side by trees in leaf all the year round. The East end is the more important, but even in Merchant Street extremes of industry meet.... There are a few good shops to cater for European wants—if that may be called a shop which rises superior to window display and wherein a set of double harness or half a pound of cheese may be had on demand. The West side of the town beyond Fytche Square is occupied almost entirely by the Eastern traders who congregate, according to custom, in quarters ruled by race, and streets determined by trade. All the hardware dealers dwell side by side; the crockery men cling together, and the dealers in cloth.[31]

Jewish shops and homes were generally on Dalhousie or Mogul Streets. Jewish merchants traded in wines and liquors, wholesale coffee or fruit, fine provisions, or antiques; some were estate agents; others were tailors, or engaged in similar commercial activities. In the late 1880s, a Jewish businessman established the city's first bioscope theater.[32] One of the most prominent liquor merchants was E. Solomon and Sons, whose store on Dalhousie Street held several exclusive contracts for fine whiskies and cognacs desired by the British.

In a letter home dated January 7, 1908, another visitor, Gilbert Little Stark, adds details to the picture above. He writes:

> As we drew near to Rangoon, the first object that lifted itself above the level land about us was the golden spire of the Schwe' Dagon Pagoda, and the next distinctive feature was the elephants piling teak logs along the shore. . . . Rangoon is broad-streeted and dusty, and has a new, unfinished appearance everywhere, except in the hotels, which appear to be of about the same date as the First Crusade. The population is even more cosmopolitan than in Singapore, and Klings, Tamils, Bengalis, Punjabis, Sikhs, Ghurkas, Jews, Chinese, Arabs, Armenians, Malays, Shans, Karens, Persians and Singhalese jostle one another in the noisy streets, where barbers and cooks ply their trades on the curb, and every third shopkeeper is reading aloud out of the Koran. The strange fact is that about one man in a hundred is a Burmese!—south India has seized the town.[33]

The latter half of the nineteenth century and early twentieth century were years of great commercial expansion for Burma. Oil had been discovered in Yenangyaung in Upper Burma, possibly by the Jewish merchant Saul Aaron, who alerted the British to the kerosene taste of the drinking water.[34] Abundant Indian labor was accelerating the expansion of rice cultivation and processing, and sawmill production, and provided labor for Rangoon's busy docks. Ships arrived from Singapore and Calcutta, from Hamburg, Kobe, Madras, Straits, Zanzibar and Bombay; they came from Trieste, Karachi and Colombo, Glasgow and Liverpool, from Alexandria and Port Said. They brought goods and news, and carried passengers all along the Southeast Asian Coast—Chittagong, Akyab, Moulmein, and farther. By the turn of the century business and personal travel within the country were made easier by a good railway and by the paddle steamers of the Irrawaddy Flotilla Company, which linked towns such as Bassein on the delta, Yenangyaung upstream, and Mandalay in Upper Burma.

In 1901, the Sarkies Brothers, builders of the Raffles Hotel in Singapore, opened the elegant Strand Hotel[35] to the many travelers and businessmen now passing through the city. The first "motor wagons" came to Rangoon in 1910, promising to bring cargo from the ports more expeditiously than by hand or bullock cart. The city now had steam trams also, carrying passengers from the busy Strand to the approach to the Shwedagon Pagoda.

Twentieth Century Impressions of Burma, published in 1910, featured significant personalities and businesses to highlight the commercial and industrial progress of Burma. Among the many businessmen profiled are several Jews:

Isaac A. Sofaer

was appointed member of the Municipal Committee in 1909. Born at Baghdad in 1867, he was brought to Rangoon by his father, Abraham Isaac Sofaer, when nine years of age. Upon leaving St. Paul's High School, where he was educated, he joined a firm of wine and spirit merchants and remained with them for ten years. In 1893 he started a business on his own account, and already the firm's premises have been enlarged six times their original size. In addition to wines and spirits, Messrs. Sofaer and Co. do a large business in oilman-stores, and export a considerable quantity of rice to the Straits Settlements. Mr. Sofaer is a large landed proprietor, and owns one of the finest buildings in the town. He is a highly respected member of the Jewish community, and has been a trustee of the Jewish Synagogue for ten years. He is also a member of the Excise Committee, of the Agricultural Society and the Burma Pasteur Institute. Mr. Sofaer married a daughter of Ezekiel Solomon of Rangoon, and has two sons and four daughters. *Mr. Meyer Abraham Sofaer*, who has recently become a partner in the firm, has served for a considerable time in the business. He is married to a daughter of Mr. David Isaac, and has three sons and one daughter. [36]

A large photograph of Sofaer and Co.'s building at the corner of Phayre and Merchant Streets—most likely the "mercantile office forming a block in itself"—accompanies this article. In a section entitled "Significant Men in Burma" are photographs of Isaac Sofaer and his cousins Kelly (Kadoori) and Sassoon Solomon.

Solomon & Co.

Messrs. Solomon and Co. have carried on business at 271, Dalhousie Street, as wholesale and retail wine and spirit merchants and oilmen, since 1871. They are sole agents for Marie Brizard and Rogers' cognacs, William Greer and Co.'s whiskeys, and the manufactures of many other European houses. The firm was founded by the late Mr. E. I. Solomon, and on his death, in 1898, his three sons, Messrs. I. Solomon, K. Solomon, and J. Solomon continued the business. Mr. Kelly Solomon is the managing partner.[37]

David & Ezra Brothers

For the greater portion of its supply of mineral waters, cordials, and syrups, Mandalay is dependent upon the output from the factory of Messrs. David & Ezra Bros. in which twenty men are constantly employed, and from where over five hundred dozen bottles of table waters are distributed daily. The machinery and plant, which were supplied by Barnett & Foster, are worked by electricity, and are the most modern pattern. The bottling and washing machines have silver-plated cylinders, and in every process of manufacture the greatest precaution is taken to ensure absolute cleanliness. The first also deals in fodder and crushed foods.

The partners in the business, Messrs. David and Ezra Saul, are sons of the late Mr. M. Saul, who was proprietor of the business of Moses & Friends, at Mandalay and Maymyo. Both brothers were educated in Rangoon, and the elder, Mr. David Saul, afterwards joined the first of Levetus, Ltd., Basinghail Street, London, in order to gain business experience. For some time he carried on a commission agent's business on his own account before returning to Mandalay, where he was employed in the Cooperative Stores. In 1904, he entered into partnership with his younger brother, who had assisted in his father's business, and the mineral water factory was started.[38]

Messrs. A. V. Joseph & Co.

This firm of timber merchants and sawmill proprietors has a "turn-over" of from ten thousand to twelve thousand tons of timber annually. The converted wood has a large local sale, and the surplus is exported to Calcutta, Bombay, Madras, Ceylon and Europe. A portion of their supplies they themselves extract from the forests, and in addition they purchase large quantities of timber from the Government and private sources. Their two sawmills at Botatoung and Dunneedaw occupy one-and-a-half and three-and-a-half acres, and are worked by engines of thirty-five h.p. and seventy-five h.p. respectively. They have a qualified office staff, and employ altogether about four hundred persons daily, and have a number of elephants and buffalos.

Mr. A. V. Joseph, the founder and proprietor of the firm, has been connected with the timber trade since 1895. He started in Rangoon by importing small quantities of timber from Moulmein. This business increased rapidly, and within three years he opened a sawmill capable of an output of one thousand tons a year, while three years later, by various improvement, and the installation of new machinery, he increased the capacity of the mill five-fold. His business transactions in other directions were also eminently successful and provided the capital necessary for starting the firm's new sawmill, which is equipped in a very complete fashion, and has a very large frontage to the river.[39]

This article is accompanied by large photographs of the sawmill at Botatoung, of Mr. Joseph, and of a working elephant.

FOUNDING A NEW SYNAGOGUE

With prosperity and increased population came the need and desire for a synagogue building that reflected the size and comfort of the Jewish community in its adopted land. Accordingly, in 1893 construction was begun on a new building and ritual bath on the same site, as well as an adjacent school,

Shaarei Yeshua, to teach Hebrew and English. The community felt confident that they could afford the new building: in 1881, they had received permission to erect stores on synagogue land along Dalhousie Street between 25th and 26th Streets. The rent from these buildings would provide a steady source of funds for synagogue maintenance. In 1896, the same year that the British erected the imposing statue of Queen Victoria, the Jewish community made a similar public statement of their rightful place in Burma and within the British Raj. In that year, they dedicated their new imposing synagogue, the present Musmeah Yeshua (figure 1.1), with its soaring ceiling and interior columns, central carved *bima* and, at the far end, the *hekhal hakosh* (Holy Ark), the small semi-circular room to house the many Sifrei Torah. Musmeah Yeshua is similar in interior style to the grand Maghen David Synagogue in Calcutta and other Baghdadi synagogues in India. Enticed by the growing, devoted community, a famous rabbi, Haham Ezra Dangoor, had come from Baghdad to Rangoon in 1894 with his wife Habiba and sons Eliyahu and Moshe to serve as religious leader, *shochet*, and *mohel*. Bad health forced him to return to Baghdad after just a year. A few years later, Rabbi Shaul Yitzhak Meir Yaakov Elisha arrived from Baghdad to lead the congregation, teach, and perform other ritual functions. His son Yaakov-Faraj became a wealthy merchant in Rangoon and followed his father as religious leader of the Rangoon community.

Figure 1.1. Musmeah Yeshua Synagogue, interior. *Credit:* **Mark Simon**

In keeping with the impressive new synagogue, thick leather registries were started to record the births, deaths and marriages of this developing community. While there were certainly Jewish births in Burma during the previous half century, the earliest entry into the birth registry is the birth of Judah, son of Abraham Gavi Raphael Judah, and Chalah, born at Bassein, October 30, 1890, corresponding to 17 Heshvan 5651 (the date according to the Jewish calendar). Both sons and daughters were usually given biblical names; daughters might also be blessed with Hebrew names indicating happiness, such as Seemah or Simha (*simcha*, "rejoicing," pleasure, celebration), and Mozelle Tob or Fortune (*mazel tov*, good luck, good fortune). In keeping with Baghdadi Jewish tradition, the full name of the child indicated the family history through the male line: the new name was "attached" to the father's name, which itself might be a string of his grandparents' names without the words "son of" intervening. Thus Abraham Shalom Jacob Meyer Abraham Cohen indicated that the new child Abraham was the son of Shalom son of Jacob son of Meyer son of Abraham of the priestly tribe Cohen. If the child was named for someone who had died, the Hebrew name Hai or Hayeem ("life") was placed before the name to be memorialized: Ezekiel Hai Solomon Khadoori. The traditional names continued to be used in synagogue records even after, under British influence, family surnames were adopted. In British records, Mordecai Saul Reuben became Mordecai Saul, and his son, Ezra Mordecai Saul, Ezra Saul. Since it was a custom to name a child after a grandparent, and especially a living grandparent, names were often repeated: Isaac Ezekiel Isaac Solomon Benjamin. When under the British the list was shortened and the third name, the grandparent's name, became the surname, the result was an apparent double name: Saul Saul, David David, Aaron Aaron or Moses Moses. In the following decade, until the end of 1899, 116 births were registered, and this number apparently does not include all of those born in outlying areas such as Mandalay.

Musmeah Yeshua's Registries for the period 1880–1900 indicate the founders and most active members of the Jewish community in Burma during this period: Ezekiel Hai Solomon Khadoori, Abraham Shalom Jacob Meyer Abraham Cohen, Mordecai Hayeem Isaac Cohen, Joseph Isaac Joseph Said, Meyer Abraham Sofaer, Isaac Solomon Abraham Sofaer, Isaac Ezekiel Isaac Solomon Benjamin, Mordecai Hayeem Isaac Mordecai, Abraham Raphael, Menahem Hai Salah Sassoon, Jacob Meyer Abraham Shemuel, Saul Isaac Meyer, and Shlomo Rahamim Levi.[40]

When Judah Ezekiel came to Rangoon, he was employed by the British East India Company, and became quite prosperous and influential in the town. By the turn of the century, there was a street named for him, Judah Ezekiel Street, in the heart of Rangoon. Although he was one of the first Jews to settle in Burma, and obviously a man of great ability, Abraham Raphael's estranged brother Judah Ezekiel seems to have been well-known also for another distinction:

Letter to the Editor,[41]
The National Newspaper
Sir:
"Old Books in Burma" and the account about Mr. Judah Ezekiel have tended to awaken old memories. Those afflicted with my reminiscences suggest that since you responsible for this frame of mind, the affliction be extended to you, so far as it concerns Mr. Judah Ezekiel.

In my youth I often heard my father and other elders speak of the people of their time. Of Mr. Judah Ezekiel it was said that he was not only a wealthy man, but a well-respected citizen of Rangoon and a known philanthropist. It was stated that Judah Ezekiel Street was not named after him solely because he paid for the metalling of the road, but also because he took a very deep interest in the civic affairs of the Town.

I doubt if there is anyone living in Rangoon today who knew Mr. Judah Ezekiel but it was said that he was a big made man and enormously fat, and that when the *gharry-wallah* spotted him coming along a road, he would whip up his pony and stampede in the opposite direction, it being rumoured that he once went through the floor of a gharry and was extricated from his predicament, with great difficulty.
Yours, etc.
William T. Wilcox

Judah Ezekiel left nine rupees per month in his will for the cleaning of Judah Ezekiel Street.[42]

NOTES

1. Travel to Burma would have been by ship (2956 nautical miles), with stopovers in Calcutta for most.

2. Hunting was such an important British colonial pasttime that several books were written about it for the edification and guidance of "sportsmen." One such book, written by the fortuitously named George W. Bird, discusses twenty-seven potential targets: elephant, rhinoceros, tapir, wild hog, sambur, brown antlered deer, hog deer, barking deer, wild goat, bison, wild buffalo, wild cattle, gayal/mit-hun, sun bear, otter, wild dog, jackel, grey covet cat, common civet cat, binturoung/monkey tiger, tiger, leopard, leopard cat, jungle cat, gibbon, monkey, hare. *Wanderings in Burma*, 51.

3. Andrew Marshall, *The Trouser People*, 55.
4. Niall Ferguson, *Empire: How Britain Made the Modern World*, xxi.

5. Within limits. The British soon objected to, and attempted to curtail, the custom of *sati*, widow burning, in India. And, when the missionary movement reached its zenith in the mid-nineteenth century, further intrusions into native practices in India occurred.

6. Ferguson, *Empire*, 168.

7. Nathan Katz and Ellen S. Goldberg, The Last Jews in India and Burma, *Jerusalem Letter*, April 15, 1988, 6.

8. Nathan Katz, *The Last Jews of Cochin*, 114. Encyclopedia Judaica, nd, B: 1526.

9. Arnold Wright, *Twentieth Century Impressions of Burma*, 1910: 253.

10. 1987, 3: 1.

11. It may be that some Jews from Baghdad and Egypt were already present in Rangoon by the 1830s. The sources for this information, Nissim A. Meyer and Avraham Ben Yehuda, do not provide details or names. Yitzchak Kerem: "The History of Jewish Settlement in Burma in the 19th and 20th Centuries," 1.

12. Pronounced "ratanapon."

13. The name Mandalay is a derivative of two Pali words: "mandala," which means "a plains land," and "mandare," meaning "an auspicious land."

14. A silver Torah filial once in the Sir Isaac and Lady Wolfson Museum in Jerusalem suggests that there may have been a Jewish congregation already established in Mandalay at the time, but there is no substantiation for this. The filial may be incorrectly attributed to Mandalay. The filial is in the shape of a protective *hamsa*, a hand, and is inscribed with words stating that it is the gift of Miriam ben Joseph Isaac in honor of Rabbi Meir Baal ha-Ness.

15. Jorg Schendel, *Trade, Identity and Imperialism in Upper Burma*, 6–7.

16. King Thibaw's father had fed one thousand pigs. When he died, the pigs were released and, as the former king's property, were considered quasi-sacred. Marshall, 42–43.

17. Marshall, 40.

18. W. R. Winston, *Four Years in Upper Burma*, 1892: 38.

19. Gwendolen Trench Gascoigne, *Among Pagodas and Fair Ladies*, 1896: 139.

20. Frank Vincent, *The Land of the White Elephant*, 1873: 85.

21. Colesworth Grant, *Rough Pencillings of a Rough Trip to Rangoon, 1846*, 1853: 34.

22. *Religion and Politics in Burma*, 1965: 40.

23. 1966, x.

24. Malcolm Howard, *Travels in South-eastern Asia*, 1850: 364.

25. Jan Morris with Simon Winchester, *Stones of Empire: The Buildings of the Raj*, 57.

26. In 1883 eighty-three thousand Indian workers came to Burma; in the 1920s, as many as four hundred thousand came in a single year. E. Pendleton Banks, *The Tragic Paradox: Burmese Attitudes Toward India and Indians*, 5.

27. Arnold Wright, *Twentieth Century Impressions of Burma*, 1910: 255.

28. Anemia could be prevented, it seems, by "Dr. Williams' Pink Pills for Pale People." *Rangoon Gazette*, June 6, 1908: 35.

29. *Rangoon Gazette* July 17, 1905: 35.
30. *Rangoon Gazette* January 23, 1905: 23.
31. E. D. Cuming, *In the Shadow of the Pagoda; Sketches of Burmese Life and Character*, 1897: 3–5.
32. This was the grandfather of Ellis Joshua of London.
33. Gilbert Little Stark, *Letters of Gilbert Little Stark, July 23, 1907–March 12, 1908*, 1908: 383.
34. Yascha Malkhoo, personal correspondence.
35. It was at the Strand Hotel that Noel Coward was inspired to coin the famous phrase about "mad dogs and Englishmen." In one of his ditties he wrote: "The toughest Burmese bandit can never understand it. In Rangoon the heat of noon is just what the natives shun, they put their Scotch and rye down and lie down . . . but mad dogs and Englishmen go out in the midday sun." Andrews, "Tiffin Time Again," *The Irrawaddy Online Edition*, January 2006.
36. Wright, 295.
37. Wright, 353.
38. Wright, 356.
39. Wright, 191–92.
40. Moses Samuels and U Aung Kywe, *Musmeah Yeshua Synagogue and Jewish Community in Burma*, 1991: 8.
41. Postwar, no date.
42. Joseph Menasseh, great-grandson of Judah Ezekiel, personal communication.

Chapter Two

Beautiful Burmese Days

I was born in Rangoon at the time when the sun never set on the British Empire. Queen Victoria had died but three years earlier. Britain's greatness shone with brilliant splendour, and the Pax Britannica spread over us like a benign umbrella. It gave us comfort and stability, and it fostered the conviction that God was in his heaven, and all was right with the world.

In the environment into which I was born I was exposed to two cultures. There was the 'public' culture of the British presence, and then again there was the private culture of the Jewish family of which I was a member. This duality did not seem strange to me, quite the contrary. Around me I saw numerous ethnic groups similarly placed, behaving at times in the British tradition, and at others in accordance with their own cultural inheritance. Besides the Burmese, there were Moslems, Hindus, Parsees, Turks, Armenians, Chinese, and others. And there were, of course, Jews.[1]

So recalls Ellis Sofaer, who was born in 1904, eighteen years after Burma was incorporated as a province of India. It is more accurate to say that the Jews were in Burma, not of Burma, and that the simple duality of identification described by Ellis Sofaer was a bit more complicated. The community was in fact several sub-communities, differentiated by social status, religious interpretation, and history.

The Baghdadis defined community standards and controlled access to the primary means of validation of Jewish identity, the synagogue. They lived in close and comfortable society on Dalhousie, Merchant, Fraser, Tseekai Maung Taulay, Phayre, Baar, and Sparks Streets, Sandwith Road and the numbered streets in the heart of Rangoon, employing Bene Israel, Cochini Jews, and Hindustanis in their stores, and Hindustanis and Muslims in their homes. Jewish children mingled freely with all of the resident populations, and might have friends who were British, Chinese, Indian, and Burmese; Muslim, Christian, and Buddhist.

Through the years, the wealthiest families of Rangoon have included the Solomons, Meyers, and Sofaers, as well as Aslan Benjamin, A. J. Cohen, who became rich in the early 1920s by investing in rice shares, and Charles Joseph, who inherited the liquor business of his Chinese employer, Sing Ching Hing, in 1927. The wealthier Baghdadis had elegant second homes away from town on Halpin and Windsor Roads. Sofaer's Building at the corner of Merchant and Phayre Streets proclaimed the prominence of the family and of the Jews of Rangoon. The Governor-General of Burma officially opened the art nouveau building with a gold key; the bright green tiles brought especially from Manchester, England, still line the entrance. E. I. Cohen and Mordecai Hayim Isaac Cohen donated the ornate cast-iron bandstand close to the statue of Queen Victoria in Fytche Square Gardens (figure 2.1), where the cosmopolitan inhabitants of Rangoon came to hear the British Army Band; and visitors to the Victoria Memorial Park and Zoological Gardens, which had been formally opened in 1906 by the Prince and Princess of Wales, passed through gates donated by the Sofaer family.

In a rare memoir of this early period, lovingly written for his grandchildren, Ellis Sofaer of London provides an intimate view of life in Rangoon during the early days of the twentieth century:

> Although the Burmese were the indigenous people and most numerous, there was remarkably little contact between them and the circle in which I found myself. They were of course to be seen everywhere, clean and elegant, dressed in their brightly coloured sarongs (called *lungies* in this part of the world). The men wore silk scarves around their foreheads, and the women coiled their rich black hair into an almost sculpted mound on the tops of their heads, often decorating their coiffure with flowers. There was nevertheless an air of mystery about them, at least for us. One heard that up in Mandalay they had had a King, a shadowy figure called Thibaw; and one heard that they could with incantations

Figure 2.1. Moses Family, at Bandstand in Fytche Square Gardens, Rangoon, 1941. Courtesy of Esther Moses Solomon.

employ the dark Spirits to perform their wills. Except for my father, we never learnt the language of the Burmese, and the mystery and aloofness that hung around them may possibly have been a consequence of this.

There was a statue of an English General in the park in Rangoon. I remember my brother Abe, eight years my senior, pointing this out to me and saying "This is the man that won Burma." I learned from the encyclopedia that although the British occupied Southern Burma since before the middle of the nineteenth century, Thibaw was finally subjugated in 1885. Burma was then fully taken over as a colony and incorporated as a province of India. This was only eighteen years before I was born, a short period for an independent people to emerge from aloofness (if indeed they were aloof), and to adjust to subjugation.

Reference to the park brings to mind the lush green foliage to be seen in this tropical land. There was (as I remember) no dry season. There was a season when it rained less and another when it rained more. The sunshine was always brilliant. I remember too that at a certain time of the year, the tree we called Flame of the Forest burst into bloom. Its bright red flowers, abundant on the long branches, looked like cascades of fire.[2]

As a young child at home, Ellis Sofaer was dressed in Arabic style like his father, with wide trousers and a long-sleeved chemise covering his knees. Outside the home, he might wear a sailor suit or even a Lord Fauntleroy outfit of tussore silk. Throughout his life, however, Ellis's father Isaac continued to wear Arabic dress:

> . . . his undergarments were made (of) a high quality white longcloth. The trousers were wide-cut and came down to the ankles, and were held at the waist with a pyjama tape. Over this he wore a kind of chemise, rather like a caftan. It had long wide sleeves and a round-cut neck, and reached well below his knees. Over this again he wore a waistcoat of cotton poplin, held together by a set of gold buttons. A gold chain hung like a festoon from the lowest buttonhole to the left hand pocket of the waistcoat where he kept his watch. His cap, which he wore constantly, was of black velvet, gaily embroidered with flowers by my mother. His shoes and socks were black and conventional, and seemed an incongruous adjunct to his exotic dress, even to my childhood eyes. For dress wear at festival times, he wore over it all a long gabardine of satin or brocade.[3]

From his vantage point on the balcony, or the verandah as it was called, above his father's shop on Dalhousie Street (figure 2.2), the child Ellis peered at a rich and inviting world. To the right, the golden spire of the Sule Pagoda seemed to reach to the bright blue sky; in the distance, a small mosque could be seen, and at Chinese New Year, the sky was filled with hot air balloons. Made of paper stretched over a bamboo frame, with a wooden undercarriage wrapped in rags soaked with kerosene, the balloons were propelled by the hot air produced by lighting the rags. As exciting as these hot flashes in the sky

Figure 2.2. Sofaer Store, Dalhousie Street, 1905. Courtesy of Tuborg Brewery, Carlberg A/S.

were to a young child, they added to the danger of life in Rangoon. Fires were frequent in this city of wooden buildings, caused not only by the hot balloons but also by the kerosene lamps that lit many homes and shops.

In the evenings, Ellis could look down on the "night bazaar"—the vendors who filled the streets after the businesses closed. Flares lit the stalls that sold a tempting variety of foods: kebabs, *nan-roti* (naan bread) fresh from the griddle, soft drinks, sherbets, *powsies*—balls of ice drenched in fruity syrups. Soda water drinks were sold in special bottles which can still be found in some antique shops today: the bottle had a small glass ball in the neck and a rubber ring in a groove near the rim. When the bottle was full of soda, the gas pressure sealed in the contents by forcing the ball tightly against the rubber ring. Basic household equipment included a wooden opener for such bottles.

Most servants were Indian. Those who worked inside the house—the *borchies* or cooks; the *ayahs*, women who served as nannies or chambermaids; and the "boys," house boys—were Muslim: Hindus would not handle meat in the kitchen, while Muslims, who observe the dietary laws of *hallah*, understood the rudiments of the Jewish dietary laws, *kashrut*. Those who performed duties outside the house might be Hindu or Muslim. These included the *mali*, gardener; the *cutchwan*, coachman; or the *syce*, stableboy. Since automobiles were rare in early twentieth century Burma, so were "drivers," chauffeurs. More commonly, one hired a rickshaw for short trips or, for longer journeys, a *tikka gharry*, a four-seater box-shaped carriage. The *tikka gharry* rattled along on iron tired wheels, drawn by a single, usually skinny horse.

The *borchies* cooked on brick stoves with steel rods imbedded as grates. Homes had cold water only, which was used for cleaning purposes. Drinking water was provided by a *bhisti*, who came several times a day with a goatskin filled with water. This water was stored in receptacles in the kitchen, boiled before drinking, and stored in earthenware jars. Given the warm climate of Burma, cold baths usually sufficed, but if a warm bath was desired, the water was heated in the kitchen in a galvanized bucket and carried to the bathroom. Bathrooms had a drain in one corner, which collected the water poured by cup over the bather. The toilet was cleaned by the "sweeper" or *methar*, a member of a caste of Indian Untouchables, who came three or four times a day to keep the toilet clean and to sweep the floors each morning. A *dhobi*, a washerman, collected the soiled clothes each week, and returned them a week later.

The "suburbs" of commercial Rangoon was the verdant area known as The Lakes, only eight miles away but seemingly far removed from the city's closely packed residential streets. Those who could afford it built private villas in The Lakes, many as weekend retreats. The Sofaers' weekend home, the Garden House, was modest compared to the palatial house of their cousin, Sassoon Solomon, at 18 Halpin Road, with its marble floors, interior marble staircase, and spacious, landscaped grounds, concrete tennis court, stables, and private artesian well. If the home was visited only for a day or a weekend, full meals were cooked at home and packed for the journey. On these special outings, banana leaves, "wide and green, and like satin to the touch,"[4] served as plates, and fingers replaced spoons and forks — a rare treat.

As luxurious as the Sassoon Solomon home was, it did not offer the extraordinary experience that Dawn Swift remembers on the estate of Abraham and Ramah Cohen, at 26A Wingaaba Road: a large zoo, complete with wild cats and large animals. The animals were held there before being exported throughout the world. Dawn recalls riding a baby elephant up the marble front steps of the house.

Most people, of course, did not own mansions nor enjoy the luxuries of the Solomon, Sofaer, and Cohen families, but lived instead in small apartments close to the synagogue. Daily life for the other Jews of Rangoon in the 1920s is recalled by Abraham Shalom Judah:

> During the early years we lived in a two bedroom flat on Sparks Street. One bedroom was my parents' bedroom, and the other was occupied by my eldest sister with her husband. My mother had five daughters and one son (me). The rest of

us would roll out our bedding on the floor of the sitting room, where we slept and each morning it was rolled up again.[5]

THE CHARITABLE CONNECTION

As in Jewish life in general, charitable giving, *tzedakah*—righteousness, social justice—was an important aspect of Baghdadi society. Through the act of giving, the Baghdadis not only fulfilled their religious obligations, but also maintained actual and symbolic communication with their past and with other parts of the Baghdadi diaspora. When the new Musmeah Yeshua was constructed, a charitable organization, Achei Sameach, was established to raise money for the needs of the local community. Emissaries—*shlihim*—from Baghdad or Palestine facilitated the connection to ideals and institutions abroad. Through these emissaries, the Jews of Rangoon supported such institutions as the yeshiva by the grave of Ezra the Sofer (scribe) in the village of Azir near Basra, the Midrash Talmud Torah in Baghdad, the Hevrat Nesuin of Baghdad led by Haham Rabi Salah ben Rabi Abdallah Somekh. After the 1941 Farhud anti-Jewish riots a Baghdadi Jew from Rangoon contributed a large sum to support community institutions in Baghdad.[6]

Emissaries, especially from Jerusalem, appear to have been a regular part of the Rangoon scene and tapped into the Baghdadis strong religious beliefs. In 1861, Rabbi Yaakov Sapir visited Rangoon and Moulmein, and noted the Baghdadis' deep devotion to Jerusalem.[7] In 1881, the community met and set a limit on the amount of money that each *shaliach* from Jerusalem would receive: twenty-five rupees for the institution he represented, and another fifteen rupees for his own use.[8] On September 21, 1888, the *Jewish Chronicle* of London reported that

> The new Jewish congregation at Mandalay has given evidence of its existence in a manner common in the East. Learning that there was in Calcutta a messenger from Aleppo who was collecting funds in aid of the Talmud Torah schools in his town, the Mandalay congregation sent a contribution for this object.[9]

In the early 1920s, Israel Cohen, a Zionist emissary from Europe, visited Rangoon while on mission throughout Southeast Asia. His journal affords a rare, outsider's observation of the Rangoon community of the time, even as it reveals the author's own somewhat jaundiced reflections on his experience.[10] On his dawn arrival in Rangoon from Penang aboard the *Ekma*, he was met at the wharf by the president of the Jewish community, A. J. Cohen, and Meyer Meyer, who hosted him during his visit. He describes the Meyer house as "palatial," with extensive gardens, including a small farmyard with cows and poultry for the household's consumption, and looked after by thirty-six Burmese servants, "but their vigilance was of dubious value, as some of the denizens of the farmyard regularly strayed to other domains and were never recovered."[11] The next day he met with the community, either in their places of business or in the synagogue, and remarked that,

> They have the unique distinction of possessing an endowed synagogue . . . which is maintained out of the rents derived from the adjacent shops, so that public worship is gratuitous, though hardly more popular on that account. Indeed, there is a disadvantage in this arrangement, as the community has only a Hazan to conduct its prayers and no Haham to expound their meaning—a deficiency that is bound to affect its spiritual welfare. It also has a day school, built about 1910 and attended by 140 children, which receives a Government subvention even larger than the amount contributed by the community.[12]

Israel Cohen also visited the glorious Shwedagon Pagoda. In his memoirs, Ellis Sofaer describes his wondrous visit to the Pagoda with his father, but the experience was more annoying than wondrous to Cohen. He was obviously distressed by having to remove his shoes to visit the shrine, and by being jostled by the crowds of children, dogs, beggars and crippled that "infested" the place. Still, his description does evoke the world inhabited by the Jews of the time, as well as the atmosphere at the Shwedagon Pagoda to this day:

> The stairs were flanked on either side with little stalls and shops, at which were sold flowers and fruit, cigars and chocolates, picture postcards, pictures of Buddha and sacrificial tapers. . . . The Pagoda itself is a very large and lofty bell-shaped structure, thickly overlaid with gilt, which shone resplendent in the sun. Around it ran a wide circular promenade, which was bordered on both sides by all kinds of smaller picturesque shrines, some of carved wood, others containing white-painted Buddhas, and some a Buddha twenty-five feet high, whilst within them were many worshippers, especially women, wither kneeling or prostrate, with flowers and lighted tapers in their hands. . . . [13]

As strange and exotic as Rangoon seemed to him so he apparently appeared to the Jews whom he met later in the day in the synagogue. They

> gazed at me with open-eyed curiosity. It was composed entirely of men and boys, many of them wearing white baggy trousers and embroidered round caps, and one or two the flowing white garb and scarlet waistband of Baghdad. . . . I spoke from the little platform before the Ark and was listened to with close attention, but in the middle of my address one of the wealthiest members of the congregation went out to keep an appointment and was followed soon

afterwards by another rich member, so that my hopes of a golden harvest began to dwindle. . . .[14]

But his mission was successful after all. Guided by a Mr. Menasseh, he made the rounds of the most affluent Jews of Rangoon, in order of their reputed wealth. His first stop was Sassoon E. Solomon, who contributed three thousand rupees. His guide helped him with the unfamiliar customs of Baghdadis:

> When a sympathizer wrote down on the list "100," (Mr. Menasseh) immediately prompted him: "Make it 101 for luck!"—a suggestion that was readily complied with: for the numerical values of that Hebrew phrase, "Who is like unto the Lord?" amounts to 101, and the giver of this sum believes that, like the quality of mercy, it blesseth him that gives and him that receives.[15]

Israel Cohen encountered an assortment of Ashkenazic Jews living in Rangoon at the time: two men from London, one married to a Burmese woman, the other to a Japanese woman; a Swedish merchant, resident in Alexandria, who was traveling between Singapore and Sumatra; and some Anglo-Jewish bookmakers who traveled regularly between London and Rangoon. Apparently satisfied by the financial success of his stay in Rangoon, Isaac Cohen stepped onto a sampan to be rowed back to his ship to travel to his next stop, Calcutta. As he endured the turbulent Irrawaddy waters, he looked back on Rangoon as it receded from view:

> The sun had set suddenly, and all around me the black waters rushed along with irresistible force, swollen with menace and fury, whilst the gloomy forms of the river-craft, with their phantom lights, flitted past. . . . A couple of hours later . . . I leaned over the side of the (ship) and gazed at the illuminated pagodas which filled the sky with a blaze of glory. . . .[16]

COSMOPOLITAN RANGOON

Despite living amid illuminated pagodas, the Jews and the cosmopolitan community of Rangoon were very much part of the Western world, with the added advantage—for the fortunate—of beautiful items from Burma and China (figure 2.3). Chinese peddlers brought tablecloths, silk kimonos, and lacquerware to the door. "We had such beautiful things: rubies, jade, mahogany furniture made by the Chinese, tablecloths, silk kimonos, lacquerware," recalled Flora Judah Jacobs. "Each girl had her own set of silver-clad combs." Business was prospering and news of the world was up-to-date. Sofaer's Building housed several commercial offices; Manook and Cohen, 106

Figure 2.3. Anna Sofaer and Her Dolls, Rangoon, 1902. Courtesy of Ruth Sofaer.

Dalhousie Street, claimed to sell the best liquor. E. Solomon and Sons advertised Edsol's Vacuum Teapot—the new marvel of technical science: "Beautiful things soothe the mind and quicken the imagination and stimulate joy in living, and the EDSOL Teapot will assist in the realisation of all these desires."[17] All comforts of living available in Britain were also to be had in Rangoon. The Maison Continental on Sule Pagoda Road and the Vienna Cafe on Phayre Street, and in Maymyo, served continental food. The *Rangoon Exchange Gazette* informed these distant Englishmen and almost-Englishmen that Iraq had been bombed,[18] that the Prince of Wales broke his collarbone,[19] and that Woodrow Wilson had died.[20] The *Rangoon Exchange Gazette* advertised the latest movies playing at the Excelsior, Olympian, Majestic and Globe theaters: *Passion*, with Pola Negri as Madame DuBarry; *Buffalo Bill*, and features with Mack Sennet.[21]

One could even bet on the Irish Sweepstakes in far-off Rangoon. In 1930, Jonah Cohen sold the winning ticket to brothers Asher and Darhood Isaac. Despite Cohen's claim that he was owed a share of the winnings, the brothers promptly took their million pounds, sold their shops, and departed for Palestine.

In the mid-1930s, the branch of David Sassoon & Co. based in Hong Kong switched its trade in rice from Saigon to Rangoon, upgrading its long-term relationship with Burma rice-exporter Blackwood, Ralli. In so doing, it established a virtual trade monopoly in that commodity. The trade through Rangoon was monitored by cable from Hong Kong, and no actual office was established in Burma.

Somewhat apart from the commercial center of Rangoon a Magen David can be spotted high on a wall of an old building. This was once the American Ice Factory Company, established in the 1920s by Haskel and Ephraim Solomon, with equipment imported from the United States. The brothers became very prosperous by providing 120 pound slabs of ice to many parts of Burma. Because it was a wholly Jewish firm, the Solomons felt free to put the Star of David proudly on its upper wall.[22] The factory was abandoned at the time of World War II.

THE RANGOON "DIASPORA"

Alone, as in Akyab, or with one or two other families, Jews were scattered in large and small towns throughout Burma. Yenangyaung, on the Irrawaddy River between Mandalay and Rangoon, was the home of several Jewish families in 1910: Saul Aaron ran a hardware store; Hardon Agasie a wine and provisions store, and Ezekiel Zion Battat and his wife Sally Namoordy owned the American stores, selling "American" goods and exporting tropical fruits. Jewish merchants and traders lived also in Toungoo, Yandon, Maymyo, Moulmein, Mergui-Tavoy, and Thayetmyo, where there was a small cemetery.[23] In the important rice-exporting delta city of Bassein, the Raphael family prospered as furniture merchants and auctioneers, and as providers of power, ice and general provisions. The Raphael family, along with the business's Jewish employees and two other families, lived a ritually correct Jewish life amid the friendly but socially and religiously distinct populations. They established a cemetery and a prayer hall; brought a *shochet*, a *shamash*, and a *mohel* to Bassein; and ensured Jewish continuity through their children by bringing in instructors of Hebrew and Talmud. Although it might seem that the Jews of the delta were far away from family and friends, in fact it was relatively easy for them to maintain contact with their relatives: the busy river traffic from Rangoon and Mandalay to Bassein carried freight, mail and passengers. Several times a week, steamers between Rangoon and Bassein enabled the Raphaels to be part of the social and religious life of the capital city. The British presence, including several missionary societies, was well established in Bassein. During the 1930s, R. A. Raphael, M. B. E., K. i. H.[24] was Mayor of Bassein. "These honors were bestowed on him by His Majesties King George V and King George VI of England for his good services before

World War II. My uncle also belonged to the Masonic Palm Lodge in Bassein," recalls Margaret Raphael Glicksohn.[25]

In Mandalay, Mordecai Saul's two sons David and Ezra and their families formed the core of the Mandalay Jewish community, which eventually included approximately thirty adults and forty children. Ezra Saul and his wife Mozelle Aaron Saul and their seven children eventually settled across from the large Anglican Church on Cathedral Street. Ezra's elder brother David, his wife Sally, and six children occupied a two-story home on Civil Lanes.

The Saul family was intricately related by marriage to the Solomon and Sassoon families of Rangoon—and many of the other families in Burma—as sisters of one family married brothers of another, and cousins married cousins throughout the generations. Such intricate relationships stretched back generations. A hint of how this played out is provided by Geoff Saul:

> Auntie Tobah seems to be pivotal to the three great families of this narrative, the Sassoon family, the Solomon family and the Saul family. Auntie Tobah is Mozelle, daughter of Ezekiel Ezra Sassoon patriarch of the Sassoon family. When she was about fourteen she married Ezekiel Isaac Solomon, patriarch of the Solomon family. There is some circumstantial evidence that Ezekiel Ezra Sassoon was a cousin of Saul Reuben Hakham Rabbi Sassoon, patriarch of the Saul family. However, Auntie Tobah's relationship to the Saul family became more direct when Auntie Tobah's sister, Seemah, married Mordecai Saul, son of the Saul family patriarch. The relationship was further cemented when Auntie Tobah's sons, Kelly and Saul Solomon married Seemah and Mordecai's daughters, Mozelle and Sally Saul. Finally, Auntie Tobah's granddaughter, Mozelle David Hai Aaron, married Seemah and Mordecai's son, Ezra Saul.[26]

The relations get even more complicated when the marriages of all the children of all the large families are considered. For instance, the daughter of Ezekiel Isaac Solomon's first marriage was Ramah, who married Isaac Abraham Sofaer. The Sofaers, therefore, were also part of the Sauls' extended family. Many years later, Isaac and Ramah's son Ellis wrote the memoirs quoted in this book.

A traditional, Orthodox Jewish community has many essential requirements, and like the Raphaels in Bassein, the Saul families built such a community among the Burmese in Mandalay. A cemetery area was consecrated which would eventually hold twelve graves.[27] Since the boys attended St. Peter's High School and the girls studied at St. Joseph's Convent School, a tutor, Mr. Howard, and his wife were brought from Rangoon to teach them Hebrew six evenings a week. Each Shabbat, each festival and holiday, religious services were conducted by David and Ezra Saul in the prayer hall they built less than ten minutes from their homes. Three Torahs, each one glorious in its solid silver and gold-clad wooden case, or *tiq*, rested in the Ark on High Holy Days. The cases had been crafted in Simla, India, by a silversmith on appointment to Lord Redding, the Viceroy of India.[28] The scrolls themselves were brought from the Holy Land. One Torah was dedicated to Ezra and David's father Mordecai; another to their grandmother Simha; the third to their younger brother, Moses. For safekeeping, the Mandalay Torahs were kept in the synagogue in Rangoon and brought by train to Mandalay for Rosh Hashanah and Yom Kippur. At this time, David Saul would blow the *shofar*, the ram's horn, in the prayer hall.

The prayer hall had additional requirements: a caretaker, *shamash*, and members of the priestly castes of Judaism, the *Kohanim*, who take precedence during the reading of the Torah. Accordingly, the Sauls brought *Kohanim* to Mandalay, as well as a *shamash* from India. The teacher and the *shamash*, known as Yakoob-Shamash, received support and housing from Ezra Saul.

As the business prospered, Ezra Saul's home expanded to become a compound, with a separate "bachelors quarters" that included a magnificent library—a large room under the stairway with lights and floor-to-ceiling shelves and well-indexed books. In elegance, the home was comparable to the finest of European homes in Burma in the early twentieth century. According to Saul Ezra Saul's son David,

> ... My grandparents' home was large but not ostentatious. It consisted of two stories and contained airy, uncluttered living rooms of polished wood with Persian rugs over marble floors. The children all lived upstairs until puberty, when the boys were separated from the girls and moved to "bachelor quarters" behind the kitchen and near the badminton court.
>
> There was no shortage of staff in the household. The children were allocated servants to look after them; the girls had individual *ayahs* and the boys had bearers, with these servants conveniently named after the children for accurate identification. Grandpa Ezra had his own special bearer ("Dad's bearer") who was paid thirty rupees a month and saw to his every personal need; which apart from the usual valeting duties of starching shirts and polishing shoes, included towel-drying and powdering after his master's daily bath. There was a head cook, usually an Indian, who was sacked regularly if the food was too oily; a *masalchi*, whose only duties were to chop, peel and clean vegetables in readiness for the head cook; an inside sweeper who continuously swept and washed the marble floors inside the house; an outside sweeper whose domain was confined to the grounds around the house which were concreted and paved, since Grandpa Ezra loathed grass; a table boy, being a middle-aged man who served the daily meals; a *dhobi* who hand-washed the family's clothes; a *dharawan*, usually a burly Gurkha, who patrolled outside the high walls of the house carrying a wooden staff which, at the first hint of trouble, would be propelled at high speed with the

fingers of one hand and could inflict serious damage to any unfortunate and unwelcome intruder; a gardener, whose responsibility was to water the hundreds of flower pots which surrounded the house (since there was no garden), and the commode man who had the most unenviable of all the various household duties, until Grandfather finally installed ensuite bathrooms in every bedroom. There were of course numerous untitled staff who "assisted" the other staff in a variety of unspecified duties.[29]

While Ezra Saul's home was luxurious and functional, his brother David Saul's home was formal and elegant, especially at dinnertime—even if in retrospect amusingly inconsistent with reality. According to David G. Saul:

Great Aunt Sally insisted on wearing white gloves when dining at home, which was every evening. The teak dining room table was always set at 6:45 p.m., on her instructions, with a starched white table cloth and freshly laundered napkins (initialed), china crockery, crystal glasses for both red and white wine (which were used to drink distilled water only, since she forbade alcohol in the house) and the day's menu, carefully scripted in her copperplate hand in black ink on thick white parchment, supported by her mother's silver candlestick holders at the table's centre. The menus, although prepared and written afresh each morning, never varied, and consisted of clear vegetable soup, roast beef with baked potatoes and apple pie with cream. The table was attended by two servants, both Indian, who wore full livery (also with white gloves, as Great Aunt Sally feared infection) and each of the children, all of whom were under the age of ten, wore evening dress; full length dresses for the girls and tuxedos for the boys. Great Uncle David, a mild man who is best remembered as never having fought with another living creature, least of all with Great Aunt Sally, endured this nightly ritual with his customary good humour and calm disposition, sitting uncomfortably in his starched wing collar, bow tie, spats and tails. In Mandalay, with temperatures constantly in the high thirties, and the barometer dripping with humidity, dining in this manner required great fortitude and discipline, despite the large *punkah* fans swaying gently overhead (which only recirculated the existing air), since Great Aunt Sally feared open windows and doors "in case of infection."

... Great Uncle David never failed to compliment Great Aunt Sally's choice of menu at the conclusion of each meal, though he secretly and thoroughly detested vegetable soup, found roast dinners too bland and indigestible, and had no tooth for anything remotely sweet. His tastebuds, from the age of eight months, until he was married at twenty-six, were more accustomed to, and craved for, fiery mutton curries, spicy eggplant *bhajis* and saffron rice fried with onions, cardamom pods and cloves.[30]

As in Rangoon, music was an ever-present part of life in Mandalay. Sons received violin lessons, and daughters learned the piano. The talented Mandalay cousins were enthusiastic amateurs who enjoyed making music and singing together. Each week, after Shabbat, David Saul's sons Maurice, Eddie and Arnold would join their cousins, the children of Ezra Saul, for a musical evening. An excellent pianist, Ezra Saul's daughter Seemah played regularly at the concerts at St. Joseph's Convent School.

By 1910, the family's aerated water factory, David and Ezra Bros., distributed over five hundred bottles a day, and soon after their ice factories in Mandalay and Rangoon were supplying ice to most of Upper Burma and the hill stations as well as to Lower Burma. Each hundred pound block of ice was placed in a hessian bag and stuffed tightly with saw dust, which preserved it for the long trip overland or by boat. The Sauls also had factories to process matches and rice. The children spoke Burmese or English with their Burmese, Muslim, Indian and Anglo-Indian friends. Together they wandered the streets of Mandalay and the Zeyjo Bazaar, and watched the boats on the Irrawaddy being unloaded by bare-chested workers, piling bundles on their heads, one after another. As they walked the countryside, they passed clay vessels of water and mugs standing outside the doors of Burmese homes, offering refreshment to travelers passing by. Yellow *thanakha*[31] colored the faces of the Burmese women they met, and bullock carts lumbered along the roads. The closed world of Jewish orthodoxy in Mandalay coexisted comfortably with the church across from the Sauls' homes, and opened its doors easily to the red-robed *pongyis*, the Buddhist monks, who came each morning with their golden bowls for donations of food. Water pots still wait outside of homes, women still draw *thanakha* designs on their cheeks and foreheads, and *pongyis* still roam the roads of Myanmar, suggesting a timelessness that belies political events that cast the Sauls and others from their homes.

As a young man, in the late thirties, Saul Ezra Saul obtained a contract to administer and service the railway refreshment rooms in twenty-one railway stations throughout Burma. For six weeks twice a year, he and his wife traveled the country in their own white railway carriages attached to the end of the train, stopping in all parts of Burma.

It is interesting to contrast the way of life of the Jews and the other European populations of Burma with that of the Burmese among whom they lived. While the Sauls were wearing fashions from Europe, traveling by automobile, and eating roast beef, the Burmese and tribal peoples such as the Padaung and Pa-o a bit farther away lived as they had for centuries, tilling the soil or hunting small game, wearing traditional dress, appeasing the Nats, drinking rice wine, and eating baby wasps, beetles, bats, snakes, anteaters, boar and bear.[32] Writing in 1968, Manning Nash observed:

> One feature of the sixty-odd years of British rule in Upper Burma, remarkable in retrospect, is the small impact the modern world made there. No revolution

of agricultural technique, no influx of machines, no burst of industry, no greatly widened mental horizons came in the wake of the British. The Burmese villager was as isolated as ever, in daily life, from the modern world.[33]

Some four decades later, another government, now Burmese, purposely keeps the Burmese villager similarly isolated: trade with China brings more material goods and more homes have electricity, but contact with the outside world is very controlled. For better or worse, the traditional way of life endures in this very beautiful land.

NOTES

1. Ellis Sofaer, *Gaya: His Childhood*, I, 1.
2. Sofaer, I, 1–2.
3. Sofaer I, 3–4.
4. Sofaer IV, 4.
5. Letter, August 9, 1993.
6. Kerem, 2.
7. Kerem, 1.
8. In 1880, Rabbi Yosef Mordechai Meyhuas visited from Jerusalem; in 1894, the Shaddar Rabbi Faraj Haim Ben Rabi Shlomo Yehezkiel and Rabbi Refael Ohana came. Kerem, 1.
9. Cowen, 181.
10. Isaac Cohen, *The Journal of a Jewish Traveller*, 223–30.
11. Cohen, 223.
12. Cohen, 224.
13. Cohen, 224.
14. Cohen, 225.
15. Cohen, 226.
16. Cohen, 230.
17. *Rangoon Gazette*, February 1, 1924, 1–2.
18. *Rangoon Gazette*, February 2, 1924, 11.
19. *Rangoon Gazette*, February 9, 1924, 1.
20. *Rangoon Gazette*, February 5, 1924, 11.
21. November 2, 1923, 1.
22. A keen horse racer, Ephraim Solomon's fortune increased when his horse, the Kaikesen Queen, won the Governor's Cup in 1938.
23. *Universal Jewish Encyclopedia*, 1911, 605.
24. MBE—Member of the Order of the British Empire, an award created by King George V in 1917 to reward individuals domestically as well as throughout the Empire who had contributed to winning World War I. K.i.H.—Kaisar-i-Hind Medal for Public Service in India.
25. Personal communication.
26. Geoffrey Saul, *The Road to Mandalay*, 4.

27. The graves have been demolished as a result of redevelopment plans by the city government. Among the graves lost in Mandalay were those of Mozelle Saul's father, Ezra and Mozelle's younger son, and Ezra Saul's younger brother.

28. Lord Redding was Jewish; Rufus Daniel Rufus Isaac, the Marquess of Reading. This is the highest rank in the Peerage achieved by a Jew in British history. *Wikipedia.*

29. Geoffrey Saul, 15.

30. Geoffrey Saul, 17.

31. *Thanakha* is a sandalwood powder, ground on a stone, which is used as a cosmetic and to protect the skin against the sun. It may be applied simply in circles on the cheeks and forehead or in creative design patterns.

32. Pascal Khoo Thwe, *From the Land of Green Ghosts*, 22.

33. Manning Nash, *The Golden Road to Modernity*, 5.

Chapter Three

Three Cheers for the King and the British Empire

To escape the heat and mugginess of Burma, and to still the nostalgia for England, the British created a series of cool retreats in the hills and mountains of Southeast Asia. These bits of England—Simla, Darjeeling, Kalimpong, Musoorie, Madhupur, Poona, and similar retreats—were a respite where English manners, English society, and even an English landscape dominated and allayed the sense of being in a foreign land. One went up, as it were, to a purer place, ordered, civilized, British. Indeed, the hill stations had an almost mythic quality, or so it would seem from the following advertisement for a new hill station, which appeared in the *Rangoon Gazette* in January 1905:

> Who does not wish for the Elixer of Life? . . . Come to Ngwe Long, where the air is the pure breath of heaven and the water like champagne 'bien frappe.' Before you have been here a week you will feel younger, better, the world brighter, and heaven nearer.[1]

In Burma, the premier hill station was Maymyo,[2] just north of Mandalay in the Northern Shan States. Maymyo had a special place in the lives of some of the Jews in Burma. Religious holidays meant gatherings in Rangoon with families from all over Burma; other times away from work or school might be spent with relatives in Calcutta. But a trip to Maymyo was different: it was a move to a different land, a different climate; it was immersion into another world. The writer George Orwell, who served for five years with the British Imperial Police in Burma, recalled the passage to Maymyo:

> From Mandalay, in Upper Burma, you can travel by train to Maymyo, the principal hill-station of the province, on the edge of the Shan plateau. It is rather a queer experience. You start off in the typical atmosphere of an eastern city—the scorching sunlight, the dusty palms, the smells of fish and spices and garlic, the

squashy tropical fruits, the swarming dark-faced human beings—and because you are so used to it you carry this atmosphere intact, so to speak, in your railway carriage. Mentally you are still in Mandalay when the train stops at Maymyo, four thousand feet above sea-level. But in stepping out of the carriage, you step into a different hemisphere. Suddenly, you are breathing cool sweet air that might be that of England, and all round you are green grass, bracken, fir trees, and hill-women with pink cheeks selling baskets of strawberries.[3]

On cool, damp days, amid the fir trees, Maymyo smells especially like England, and people remained warm before the fireplaces in their brick homes as the quick-moving fog closed in.

With its broad streets and large estates lined with poplars, pines, oaks, chestnuts, and rhododendrons, Maymyo was "paradise," to Saul Ezra Saul, whose family frequently drove up the hills to Maymyo from their home in Mandalay. Their journey took them by the fields of chrysanthemums that decorate pagodas throughout Burma, and past poinsettias that grow wild by the roadside. Large, juicy pineapples lined the road at the entrance to the town, which was "clean and beautiful," with fresh, cool air and homes with fruit trees—plum, peach, apple, orange.[4] As the British "summer capital" in Burma, Maymyo had—still has—English-style red brick Tudor homes, a golf course, a polo ground, tennis courts, private clubs, missionary schools, a beautiful lake and a lovely botanical garden. On Sundays, in an open-air market, the Shan came to sell vegetables, fruits and sweets. Although no longer owned by the Sauls, their home in Maymyo, called Floren Villa after the youngest daughter in the family, still stands on Circular Road, close-by the grand British hotel, the Candacraig, which was built in 1905 by the Bombay Burma Trading Company.[5] It was in Maymyo that cousins Ezra Solomon and Saul Ezra Saul began a life-long friendship that continued well after the former was established in Palo Alto and his friend in Sydney.

As in the hill stations of Vietnam and the Philippines, there was a military academy in Maymyo, which was occupied by the Scottish Black Watch and the British Manchester Rifles. From the age of fifteen, for three months a year, Saul Ezra Saul trained with the regiments. Despite his parents' initial objections to his infatuation with the military, Saul was commissioned into the British Army at the age of eighteen. This was a rare step for a Jewish man at the time. Indeed, few Jewish officers were found in the British army since the officer corps as a whole was very anti-Semitic. Lord Baden-Powell, who had served as a soldier in Africa and India before founding the Boy Scouts, once remarked that he could not blame the younger officers, who

> cannot help feeling that the average Jew who comes into the service does not do so for love of soldiering so much as to gain position in society. (Jews without

money do not join the army.) . . . A Jew is as a rule not an English gentleman and very often not even an English public school man—so he cannot well amalgamate.[6]

But Saul Ezra Saul did "amalgamate," and served as an officer in the British Army until the end of World War II.

Kalaw, three thousand feet in altitude and seventy kilometers west of Taunggyi in the Southern Shan States, was another, more tranquil hill station where Jews joined the other "European" populations to breathe the cool air and hike amid gnarled pines, bamboo groves and rugged mountain scenery. Kalaw was less fashionable than Maymyo, especially for the class-conscious British, but roses and fruit trees were abundant, and the natural lakes, with crystal clear water, were beautiful. Saul Ezra Saul's uncle David had one of the homes scattered through the area, set amid large gardens, and the family spent many happy days there.

THREE GOLDEN LANDS; TWO PROMISED LANDS

For the Baghdadis, the British and Jewish dimensions of identity were all that mattered; the Burmese context was irrelevant to the realization of who they were and who they could be. Despite generations in a land often called "golden" because of its brilliant golden pagodas and countless gilded Buddhas,[7] this actual home had less power over Baghdadi minds and souls than the ideal homes in which they also lived: Jerusalem and the British Empire. Jews and British alike envisioned a distant home in myth-like terms: the Jews conceived of the Promised Land as Jerusalem of gold, where the sunlight coming from the East over the Temple Mount suggested God's presence; the British visualized their vast empire ever shining in the golden light of the sun. The concept found words in 1743 when Sir George Macartney wrote of "this vast empire on which the sun never sets and whose bounds nature has not yet ascertained."[8] In recalling his childhood, historian Niall Ferguson says simply, "To the Scots, the Empire stood for the bright sunlight."[9]

For the Baghdadis, these two ideal worlds were easily reconciled. Jewish law and the Hebrew language reinforce the realization of Jewish identity as inherently international and eternal. The international language and apparently enduring and desirable culture of the British Empire seemed compatible with this essential Jewish identification. The English, as well as the Jews, were aliens in Burma, and interacted with the local population only when necessary for the transactions of business and daily life. The Burmese language they learned at school was rarely needed: they spoke Hindustani to the servants,

English in school, Arabic to their parents (especially during the early years), and Hebrew in synagogue.

For the Jews in Burma, Hebrew was the intimate language of religion, home and heritage and English the language of passport and political future, as well as the language of an elusive ideal. Although they turned their face toward England, this was a land they never actually experienced, a promised home presented through the paradox of only partially opened doors. Yet together, English and Hebrew formed a comforting cocoon around the Baghdadi Jews in their Burmese home.

While the two languages were essential for each Jewish child, there was a different emphasis on the need to understand the culture represented by the language. It was necessary to be able to read Hebrew in order to take one's place in the synagogue, but there was little stress on understanding the meaning of the words or the history and heritage they embodied. Judaism became a "natural," indelible state of being born into a Jewish family. The compelling, proud memories of Baghdadi history and tradition, so operative in the first generation in Burma, became anemic in the second generation: devoid of meaning other than the immediate emotional connection to family and community, for many—though not all—the Baghdadi tradition lost much of its power to compel when the community was torn apart. The English language and an English education, on the other hand, were keys to a seemingly glorious future, an identification with an illustrious history, as well as a political necessity. The Baghdadis were adopting the British narrative, writing themselves into British history—if not in the notes of the past certainly, it seemed, in the accounts of the future. A child of the second generation in Burma, Ellis Sofaer recalls:

> In common with countless generations of Jewish children, these (religious) influences operated on me. I can remember the pride I felt at quite an early age in belonging to 'God's chosen people,' even though at the time I had already begun to disobey the ordinances of community life. The taboos designed to secure the absolute sanctity of the Sabbath had little effect on my actions . . . The grown-ups who had care of me could not have thought my deviations very serious, for I cannot remember ever being chastised for them. . . .
>
> The influence of British culture was more direct. Everything we did at school was tilted in that direction. We were taught English as if it was our mother tongue, irrespective of our origins. The teachers were English, and the lessons were based on the lessons taught in schools in England. We played cricket and football. We joined the Scouts. Our characters were developed with canings and Latin impositions. We were shown proof of Britain's greatness on world maps, where the areas in pink, signifying British-owned territories, outspread all others. The effect of an upbringing in the glow of the effulgent glory remains with

me today, undiminished by Britain's adumbration. It has made England in my eyes a better country than any other in the world.[10]

This duality of identification and aloofness from the context in which they lived marked the diaspora experience for Baghdadis throughout Southeast Asia. It is easy to understand the similarity of community patterns and orientation when comparing life in Rangoon with life across the Bay of Bengal in Calcutta or even in Bombay, but it is even more revealing when considering experience in a vastly different context, China. Close to two thousand miles away, in prewar Shanghai, Rebecca Toueg inhabited the same world as the Jews of Rangoon:

> (We) lived, one might say, a double life—inside the home there was the warmth of oriental customs and loyal family ties. My grandmother never spoke English, and knew only Iraqi Arabic, so that I was forced to speak it in spite of my terrible anglicized accent. She dressed and comported herself in the traditional Baghdadian manner. . . .
> Shanghai was a city of tremendous opportunities, an international city open and free to all who wished to come there and make their fortunes. The Babylonian Jews took full advantage of this and were extremely successful. . . . One could see (in the Shanghai Jewish newspaper) the close ties maintained among the Babylonian communities in the Far East. Learned and pious men were often brought over from Baghdad to serve these communities as spiritual leaders or to fulfill the function of *hazan*, *shochet*, or *melamed* (teacher). They spoke Iraqi Arabic among themselves, but educated their children in British schools, and many of the wealthier families used to send them on to complete their studies at universities in England. Besides the clubs and social centers, the community also set up their own schools, hospitals, and shelter houses for the aged poor. Yet most of the families sent their children to British schools rather than to the Jewish school.
> It was the British who set the tone in the International Settlement in Shanghai, and the Babylonian Jews quickly adapted themselves to their style of living, and the family style was similar to that of a well-to-do English family. The homes of the richer members were often built like estates with large buildings and wide stretches of garden surrounding them. And the servants lived with their families in their own quarters within the compound.
> I realize now that the community had gradually patterned itself on the English model of the class system, and that there was a certain amount of social snobbery in the way the wealthier members adopted a grander style of living, owning racing horses and enjoying all the pleasure of high society. But this did not prevent the creation of a traditional orthodox life within the family circle and the maintaining of close ties with the community both in the synagogues and in other social gatherings on festive occasions. Families would enjoy both styles of living at the same time. They would go to the synagogue on Saturdays, study

Torah together, and enjoy their meals with all the traditional blessings and hymns around the family table, and on Sundays they could go riding or sailing in the daytime, engage in sports activities, and then go to the cinema or nightclub dancing in the evenings. Children were given piano and ballet classes, and encouraged to participate in scout activities. Today, it seems as though there should have been conflict between all these things, but at that time it was quite natural for our families to live that way.[11]

BECOMING ENGLISHMEN

The most prosperous Baghdadis in Burma sent their children to the English mission schools, where they learned Shakespeare and Shelley, played cricket, and ate kosher *tiffin*—lunch—carried to the schools by servants.[12] The curriculum was closely coordinated with that in Britain to assure fluid transition in school from the Empire to the home territory. The Diocesan or Baptist Schools were preferred because the Catholic mission schools were in session a half-day on Saturday. In Mandalay, Bassein, or other outlying towns, Jewish girls went to convent schools and boys to local church schools for the primary years, and moved in with relatives in Rangoon to attend Protestant high schools. While some recall jibes about being Jewish by their classmates or teachers, these mild affronts never amounted to much and, all in all, the children received an excellent education without proselytizing, and with allowance for their own religion.[13]

Hebrew was taught at home by private tutors before or after school or on Sunday. Jews competed against each other on the teams of St. Paul's, St. John's College, and especially the Protestant English Diocesan Schools, and performed in Gilbert and Sullivan plays. Ellis Sofaer played Katisha in *The Mikado*, which charmed his grandchildren who saw the photograph many years later, and Abraham Sofaer anticipated his future success on the stage in the same production:

> The heaviest part of the performance falls on Ko-Ko . . . and all the quaintness and rich comedy of the character were most admirably represented by Mr. A. Sofaer who sang and acted in excellent fashion. As he had also the responsibility of the "production" of the opera his success in an exacting part is all the more credible.[14]

Despite their name, the English Diocesan Schools taught few "pure" English boys or girls; classmates were more likely to be Anglo-Indian, Chinese, Anglo-Burmese, or other members of the "European" or "foreign" population: Russians, Germans, French, etc. Nevertheless, writing in 1916 in *The Fleur de Lys: The Magazine of the Diocesan Schools*, editor Abraham Sofaer states:

> This School is vastly different from the other schools in Burma. The boys are all British, all speak English habitually, and indeed live in an absolutely European manner. Consequently patriotism, which is a feeling and not a science that can be taught in the classroom, is present in the School and needs only to be developed.... We have a Company of Cadets ... whose smartness and efficiency on the parade have earned them a high reputation.... On Empire Day and on other days of national import, "D" Company turns out to do honour to the Flag and to give three cheers for the King and for the British Empire.[15]

He goes on to say:

> We have had this term a series of lectures on the Empire. Each member of the Staff has lectured on one portion of the Empire and how it came to be won, and there can be no doubt that it is a great incentive to a higher Patriotism on the part of the boys when they are told of the deeds of great Empire Builders.
>
> In our Library and Art Room we have a finer collection of Historical pictures than any other School in Burma can boast of; and the youthful and imaginative mind is here delighted with impressions of Britain's early barbarism and of the civilizing influences of the Romans, of Norman feudalism and of royal tyranny, of the pageantry of the Armada and of the pomp and glitter of the Stuarts, of the beginnings of Empire abroad and of the efforts of brilliant Statesmen at home to maintain its glory; and so he comes to learn in another forceful way what the Empire really means....
>
> Last, but not least, we have sent more people to the War than any other School in the province.... Within the last year boys in the School have been four times reminded of the seriousness of the Great War and of the necessity to grow up as good citizens of the Empire.[16]

Abraham Sofaer makes an interesting observation in these Kipling-like passages. Patriotism is a primordial national feeling that is developed through education and through public rituals, such as the school's military parades and the cheers for King and country. While English patriotism was attaching itself to Jewish students' hearts, the "national"—Baghdadi—context for the religion was fading. Substitution of another national framework in which to practice Judaism is a common aspect of diaspora experience and of assimilation, and was fostered and accepted by the Baghdadis. However, they overlooked one thing: to be truly British, cheers and parades notwithstanding, one had also to be purely "white" as well as Christian. As Albert Memmi has pointed out, "The Jew has always assimilated ... but assimilation does not go far enough: in a society that is still religious, true assimilation would be conversion,"[17] and this the Baghdadis would not entertain. In his youthful optimism, Abraham Sofaer had not yet understood another of Memmi's realizations:

> I have longed with all my might for that integration. I have longed to become a citizen like other men. Yes, on this point I confess my humiliated disappointment.

... Whether I like it or not, the history of the country in which I live is, to me, a borrowed history. How could I feel that Joan of Arc is a symbol for me? Would I hear with her the patriotic and Christian voices?[18]

British colonialism thus brought to far away Burma the dilemma that Jews in Christian Europe had been facing for centuries.

Attendance at English schools required expensive tuition. This effectively separated the wealthier children from the other Jewish children (figure 3.1). The less advantaged Jewish children attended the community's Jewish English School at 22 Sandwith Road, near the Scott Market Bridge (figure 3.2). As at the elite schools, students at the Jewish English School also studied subjects useful for the education of a citizen of the Empire. Faces turned toward the Union Jack in the corner of the assembly room, the students began each school day with the robust singing of "God Save the King!" Events such as the death of King George V in 1936 are vividly recalled, and students were on their best behavior for the annual classroom visits by the Inspector of Schools, and sometimes by the wife of the Governor of Burma. Hebrew and other religious subjects, but not general Jewish history, were also in the curriculum. Yearly examinations were based on material taught throughout the year, and the excellent education received during these early years is evidenced in the strong writing skills and wide knowledge of the graduates.

Figure 3.1. Solly Saul as Schoolboy, Jewish English School Rangoon, 1930s. Courtesy of Solly Saul.

Figure 3.2. Jewish English School, Sandwith Road, Rangoon, 1937. Courtesy of Esther Moses Solomon.

Philanthropists, the Aaron family supplied a substantial lunch for the students, which was especially important to the poor students. Lunch was usually chicken, curry and rice, but sometimes a different menu was provided by a mourner or a person observing the anniversary of the death of a relative. While the occasion for this special meal was solemn, students were excited at the prospect of "outside food." At the conclusion of the meal, the Hebrew teacher, Mr. Einy, and the male relatives of the deceased said *kaddish* (the mourners prayer). Mr. Einy was also a *shochet* and the children watched as he slaughtered fowl brought to him by household servants or in preparation for the afternoon school meal.[19]

Boys and girls studied together until sixth or seventh grade, but as they grew older, girls received separate schooling. Unlike in Calcutta, the community was not large or affluent enough to support separate schools for boys and girls, and therefore the girls were sent to the missionary schools. At the Methodist English School, Seemah Saul Betz recalls receiving an excellent education, the same as the Cambridge curriculum, among classmates of diverse nationalities—Russian, French, Japanese, Chinese, and others. Jewish students were released from classes in Christianity, and studied nutrition instead. Jewish education and the study of Hebrew were not part of the curriculum nor were they provided at home for girls: it was not considered important for Jewish girls to be further educated in their cultural history. Theirs was to be a practical and affective, not an intellectual, understanding of Judaism.

As they became English and European by education and culture, the children understood the Baghdadi Arabic of their parents and grandparents less and less. Ellis Sofaer remarked that it became difficult for the younger generation to follow the Passover Seder when the parents, clinging to Baghdadi tradition, recited the *haggadah* ("narration") in Arabic. Despite this obstacle, he emphasized, the children understood that they were participating in a great and meaningful celebration.[20] As time went by, the prayer books also had to be replaced: the first *siddurim* (prayer books) were in Hebrew and Sharak (Arabic written in Hebrew letters); gradually, as the spoken Arabic became unintelligible to the generations born in Burma, English was introduced into the prayer book.

Through time, however, the strict religious orthodoxy of Baghdad, still practiced by the elders, was insufficient to transmit the specifically Baghdadi history and culture to children born in another place, receiving an excellent English education, and a weak Jewish one. The Baghdadi gloss on Jewish values, experience and perspectives was "natural" in the old country: it was reinforced by casual conversation, artifacts, education, and interaction with family, friends, and social institutions. Above all, it was transmitted each day through language, the storehouse of memory. The idioms and nuances of Hebrew and Judeo-Arabic conveyed attitudes as well as information, and the tales told over dinner could conjure up worlds. As long as the language lived, the past colored the present, but it dissipated when, as in Burma, English intruded into the home. Early in the century, the Sofaer family Passover Seder, in Arabic, seemed "majestic" to Ellis Sofaer; by the late thirties, the Saul family Seder, in Hebrew, was hardly majestic to Seemah Saul Betz. She recalls her very religious father chanting the Passover *haggadah* totally in Hebrew, with no explanation, in the company of non-comprehending and impatient children. By then, the Baghdadi way of life appeared limiting and opaque to students imbued with the glorious history of the British Empire and the attractions of the modern world around them.

BAGHDADI WORLD VIEW

Imagine, then, the Baghdadi world view, whether they lived in Rangoon, Shanghai or Bombay, Hong Kong or Singapore: they looked to Iraq for rabbinical guidance, family history, tradition, religious books and, in the early days, for dress and language; for eternal, spiritual values, they looked to the Torah and thus to an ideal Jerusalem; and for nationality, culture, and a future, to Britain. They looked to two promised lands: Jerusalem the ideal, and Britain the apparently attainable.[21]

The families carried British passports and therefore lived as though their future belonged in Europe, even though their past was Middle Eastern and their present Asian. Over time, the Hebrew or Arabic names bestowed on their children by the first generation were replaced by English names, and sometimes English names were the first choice. Around the turn of the century, the name Victoria was bestowed on several girls with a long list of Baghdadi surnames. Eliahu Sofaer became Elias and then Ellis; Saleh Saul became Charlie Saul; Ramah Aaron, Rose Aaron, and her brother Ezekiel Aaron, Edward Aaron.

The declaration of the state of Burma in 1948 was recalled by Judah Sassoon, now living in Los Angeles, in these words: "I became a stranger in the land of my nativity."[22] Yet the land he is talking about—Burma—was never truly his home; his home existed within the international community of Burma, the transnational community of Baghdadis, and within an England he had never visited. Even so, these Jewish Englishmen-in-exile were denied entry into the Gymkhana Club where, as Ellis Sofaer describes it, "The worthy gentlemen who carried the burden of the Empire went for relaxation and company."[23] He suspected that his uncle Sassoon Solomon built his palatial mansion facing the Gymkhana Club as an affront, a rebuke to British snobbery (or, as his cousin Ezra Solomon put it less diplomatically, "to cock a snook"[24] at the British). Within his home, Sassoon Solomon's life style was British. His three sons were sent to school in England,

> and his daughter Hanny was given the genteel training of the English upper class. She studied painting under Mr. Raj, and was competent at both the piano and the violin. During a certain period (we) would visit them every Sunday.... We had musical evenings in which Hanny presided at the piano or played the violin. They featured the lighter classics, excerpts from the latest Franz Lehar operettas, or popular songs.[25]

Although England "existed" within Sassoon Solomon's home, it was more elusive when he stepped outside. From the upstairs windows of his uncle's mansion, young Ellis Sofaer watched the evening dances at the Gymkhana Club, listening to the music that floated through the lighted windows, and seeing "the couples drift from window to window like figures in a peep show."[26]

Despite his outstanding record at the English Diocesan School, Abraham Sofaer was passed over for the prize he coveted—the Burma Medal—which guaranteed a place at Oxford for an exceptional gentleman-student from Burma. He suffered a second slight when he was denied a commission in the British army, given almost routinely to his classmates during World War I. Still smarting because of these affronts to his patriotism, Abraham Sofaer nevertheless left Burma for England shortly thereafter to become an actor on the London stage.

These were not isolated instances of exclusion; they were reminders of the limitations of British identity for the Jews in Burma. The Baghdadis were defining themselves by aspiration, while the British continued to define them by occupation. As long as such minorities were "purveyors to the Crown" or in any capacity that served the British—and, as non-Christians—they were indelibly inferior. Paradoxically, exclusion also strengthened Jewish identity by cementing an illusory porous barrier. Still, life was good and the slights tolerable, because as Jews the Baghdadis had another identity which offered them stability and security.

NOTES

1. January 16, 1905, 24.
2. "May Town." The town was named after a British officer, Colonel May, who suppressed a rebellion in Upper Burma in 1889.
3. *Homage to Catalonia*, 108. Orwell's two references to the Jews of Burma in his novel, *Burmese Days*, are curious and defamatory, especially this one. Discussing a young Briton's first days in Burma, he writes: "They swilled whisky which they privately hated, they stood round the piano bawling songs of insane filthiness and silliness, they squandered rupees by the hundred on aged Jewish whores with the faces of crocodiles." 65.
4. Saul Ezra Saul, letter, September 27, 2002.
5. Maymyo remains much as it was, although the population has, of course, changed. The red brick buildings have stood the test of time, and the landscape is as it was. Once an elegant destination, the Candacraig Hotel is well preserved, but has few occupants these days. Yet the sense of being somewhere else, smelling the pines and watching in amazement as the fog quickly advances, makes it easy to conjure up the days of Maymyo's glory.
6. Byron Farwell, *Armies of the Raj*, 102–3. Lest it seem that the British looked down especially on Jews, consider the following lines by John Forbes in his 1878 book, *British Burma and Its People, Being Sketches of Native Manners, Customs and Religion*: "Unlike the generality of Asiatics, the Burmese are not a fawning race. . . . Free from prejudices of caste or creed, they readily fraternize with strangers, and at all times frankly yield to the superiority of a European. . . . On the whole amiable and pleasing, but with no noble points; the character of a race which is not destined to advance far on the path of civilization, nor to profit much by intercourse with the superior genius of their European conquerors . . . the Elders tell with sorrow the common tale, that English spirits and opium are gradually destroying their native good qualities in the rising generation." 44–46. In a similar vein—despite his harsh portraits of the British in Upper Burma—George Orwell's depictions of the Burmese and Indians in *Burmese Days* are just as unflattering. He repeatedly describes ugly physical characteristics, depicting the Burmese as almost less than human and without inherent dignity.
7. King Mindon's palace in Mandalay was considered the "Golden City." It was destroyed in 1945 by British shells trying to rout the Japanese and Burmese soldiers who had taken shelter there. To this day, fine gold leaf is crafted in Mandalay and elsewhere to enable acts of devotion by Buddhists who affix the thin sheets to the figure of the Buddha.
8. Ferguson, *Empire*, 35.
9. Ferguson, *Empire*, xvi. Ironically, like the Scots and British, the Padaung tribe of the southern Shan States also recalled the British Empire as a golden period. Writing in *From the Land of Green Ghosts*, Pascal Khoo Thwe says, "There was the idea of another paradise at the back of my mind: but this was a paradise lost. My grandparents would tell me of a golden age, the age of the rule by the British in Burma. . . . 'The British have all gone home now,' said my grandmother with fond longing, as

though she were talking of long-lost relatives. 'We were prosperous under the British, but when they went they took the prosperity with them.' I felt the genuine sadness with which she spoke." 37.

10. Sofaer I: 6–7.

11. Rebecca Toueg, "The Jewish Community in Shanghai," *Points East*, Vol. 20:1, March 2005, 4–5.

12. In her novel, *Flowers in the Blood*, Gay Coulter describes how school and office lunches were delivered: "*Tiffin*—the colloquial name for luncheon—was always prepared at home, not only in Jewish households where dietary laws were followed, but in almost every Indian household. Before eleven each school day, the tiffin-wallah called at our kitchen where he received the tiffin-carriers. . . . On the bottom of the five-sectioned tiffin-carrier was a bed of hot coals. The next two layers were perforated to keep the meal hot. The top two layers contained bread and fruit. The cook helped load these on a wide board, which the tiffin-wallah, balanced on his head. He made the rounds to various other families until he had more than twenty of the stacking tin containers. Then he went from school to school and to the offices. Around three in the afternoon he reversed his order, picking up our empty tiffin-carriers and returning them to each scullery by the end of the day." 1991: 119–20.

13. This allowance is all the more curious since the stated purpose of these schools was: "to make Christ's work and Gospel known in every part of the world in its best form . . . " *Rangoon Gazette*, June 22, 1908: 5. Ellis Sofaer makes a wry comment on the reprimand he received from a teacher. As a young child, he yawned loudly in class. She said, "I want none of your Jewish tricks here." He remarks, "Clearly she shared the attitudes of the members of the Gymkhana Club." V3.

14. *Fleur de Lys*, 7.

15. *Fleur de Lys*, 1–2.

16. *Fleur de Lys*, 2.

17. *Jews and Arabs*, 86.

18. *Portrait of a Jew*, 197.

19. Other teachers recalled are Flora Einy Raymond, Alisha Solomon, Rachel Halwega, Miss Hainault, Miss Zaccai, Miss Legois, and Mrs. Rosario. School principals were Miss White and Raphael Isaac, who was the principal in 1942 when Rangoon was attacked and the Jewish population dispersed to India.

20. Sofaer 111, S, and personal communication, 1992.

21. The Baghdadis in India tried repeatedly to be classified by the British as "Europeans," to distinguish themselves from the Indians and other foreign populations in India who might also seek British citizenship. To no avail.

22. Personal communication, 1991.

23. In Akyab, with its much smaller British and European population, the Samuel family was included in the English social circle, including events in Gymkhana Club and Christmas parties. The Samuel family in London has photos of their mother, in fancy dress, on the lawn of the Club.

24. Ruth Sofaer, personal communication.

25. Sofaer, V, 2.

26. Sofaer, V, 3.

Chapter Four

The Comforts of Home

Jewish identity can be conceived of as a refuge, a home, a place of security in an alien world. Distanced spatially from relatives abroad, the Jews in Burma were nevertheless close to them through the orthodoxy of home and synagogue ritual. The rules of Jewish law formed an apparently eternal framework for the society. The Law kept them true to their past, conforming to Jewish communities elsewhere. The continuity of tradition was ensured by a ritual director from Iraq, who served as rabbi, cantor, ritual circumciser, overseer of ritual slaughter and arbitrator of questions about Jewish law. That the authoritative voice about Jewish law and practice was vested in a representative of Iraqi Jewish tradition was significant for the community. Decisions about religious practice are also implicitly decisions about community definition, since the laws of Judaism also serve as boundaries for the society: the dietary laws not only express consistency with God's will, but also encode the limits of social interaction between the Jew and others. In strict tradition, to break a law is to break a barrier between the community and the outside population, even as a barrier is erected between the Jewish community and God.

Each Sabbath, each Passover, each Yom Kippur, the Baghdadi in Rangoon knew that his cousins in Iraq and elsewhere were lighting oil lamps the same evening, eating matzah when he did, and experiencing with him the fast of Yom Kippur. As heavily laden, multidimensional systems of meaning, these rituals and their objects are dense vehicles of communication about Jewish history, values and perspectives. They unite body and soul, individual and community. Lifting the wine of joy, eating the matzah of the desert, the exile, enabling God's light by kindling the oil's wicks, or feeling the pangs of the fast—always among family and community—makes implicit understandings tangible, and incorporates them physically and emotionally as well as spiritually. Especially during the early years in Burma, the Jews were united with their past and with their relatives through the special in-group language of Baghdadi Arabic. And the holy language of Hebrew lifted the Baghdadi even more firmly across time and space, reinforcing his relationship with God as well as with the worldwide holy kinship community. This was, of course, also true of the other Jewish groups, for although the synagogue ritual was Iraqi in practice, the calendar and celebrations are essentially the same for all Jews.

The traditional way of life continued throughout the 1930s, until World War II. It is described by Abraham Shalom Judah:

> My father had a brother in Rangoon, a sister in Singapore, and a sister in Calcutta. He always dressed in the form of clothing of the Jews of Baghdad. This form of clothing was adopted by only a few Jewish men, since the majority had adopted European dress. My father, as also nearly all the Jews of Rangoon, was deeply religious—the rich and the poor. The Sabbath was strictly observed—no cooking, no touching of money, no activating a light switch. We had neither radio nor television those days. My father and I attended synagogue services three times every Saturday, for *Sharith*, *Minha* and *Arbith*. After returning home from the morning service, we had lunch, rested for an hour, and I then had to spend about two hours with my father reading *Nevi'im* and *Ketubim* (sections of the Talmud). After that it was time to go back to the synagogue for *Minha* service. My sister and I would converse with our mother and father in Arabic, and later, in English, to a small extent. English was the medium of education in the schools we attended.
>
> We had more than one *shochet* in Rangoon, and they could only slaughter fowls. We never saw red meat except when a Haham, who was also a *shochet*, would visit from Baghdad. He would slaughter goats and sheep for the community. We also had two *mohels* in Rangoon.
>
> During these school years, I could speak fluent Arabic (the Iraqi dialect), fluent Hindustani because of our Indian servants, and could read and write Burmese since I studied this in school but did not have much opportunity to converse. In Hebrew, I was much advanced where the Bible and prayers were concerned. My studies in Hebrew continued through Mishnah and the Gemarrah, but I could neither write nor converse in Hebrew.[1]

Life has a dark side, also, but such memories are often excised when reconstructing a childhood through narrative. Whether purposely unspoken or suppressed, this omission yields only a partial view of a life that was. Mr. Judah is one of the few who included bad memories along with sweet nostalgia. His recollection of the death of his eldest sister suggests similar events throughout the community:

She underwent a gall stone operation, after which she had to lie in the hospital with both the front legs of the bed raised on wooden blocks. One leg slipped; the stitches burst; she hemorrhaged and died. My mother in her grief kept hitting her face and head with her hands. Maybe this caused a blood vessel to burst, and she got seriously ill. We were told that she could lose her eyesight or become paralyzed, but within six weeks from the death of my sister, she passed away.[2]

RELATIONSHIPS WITHIN THE COMMUNITY

As a community, the Baghdadis fulfilled their responsibility to care for the poorer Jews. The community as a whole supported those in need through the synagogue's charitable funds, and each Passover and Rosh Hashanah wealthier Jews donated to the less fortunate. Nevertheless, the wealthier Baghdadis kept their distance socially from those of a "lower class." One woman was told that early in the century her grandmother had a caretaker, a poor Jewish woman, whose children were not permitted into the house, while the children of the poor Hebrew teacher were permitted. Some forty years later, another woman, now living in Los Angeles, recalled with mature embarrassment how the family stayed upstairs when the poor came to the door.

The Baghdadis were discouraged from marrying the Bene Israel, although such weddings did take place. Nor did they intermarry with any of the other groups who lived as neighbors on the densely populated streets of central Rangoon—if they wanted to stay a part of the Jewish community. There were a few cases of intermarriage with conversion, but marriages without conversion meant severing ties. This was especially true if the woman was the one who was not Jewish, for according to Jewish religious law, Jewish identity is carried through the mother. An entry into the synagogue's Birth Registry in January, 1931, lists the child as "Christian"; on the lines for parents, his Jewish mother's name is written, but the line for the father's name is blank, except for the "x" placed next to it. Conversely, when a member of the prominent Solomon family married an Anglo-Burmese, his son's name was never recorded in the Registry. The father had died before his son's birth, and although mother and child maintained social connections, they were effectively "outside" the religious fold. This "refusal" to assure the continuation of the Jewish community through legally sanctioned marriage to a Jewish woman would seem to be the fundamental affront. Similarly, when in 1924 David Hai Aaron's daughter Ramah (Rose) defied her family to marry a Roman Catholic physician from Goa, she was no longer considered part of the community. Although she did not convert, the wedding took place in St. John the Baptist Church in Rangoon on condition that she raise her children as Catholics. In a sense, Ramah had acquired another, a professional, community: in 1922, like her sister, she had become a physician—a rare step for a woman at that time, but this community hardly substituted for the near loss of her close family. Some of her relatives continued to visit with her, and she occasionally saw her mother, but when in 1929 she went to see her father as he lay dying, he turned his face to the wall.[3] Stories are also told of hidden Burmese "families," mistresses and children, who existed in a world completely separate from and seemingly "invisible" to proper life in Rangoon.[4]

Although Jewish tradition was the core of existence, the climate and color of the land in which they lived touched the Jews deeply. Memories of Burma are rich with images of picnics and boat parties in the Rangoon harbor, of life lived in the open air. They played football, tennis, cricket, and badminton, and rowed boats on Inya Lake. They watched Burmese and Chinese street festivals from the balconies of their homes or in chairs on the sidewalk; they enjoyed the beautiful Chinese weddings, with a carpet-lined street for the groom and fresh flowers veiling the bride's face. They gathered at the marionette street theater, and looked to the skies mornings and evenings to see the hundreds of paper and bamboo kites, red, yellow, green, blue, hovering over the Burmese quarter. Memories linger of luscious fruits—the durians, the mangos, the custard apples—and the coconut street foods and, of course, the Middle Eastern foods their mothers served. Most meals were of vegetables, fish, chicken and rice strongly flavored with spices—garlic, onions, turmeric, cloves, cardamom, ginger, cinnamon, coriander and black pepper. On special occasions they feasted on goat. Above all, they remember the friendliness of the people, and the sense of well-being and contentment life provided in prewar Burma.

This pleasant life drew Alan Solomon's father back to Burma from Australia in the 1930s, to a beautiful home, amid lakes, lemongrass and roses, on Windsor Road. Reflecting on his life in Burma long ago, Abraham Shalom Judah says,

> I certainly look back at the peaceful years, without turbulence, as a time when family life was very close, and we in our unsophisticated way could enjoy simple things and lead simple lives, when the pivoting point in our lives was the synagogue, the festivals, and our strong belief in the Jewish religion.[5]

THE COMFORTS OF HOME

Affective reinforcements of identity are transmitted at home, a concept even more than an actual place. "Home" not only suggests a place of refuge and security: even more fundamentally it indicates a comfort, easy acceptance, a place where the person fits naturally. At the quintessential home ceremony, the Passover Seder, the child is initiated into the abstract concepts and fundamental realities of the society through highly sensuous and emotionally charged materials and actions. The *haggadah* presents the ideals of exiled community in an eternal and paradoxical relationship with God, but similar messages are carried in the wine the child must drink and the bitter herbs he must swallow. Community is first experienced as extended family and friends. At this level, foods, ritual, and even personal identification are not Baghdadi or even "Jewish": they are home and family. Children, entering a room, lowered their heads to kiss the hands of their aunts and uncles, in this simple greeting expressing the respect, love and honor due members of the family both as relatives and as bearers of Jewish tradition.

The synagogue, Musmeah Yeshua, was a home above all homes, and a glorious statement of Jewish identity. The synagogue belies its modest exterior: inside it is grand, its pillars reaching up past the women's gallery, and illuminated by great chandeliers. Boxes at the entrance invited the congregants to donate monies for the needy, and so to fulfill the *mitzvah*, the good deed, of *tzedakah*. At the far end of the synagogue is the *hekhal*, draped with beautiful velvet or silk curtains, *parochets*. As is customary in Sephardic tradition, the congregation sat in pews that surround the central *bima* where the Torah is read. It was an honor to be called to read the Torah, not only emotionally and socially but also financially. On major holy days, individuals bid on honors, that is, on the right to read the portions of the Torah; the monies so collected helped to support the synagogue and its charities. This had the unfortunate effect of limiting the reading by the poorer Jews to ordinary days, but because there were no membership dues for anyone, they were also the beneficiaries of the custom.

Ellis Sofaer notes: "The ability to read Hebrew was necessary if one wished to take part in the synagogue. Each repeated attendance at the synagogue was not so much an act of worship as an assertion of one's Jewish identity."[6] Each person had an assigned place within the building; to this day people raised in Burma remember exactly where their fathers sat, and relive their pride in locating their fathers from the heights of the women's gallery or, for a boy, in sitting with his father in the special family pew. On the eve of Yom Kippur, and at Simchat Torah, the synagogue's 126 silver- and gold-clad Sifrei Torah were displayed around the *bima* so that everyone could touch and kiss them. As was traditional among Baghdadi communities, it was the custom of families to donate Torahs to the synagogue in memory of a loved one, and so the number of Torahs increased throughout the years.[7] Torahs were read in rotation throughout the year, but on the anniversary of the death, the scroll donated in memory would be read. Families also donated the beautiful *parochets*, embroidered with gold or silver thread, to grace the *hekhal*, and bearing an inscribed silver plaque in memory of a deceased member of the family. Each Yom Kippur and Simchat Torah, all of these beautiful cloths covered the tall pillars of the synagogue, thus tangibly and gloriously linking individual families, their heritage and the proud place of the Baghdadi Jews within the British Empire in Burma. The synagogue caretaker knew exactly where each *parochet* was to be placed each Yom Kippur; as though it were yesterday, the caretaker's son Maurice Shamash, in his home in Los Angeles, could picture his father hanging each silver or velvet cloth on the pillar closest to the family's pew. Within this beautiful setting, the community expressed the range of emotions that marked its devotion to family and tradition: the solemnity of Yom Kippur; the joy of Simchat Torah; the sadness of Tisha b'Av; the delight at marriages and pride at bar mitzvot.

Musmeah Yeshua was much more than a temporal place of meeting: it was a *makom*, a space, a place where eternity was captured, where the individual became one with his historic community and his forefathers through the media of the holy language, Hebrew, the timeless Torah, and Baghdadi tradition. This unity with the past was dramatically evident on Tisha b'Av, which commemorates the fall of the second Temple in Jerusalem in 70 C.E. This is a twenty-four hour period of deep, personal mourning for an event that happened close to two thousand years ago. On the eve of Tisha b'Av, all the benches were removed from the synagogue, and the entire floor was covered with carpets on which the community sat to chant *kinot*, the lamenting elegies recited this sad day. When the congregation reached the portion enumerating the number of Jews killed at the time of the destruction of the Temple, the lights would be switched off and in the darkness the congregation would mourn and weep. The community also gathered in darkness for the first prayers of the penitential period, the *selihot* (forgiveness) prayers, which started at four a.m. a few days before Rosh Hashanah. The caretakers of the synagogue would ride through the streets in a rickshaw, traveling from house to house, to awaken people to come to synagogue. The period of repentance, beginning before Rosh Hashanah through Yom Kippur, thus started in darkness and finished in light, metaphorically mirroring the community's hope for forgiveness and renewal.

If Musmeah Yeshua represented the community's devotion to its eternal religion, it is fitting that it was the place where actions denoting purity took place. At appropriate times, women came to the *mikveh* to purify themselves in anticipation of sexual relations and to create a pure "context" in which a new child might be conceived. On the afternoon before Yom Kippur, men would bathe in the *mikveh* so that they might address God in a purified state.

The synagogue as the seat of ultimate Jewish identity had another, unforeseen, legal outcome. Each newborn was registered both with the civil government in Rangoon and in the synagogue's birth registry. Because Jewish boys are not given a name at birth but eight days later at the *brit milah*, the covenant of circumcision, or at a Torah reading in synagogue for girls, birth certificates issued by the municipality do not bear the person's first name: they state only that a male or female child was born on this date to these parents. The birth certificate from the synagogue includes all names. At the time of Burmese independence, when Jews could opt for British nationality, birth certificates from the municipality were unacceptable, but the one from Musmeah Yeshua solved the problem.

RITES OF PASSAGE

On major holidays or for significant family events, Jews from small towns throughout Burma convened in Rangoon to celebrate or cry together. Intertwined family marriage relationships, inclusive concepts of extended family, and residential proximity meant nearly everyone was related to everyone else, or a friend or neighbor, and therefore family events were more exactly community events.

Even as they rejoiced or mourned together, these close and distant relatives were validating the change in the community's composition, and publicly recognizing the new status of the individuals involved—a change that implicitly carried communal as well as familial obligations and responsibilities. They danced around the celebrant, broke bread with him or her, sang and prayed with the family, and implicitly acknowledged the community's expectations of fealty to tradition and of children to perpetuate it. Similarly, at a time of mourning, they clustered around the new widow or widower, comforting and also healing the breach caused by the loss of a member.

Such periods of personal and social transition were understood by the Baghdadis—as they are by peoples throughout the world—as times of special vulnerability. The newborn child is not yet a full member of society (this comes at the *brit milah*); the engaged couple—the potential bride and groom—are not single, not married. As in other societies, customs developed to protect the vulnerable, "ambiguous" person from evil forces: demons, the evil eye, magical contagion. In Judaism, these customs complemented, supported, "assisted" the religion in keeping the individuals safe from harm.

Weddings

It would seem that the community's cup overflowed with each new union of woman and man, family and family (figure 4.1). Weddings were weeks of

Figure 4.1. Wedding of David and Sophie Aaron, Rangoon, 1923. Courtesy of Scott Aaron.

parties, celebrating with relatives who arrived from Calcutta, other parts of Burma, and even farther away. People were generally confident that the new marriage would be a good one: the couple had been carefully screened by matchmakers and parents, who operated with the assumption that if the conditions for a peaceful and productive marriage were met—economic stability, good character, and religious adherence—love would follow. Appropriate partners could be sought throughout the Baghdadi Jewish world, but existing family relationships were a good starting point. Many of the new partners knew each other from childhood or, at the very least, the worthiness of their families could be vouched for by others in the extended networks of relations and friends. During the very early years of settlement in Burma, brides were sometimes sent from the Middle East, and girls were considered eligible for marriage at thirteen.

The engagement was announced in the synagogue. Since Musmeah Yeshua did not have facilities for grand celebrations, the parties that followed were held in a home or a hall. After the announcement, the party was held in the home of the future bride's parents. The groom's family arrived bearing a tray of flowers and candy. The climax of the party came when the future mother-in-law or father-in-law placed a ring on the girl's finger. The fiancé could not do this, for the giving and acceptance of an item of value from groom to bride formally constitutes the betrothal, or *kiddushin*, one part of the binding marriage ritual; if the engagement were to be broken, a divorce would be necessary. In contemporary America, the *kiddushin* has been folded into the wedding ceremony itself, with the giving of the rings, but in early twentieth century Rangoon and Calcutta, it was strictly enforced.[8] To prevent the contagion of sadness or misfortune from touching the couple, a widowed father or mother-in-law could not take part in this ceremony; his or her place was taken by another close relative.[9]

From the engagement to the marriage, the couple was always chaperoned by a member of the family. During this time the *ketubah*, the marriage contract, was written, specifying the amount each family was to provide for the wedding, as well as the bride's dowry, and other issues. If the engagement was broken, the person, i.e., the family, breaking the engagement paid compensation to the other. About three days before the wedding, the bride and groom were celebrated at the henna party, the *khadba*. The whole neighborhood participated in the celebration, if not in the home then through the music in the streets. Accompanied by traditional Baghdadi musicians shaking tambourines, drumming tablas, plucking kanuns, and filling the night with the sweet wail of the clarinet-like zirnah, the groom and his family came in procession through the streets to the home of the bride. Inside the home, women sang and ululated as they danced around the seated couple, their loud kilililis announcing that this was a time of ultimate rejoicing. The bride's friends and relatives approached the bride and groom carrying the henna on a gold leaf tray. Eager young girls lined up to decorate the couple's fingers and palms with the green henna, which would dry to a bright orange/red. This was a joyous celebration with a serious purpose: to protect the couple against demons and against the evil eye, in accordance with long-held folk associations of red as protective in Islam, Judaism and other cultures.[10] At the end of the evening, a fine bracelet or similar piece of significant jewelry was presented to the bride by her future mother-in-law.

The wedding was held in the synagogue, followed by a reception in the courtyard. Because there were no Jewish caterers in Burma, the food at this reception was simple: fresh fruits, sandwiches, pastries, wedding cake, ice cream, soft drinks, tea, coffee, and a variety of liquors. But then, about 10 p.m., a more elaborate party followed at the bride's parents' home. Tables were piled with traditional Baghdadi pastries—date *babas*, cheese or almond-filled *samboosaks*, molasses and coconut milk *dol-dol*. Before they entered the home, the newly married couple participated in a traditional folk practice more commonly performed at Yom Kippur: *kappara* (atonement). At the door, they were met by a *shochet* who held two white fowls, which were to serve as scapegoats for any afflictions or sins that might endanger the couple as they began their new life together. The fowls were circled over their heads three or seven times. In this way, the sins were transferred to the fowls, which were then killed and the meat given to the poor.[11] This was the Rangoon version of a similar practice observed in Calcutta: The Saturday night before the wedding, the groom again sent trays of sweets and flowers to the bride, and both families came together. Rabbi Ezekiel Musleah recalled that the couple stepped over a goat or sheep as *kappara* (atonement), and then the animal was killed and its meat distributed to the poor."[12]

The new couple now entered the home and their new life in a state of purity. Inside the home, dinner guests who had been awaiting their arrival had been admiring the wedding presents displayed with the names of the people who gave them. The bride and groom changed into evening dress and joined the music and dancing, which continued until the early hours of the morning. As is customary in traditional Jewish practice worldwide, the wedding celebrations lasted for seven more evenings, seven more dinners, as guests came to observe the *Sheva Berakhot*, the Seven Blessings. On Shabbat, the bridegroom was called to the Torah and a party given in his honor. Afterward, the families of both parties recognized their new relationship by eating together at a Shabbat meal.

In Calcutta and in prewar Rangoon, the newly married couple did not leave the home for a week except to go to the synagogue, nor were they left unattended. Each day during that week trays of sweet baklava were sent by the groom's mother and other relatives, to further increase the sweetness of the household and of the new marriage.

Brit Milah

The birth of another member of the community is a time of greatest joy. Each birth was announced in the synagogue. For the first forty days of life, a child was considered especially vulnerable to harm from demons and the evil eye, and the baby was surrounded by specially-written charms and amulets: garlic, amber beads, nutmeg strung with a turquoise disc, pierced with seven holes or "eyes," as protection against the evil eye, or a silver hand with the name of God on it.[13]

If the newborn was a boy, everyone was invited to the *brit milah*, eight days after his birth. At this time, the child is entered into the covenant with God through the act of circumcision. The sixth night and the evening before the eighth day were considered exceedingly dangerous, in Rangoon as in Europe. It was believed that the demons, already associated with dark and with the night, were especially incited at this time to prevent the child from entering into the covenant with God. In Europe, this evening was called *Washnacht*, when the child was watched carefully by men who came to pray, study and feast by his bedside.[14] In Rangoon, the anxiety before the *brit* was alleviated by the joyful procession that took place that evening, when the special chair in which the godfather sits to hold the child during the ritual, Elijah's chair, was carried from the synagogue to the home to the accompaniment of songs in Hebrew and Arabic. Branches of myrtle decorated the chair, perhaps because the plant's name in Arabic, *elyas*, suggests Eliahu, the prophet, the forerunner of the Messiah and the protector of children, who is thought to be present at the *brit*. The similarity of name might be coincidental, but the function as a protection against malevolent forces has a long history in Jewish folk practice: Since Talmudic times, myrtle has been used in burial, wedding and birth ceremonies to protect against demons. It was also the preferred spice for the havdalah ceremony, which marks the "demon-infested" transition from the peaceful and protected Sabbath to the rest of the week.[15] Dancing, singing, and feasting followed the procession: musicians were hired to entertain, candles were lit, portions of the Zohar, mystical texts, were read, and everyone sang, "El-Eliyahu, El-Eliyahu, Bizcouth Eliyahu" (God of Elijah, send Elijah to us).[16]

The *brit* might be performed in the synagogue, but more often it was held in the home of the father's parents. It was held in the protective morning light,[17] in a room filled with friends and relatives, who stayed on to celebrate with music and food. During the 1930s Aslan Benjamin served as *mohel*.

If the baby was a firstborn son of neither a *kohan* or a Levite, the *pidyon ha-ben* (redemption of the first born)[18] ceremony took place on the thirty-first day of his life in the home of the maternal grandparents. Again, there was a general celebration, with music, dancing, food. And then, when he became a *bar mitzvah*, a "son of the commandment," the boy approached and left the synagogue similarly accompanied by music and singing, was showered with sweets after he read his portion of the Law, and returned home to a party.

An indication of the "invisible" Jewish presence in Burma, that of the overseas or non-Baghdadi Jews in the country at that time, is this special entry into the Birth Registry, placed on a page apart from the regular listings: "Certificate of Birth: Michael Spencer Pimley, son of Henry Pimley and Elizabeth Pimley, born at Rangoon on 27th of May 1929. Circumcised by me (signed) A. Benjamin, at 90/91 Merchant Street, Rangoon, on (blank) of June 1929."

Death

A death is an injury to the community, and requires communal action to heal the rift as well as to provide comfort to the immediate family. And, given the intricate and extensive family relationships in Burma, a funeral was often a community-wide event. The coffin was carried in public procession on the mourners' shoulders, accompanied by loud prayers which continued until the procession reached its destination. Burial was in-ground, and a rounded, inscribed tomb placed over the grave eleven months later. Throughout the seven days and seven nights which constitute *shiva*, the period of intense mourning which follows Jewish burials, mourners filled the home with the sound of *kaddish*, the prayer of mourning that affirms God's eternal goodness even in these dark hours.

FESTIVALS

Shabbat

In prewar Burma, the Sabbath was truly the day of rest, a time when the community put aside its business to gather together in the home and in the synagogue. It was inaugurated by the special, more formal Shabbat dinner on Friday evening. The father was the master of the evening: he sat at the head of the beautifully laid table and proclaimed the Hebrew blessings over the wine and bread that preceded the meal.

> The bread would be piled in front of my father's plate at the head of the table and covered with a cloth embroidered by my mother. At the corner of the dining room hung the metal carrier that held the Sabbath lamps, *teriya*. They burned bright and steady in the still air, proclaiming that the day was special.... The Sabbath lamps consisted of glass tumblers containing oil, in each of which stood a wick. The wick was a thin stick, no thicker than a grass stem, around which my mother had twisted a layer of cotton wool. The wick was soaked in oil and made to stand in the tumbler on a tin base shaped like a candle holder, but with the ferrule narrow enough to take the wick. The oil used was (I believe) coconut oil. The tumblers were half-filled with water and topped up with oil to the depth of about an inch, enough to keep the lamps burning through the night. The carrier for the tumblers was a sheet of tinned copper in the shape of a hexagon, with seven holes in it to accommodate the seven lamps. It hung by three chains that met in an apex, like the chains that hold up the pans of a pair of scales.[19]

Late on Saturday afternoon, after worship in the synagogue, families would stroll along the jetties, enjoying the evening air, meeting friends, watching the sampans and ships moored along the docks, and listening to a military band.

Purim

The festival of Purim ("lots") recalls the triumph of the Jews over the tyrant and their would-be killer Haman in Persia long ago. As such, it is a time of reversal, of joy, of celebration, an exceptional time when excessive drinking and gambling are permitted. Playing cards in the synagogue courtyard was a common way of passing the day, even while an effigy of Haman hung in the schoolyard.

The sweetness of this time, and community solidarity, are manifested in a lovely custom celebrated in many parts of the world which was practiced in a special way in Burma. *Shaloch manot*, trays of home-baked pastries exchanged at Purim among relatives and friends, metaphorically create sweet lines of communication among households. In Burma, the housewives would start their baking preparations days in advance, and there was indeed much to prepare: *sambusuks* (turnovers), *luzeenas* (fruit cheeses of guava, quince, or pumpkin, cut in diamond-shaped pieces), *nankhatais* (shortcakes), *kuleechas* (coconut cakes), and numerous other variants of the confectioner's art. It was essential that all the delicacies in these exchanges should be sweet. No savoury, however tasty and appetizing, was appropriate for Purim. The houseboys, dressed in their festive best, would act as porters, and on the day itself the trays, looking sumptuous in their lace and satin drapes, with perhaps a rose nestling coyly on a square of gold leaf among the sweets, would be sent singly to their various destinations. It was a great day for the houseboys as well, for they were tipped generously at each place of call.[20]

During the first year of marriage, this traditional exchange of *shaloch manot* at Purim was elaborated to enhance family relationships. The bride received elaborate trays of *shaloch manot* from her mother-in-law and her mother. These beautiful trays, covered with a silk cloth and heaped with flowers, were carried through the streets by the whole family, accompanied by music. In the center of these festive trays sat a piece of jewelry on a velvet cloth. This then was more than the customary statement of social relationship: the procession, the music, the silk and flower-covered tray announced to the public at large the sweetness and joy both sides of the family felt at the creation of this new household. This first year only, the bride would return the trays with pastries she had made. In subsequent years, she initiated the exchange with her parents and in-laws. The happiness of Purim was marked also by gold sovereigns given to children who carefully saved them in a jar.

Passover

In Burma, as elsewhere, the long preparations for Passover began just after Purim, and required community cooperation to ensure that all the laws governing the period were precisely followed. Without stores or bakeries to provide the necessary foods, all provisions had to be generated within the community or in homes. Such preparations were arduous and yet exciting, since they took place within the context of great anticipation. Passover, the great festival that sums up Jewish—especially diaspora—experience, is a joyous, serious period, a time to enact and reflect on the meanings of Jewish tradition. Passover also implicitly meant "family," for relatives and friends came great distances to enjoy the Seder ritual together.

While homes were being thoroughly cleaned in preparation for the holiday period, those in charge of making the community's matzah took orders from each household. Matzah was baked in a clay oven on the synagogue premises. Matzah, which is similar to the dry, lasting bread still eaten by desert nomads, was the food the Hebrews took with them as they fled from Egypt into the desert on their way to the Promised Land, according to the Book of Exodus. It thus suggests the transitional, liminal state of the Jew, ever between the darkness and despair that was "Egypt" and the light, hope and eternal promise of "Jerusalem." On a more immediate and tangible level, matzah suggests the diaspora state of exiled Jewry, in this case, the situation of also being somewhere between Baghdad and England.

The synagogue courtyard was cleaned of dirt and any possible bit of food that was prohibited on Passover. About six weeks before Passover the dough was prepared by women and baked by men. The large, circular matzahs were rolled very thin and baked until they were crisp. Families bought enough to last the eight day Passover period. The matzah was stored in large baskets lined with bed sheets, and then covered over with the sheets. To keep the matzah secure from mice, ants and other vermin, and separate from *chametz* (food prohibited during Passover), the baskets were hung from hooks in the ceiling, and raised and lowered as required. *Shmurah matzah*, the especially "guarded" matzah used at the Seder, was delivered the afternoon before Passover, just before the holiday began.

Similarly, special kosher wine was made for the community and delivered by very religious Jews, as was the date juice used for the *haroset*, the sweet mixture of fruits, nuts, spices and liquid that is on the Seder tray. Rice, which is permissible for Passover among Baghdadi Jews, was picked clean of impurities and set apart from prohibited grains. Coconut oil,[21] sugar,[22] salt,[23] and coffee[24] were specially prepared for Passover use. Dairy products were not used during Passover, since it was impossible to assure that cows had not been fed on prohibited grains. The only treat was ground walnuts on matzah; the only sweet *halaik*, a thick liquid made from the juice of dates.

The home was extensively, exhaustively cleaned, creating an environment of total purity for the festival. All dishes, cutlery and cooking vessels that had come in contact with leavened products were put away, and similar items used only for Passover were retrieved from storage. To underscore the complete compliance with the laws and customs of Passover, a ritual "search for the leaven," for impurities, was conducted the evening before the holiday began. Whereas in contemporary Western practice, the ritual enactment of the search has become a child's game, in Rangoon it was a semi-serious matter. The woman of the house would place ten pieces of bread throughout the home, and the master of the house would search for them with a candle and feather. Once gathered, they would be collected and burned outside the home early the next morning. In this way, the master of the house, the father, would satisfy himself that his home had been properly prepared. And now the stage was set for the grand, important Seder that evening.

When all the preparations had been completed and Seder night had arrived, we were dressed in festive clothes and took our places at dinner. The table was sumptuously laid. In front of my father's plate where on Friday nights the bread was placed, were the matzos, covered with a cloth even more resplendently embroidered by my mother. At each of our places was a small silver tumbler about two inches tall for the wine we were to drink in the course of the service. My father would start the chanting, reading first the Hebrew, and then again the same passage in Arabic. This procedure was doubtless customary in the Jewish community in Baghdad, where Arabic was the language of everyday speech. It enabled the children of the family who had not yet mastered the Hebrew to follow the service, and more importantly, absorb the Jewish tradition. Alas, it failed in its purpose with us, for we knew neither Hebrew nor Arabic. But although the ceremony was long, lasting perhaps two hours, my father always seemed to be doing something, with the matzos, with the herbs in little dishes on the table, or with the wine. We were both audience and participants, now and again sipping our wine as prompted. It all summed up to a great occasion.[25]

The beautiful Seder in the Sofaer home was linked to all other households celebrating that evening through the image of the mystical prophet Elijah, the emissary from God, whose travels from community to community certainly exceeded but recalled those of the earthly *shlihim*. Through the image of Elijah, and through the timeless biblical laws that govern Passover among Jews worldwide, the eternal was brought into everyday life. Each household in Burma understood itself as an element of an everlasting if extended community, all making the same efforts to assure the purity of the Jewish people and compliance with God's laws. A grand, community-wide picnic at the Zoological Gardens celebrated the end of this strenuous period, with children riding the camels, elephants and donkeys while the parents relaxed.

Shavuot

Shavuot, which commemorates the giving of the Torah at Mt. Sinai, followed soon after, and was ushered in with midnight prayers at the homes of mourners or at the synagogue. In the morning, the sweetness of receiving the Torah was embodied in a special treat eaten only at Shavuot: *kahee*, a puff-pastry-like sweet, eaten with semolina cooked with raisins, almonds and rosewater, or spread with sugar, jam or honey.

These spring holidays were quickly followed by a flurry of weddings, before the monsoon season started in earnest.

The New Year: Rosh Hashanah and Yom Kippur

After the monsoons came Rosh Hashanah and Yom Kippur, the period of repentance. Although it ushers in a time of introspection, Rosh Hashanah was a happy time in Burma. Friends and relatives from distant towns joined the crowds in the synagogue, all in their best clothing to start the New Year with beauty and freshness. Year after year, there was a problem in the women's gallery, as families argued over infringements into their traditional seating space. More relatives, growing families required or wanted more chairs in their location, and it took the arbitration by the *shamash* to settle the issue and ensure that the good spirit of the New Year prevailed in the gallery as well as in the men's pews below. The morning religious services were followed by a grand meal, by mourners' prayers in the homes, and then by Tashlikh, the ritual "casting of the sins" in the waters of the Irrawaddy River.

Dressed in white, the whole community assembled in Musmeah Yeshua for the Day of Atonement, Yom Kippur. This is remembered by Jews from Burma as a deeply spiritual, soul searching time, when people had tears in their eyes as they prayed for atonement and to be written in the Book of Life. Those living near the synagogue went home after the evening prayers and returned the next morning; those from afar slept overnight in the synagogue, since no one would ride on this holiest day. The young Ellis Sofaer wondered at a ritual that appeared to be so satisfying to others:

> Children were not called upon to undertake the twenty-four hour fast which is the act of penance, and a sacrificial method was devised to purify them of any sins that burdened them. This ritual is *kappara*, and it is performed by a member of the community competent in kosher butchery. The child is seated. The butcher takes a chicken by the wings and rotates it round and round the child's head while he mumbles the appropriate prayer. He then slits the jugular vein of the chicken and throws its bleeding body to one side of the floor, where it flops about in its death throes for a few seconds. The sins of the child have by this means passed to the chicken, which is now considered unsuitable for eating and is given away in charity to the poor. It puzzled my childish mind that these chickens should be so welcome to the impecunious although they were unfit for our table.[26]

Succot

During Succot a few days afterward, a large *sukkah* (temporary shelter) was built in the synagogue's courtyard. Since most families lived in apartments or homes close to one another, they could not build their own *sukkah*. The courtyard therefore became the focus of the festival, and the *sukkah* was always filled with families who brought their meals to eat in the *sukkah*, as prescribed, or to play cards or backgammon. Simchat Torah, the Rejoicing of the Torah, falls immediately after the Festival of Succot and it, in turn, was followed by a community picnic at the Zoological Gardens.

The more fortunate families, such as the Sofaers, were able to build their own *sukkahs*, perhaps on the terraced roof of their house.

> (The sukkah) was constructed of bamboo poles lashed together with coconut rope, and it covered an area large enough to hold a dining table and chairs for the whole family. It was thatched over with leaves of the coconut palm to protect us from the direct sunlight, and also to keep off the rain. It was gaily decorated with baubles and tinsel. Every meal there was a picnic, but the thatch was not equal to a tropical downpour, and when it rained we would have to abandon the tabernacle and return to the dining room.
>
> It is interesting to record that it was from this terraced roof that we observed Halley's Comet in 1910. We were an augmented family gathering with aunts and uncles and their offspring. The grown-ups spoke to each other with grave apprehension about the possibility of some world-shaking disaster that would follow this visitation, and we were left with a deep sense of foreboding.[27]

Hanukkah

Beautiful memories of Burma were created during the December celebration, when the weather in Burma is at its best. Hanukkah, "dedication," commemorates the rededication of the Temple after the desecration by the Syrians in 165 B.C.E., and the miracle that occurred when oil sufficient for only one day lasted eight days. It is, therefore, a time of joy and appreciation, one enhanced by the lights that are lit each evening for eight days. Local smiths made the triangular tinned copper Hanukkah lamps used in Burma. At the bottom of the triangle was a small shelf with eight receptacles for oil and wicks; near the apex was a place for the *shamash*, the "helper" lamp, as well as a hook to hang the Hanukkah lamp on the wall.

Hanukkah lamps were not the only lights to brighten the Burmese night. Hindus, Christians and Burmese also celebrated festivals in December, and groups might borrow from their neighbors to enhance their own festivities. In Mandalay, in addition to their Hanukkah lamps, the Saul family lit Chinese paper lanterns, which floated into the night sky. Margaret Raphael Glicksohn reminisces:

> Hanukkah, the Jewish Festival of Lights, always coincided with the festival of lights of the Hindu people. The streets were lit like fairyland. Sometimes, Christmas also came at this time, and you could see Christmas trees in Christian homes; Hanukkah lamps, lit with oil, in Jewish homes; and candles on the balconies of Hindu families. During this period also, the Burmese celebrated the Harvest Thanksgiving with a big carnival. Beautiful floats passed through the streets for hours, each float decorated with lights and flowers. There were Hanukkah parties, with much food and drink, and parties in the school, with food donated by the wealthier Jews.

We lived in a country ruled by the British and we did take in some of their culture. Also living with Burmese people, Hindus, Muslims and Christians we sometimes joined in their (non-religious) celebrations. The English New Year comes on 31st December night. The New Year was celebrated by all. At the stroke of midnight, bells rang from the churches, the trains whistled, and many other noises were made to bring in the New Year. The famous song Auld Lang Syne was sung wherever there was a crowd of friends, in the dance halls, at parties. At that moment it made no difference if you were a Jew, Christian, Hindu, or Burmese. Every 1st of January the Jewish community hired a launch—a paddle boat; people contributed to the cost, brought some food and musical instruments and had a marvelous time, year after year.

Life was wonderful. We mixed with the Christians, Burmese, Hindus, Muslims, and Chinese, and we all got on very well together. There was no anti-Semitism out there. I miss Burma very much.[28]

NOTES

1. Letter, August 16, 1993.
2. Letter, August 16, 1993.
3. Rose van Camp, personal correspondence, July 17, 2003.
4. The community also kept apart from the tribal Jews of the remote northwestern border, who claim ancestry from the "lost tribe" of Menasseh. Currently called the Bene Menase, they are comprised of groups from the Shinlung tribes of Mizoram and Manipur in northeast India, who trace their origins to an area called Shinlung in Sichuan province of China. The Bene Menase believe that the tribe of Menasseh arrived in China after their exile by the Assyrian King, Shalmaneser V. Simon Aaron, who was born in Mandalay in the mid-1930s, recalls his father telling him of his encounter with this "lost tribe" during trading missions to the interior.
5. Letter, August 16, 1993.
6. 1985: I, 5.
7. In Calcutta, one person questioned the wisdom of spending so much money on even more Torahs, and suggested that the money be used instead for other charitable purposes. "The proposal was too revolutionary an innovation, and the age-old tradition continued." Ezekiel Musleah, *On the Banks of the Ganga,* 199.
8. Musleah, 203–4.
9. Musleah, 203.
10. Trachtenberg, *Jewish Magic and Superstition,* 133, and Musleah, 204. This may be the origin of the use of red to indicate danger to this day, as in the matador's cape or the stop sign.
11. Margaret Raphael Glicksohn, letter, November 2, 1992. The custom of *kappara* apparently had its origins in Talmudic times, a version of scapegoat rituals common to many peoples. The Jewish religious authorities tried unsuccessfully through the years to eliminate the practice, and it is still performed among some groups to this day. A white cock stands in for the male, a hen for the female. They are circled three

or seven times of the individual's head, accompanied by the words, "This fowl is my substitute, this is my surrogate, this is my atonement." Trachtenberg, 163–64.

12. Musleah, 205.
13. Hyman, 108.
14. Trachtenberg, 170.
15. Musleah, 200–201.
16. Hyman, 110.
17. Light, especially morning light from the East, from the direction associated with God, carries associations of protection and divinity. "The soul of man is the light of the Lord," Proverbs, 20:27. Cernea, *The Passover Seder*, 37; Trachtenberg, 171.
18. The ceremony of redeeming the firstborn son on the thirty-first day after birth has its origin in Exodus 13:13 and Numbers 18:16. This precept was originally designed to counteract the heathen practice of sacrificing the firstborn, of man or of beast, to the Semitic gods. The firstborn sons in Israel originally belonged to the service of God. Later, the Levites were chosen to replace the firstborn of all other tribes for service in connection with the sanctuary. In return for this, every firstborn Israelite was to be redeemed by paying five shekels to a *kohen*, descent of the priestly family belonging to the tribe of Levi. If the child's father is a *kohen* or Levite, or if the mother is the daughter of a *kohen* or a Levite, the ceremony of Pidyon ha-Ben does not apply. Philip Birnbaum, *A Book of Jewish Concepts*, 499.
19. Sofaer III, 2.
20. Sofaer III, 7.
21. Cooking oil was bought in sealed tins, but the most religious persons made their own coconut oil for frying and baking. The white part of 20 dried coconuts was ground and placed in boiling water. It was squeezed two or more times to express all the milk, which was then boiled down over a slow fire for 12–14 hours, until all the milk evaporated and only the oil was left. This yielded about six bottles of oil. The coconut that might be stuck at the bottom of the pot was used in curry and with rice.
22. Sugar was prepared from white rock candy or by squeezing the juice of cane sugar. It was cooked until hard, poured into a tray, and when set, cut into cubes.
23. Rock salt was pounded fine.
24. Raw coffee beans were bought and roasted at home, and then pounded to make a powder.
25. Sofaer III, 4.
26. Sofaer III, 6.
27. Sofaer III, 5.
28. Letter, July 29, 1992.

Chapter Five

Bene Israel vs. Baghdadis: The Court Case

Three Jewish peoples coexisted uneasily within British India, at least according to the Baghdadis. And one group especially seemed to threaten Baghdadi aspirations for status as "Englishmen," although the argument was never openly expressed in these terms. The language of discord was "religion," not social status, but the effect was the same.

When the Baghdadis arrived in Bombay, they found a large, indigenous community of Jews, the Bene Israel, who far outnumbered them. For many Baghdadis, this was the first time they had encountered a community of Jews whose way of life differed from their own and who did not look to Baghdad for religious authority. To the light-skinned Arabic-speaking Baghdadis in their Arab dress, the Bene Israel appeared to be Indians: they spoke an Indian language, Marathi; the women wore saris; and although they observed Jewish dietary laws, their diet was usually vegetarian like their Hindu neighbors.[1] A few of their religious practices were different and, because many were poor, some worked on the Sabbath. And yet, and yet—the Bene Israel seemed to exhibit the same devotion to Torah. At first, the Baghdadis were cordial but distant, recognizing the Bene Israel as a different kind of Jew, with a different history, and accepting them into their synagogues. It was not long, however, before the Baghdadis tried to erect religious and even physical walls between the communities, questioning their religious status and even their right to be buried next to Baghdadis in consecrated ground. In 1836, David Sassoon and nine other Baghdadis tried unsuccessfully to have a partition erected in the Bombay Jewish cemetery to divide the Baghdadi and Bene Israel dead.[2] In Calcutta the community was overwhelmingly Baghdadi, with few Bene Israel and even fewer Cochini Jews; there the cemetery was partitioned to separate Baghdadis, Bene Israel, Cochinis, and Westerners. In the Rangoon cemetery, however, it does not seem that the populations were segregated. Former Calcutta rabbi Ezekiel Musleah has noted,

> While English came more and more to form a common basis, the mass of the (Jewish) communities had different backgrounds: Arabic for the Baghdadis, Marathi for the Bene Israel, and Malayalam for the Cochinis. It is understandable, therefore, that no tradition or organization developed for the exchange of views or the sharing of experiences on political, economic, religious or cultural issues. The three centers developed disparate ways of life based on varied historical and local circumstances with little affinity for each other.[3]

It was not, however, like recognizing the difference between apples and oranges, even though both are classified as fruit. The divisions among Jews were not seen by the Baghdadis as separate but equal, but rather were understood in the context of the British class system and influenced, especially in India proper, by the pervasive Hindu caste system; both were world views that accepted social hierarchy as inherent in the structure of reality. These systems, in turn, were compatible with the Baghdadi understanding of religious orthodoxy, as defined in Baghdad, as the superior, true and necessary way of life. For the Baghdadis, Jews were what *they* were. Their contact with other Jewish populations was minimal, if not nonexistent. A few Ashkenazim who had moved to Burma as individual entrepreneurs had married Baghdadis and quickly assimilated to the Iraqi way of life. The other Ashkenazim in Burma at this time—most likely representatives of foreign governments or corporations, or in the military—stayed apart from the Baghdadi community and therefore had no impact on their practices and politics.[4] How, then, could the Bene Israel, whose history was murky and whose lifestyle was different, be equal?

The cautious rapprochement between the Baghdadis and the Bene Israel, and Cochinis, is reflected in the pages of Musmeah Yeshua's birth registry. New sons and daughters born to these groups were entered into the registry just as births among Baghdadis were, but with the notation "Bene Israel" or "Cochinee" next to the parents' names. Often just one parent is so marked, suggesting the intermarriage occurring between Baghdadis and Bene Israel or Cochini.

The degree of strain between the Baghdadis and the Bene Israel in Rangoon appears to be in direct proportion to the Baghdadis' anxiety over political and social acceptance by the British. Although the arguments between the communities were posed in religious terms, they masked this fundamental anxiety over caste and color. It was also a question of status, and a means through which the more aristocratic, fair-skinned Baghdadis might further distance themselves from the darker-skinned Bene Israel and thus ensure their own position within the ranks, according to the codes, of the colonial empire. The highest status in Burma, of course, belonged to the British, who defined its terms. The Baghdadis approximated the British as best they could, retaining an elite Jewish identity while acquiring the British language, schooling and passports. The Baghdadis measured themselves against the British at one pole and against "lower class/caste" Jews at the other. To be identified with these less sophisticated populations seemed to threaten their acceptance as British.[5]

The British acknowledged the Baghdadis' sophistication and used their abilities to enhance trade and civil administration, as well as their own way of life. Yet ultimately the British locked the doors of the country club. The Baghdadis' position was pleasant but also ambiguous and insecure, dependent upon British grace.

During the early years of the twentieth century, tensions between the Baghdadis and Bene Israel increased, especially in Bombay and Rangoon. By this time, the Baghdadis had become firmly identified with the British in lifestyle and yearning, and the Bene Israel were even more identified with India. This view was clearly stated in a 1909 article in the *Jewish Chronicle* of London, in which Sir Jacob Sassoon claimed that the Bene Israel had drifted away from Judaism and had assimilated with the Hindus. He said also that the Baghdadis considered themselves a superior "caste." The Bene Israel response was pointed: they asked how many English Jews had managed to "keep themselves free" from English ways.[6]

Try as they may, the Jews were still not "white enough" in this color-conscious society. Ellis Sofaer commented, "In that Black-and-White era, White was taken essentially to mean European-white. By this convention, the Jews were excluded: but they were also not Black. This left them in a kind of social limbo, hence their frustration."[7] In this situation, the Baghdadis apparently felt the need to "purge" from close identification any group that might lower their status vis-à-vis the British. Placing greater distance between themselves and the Bene Israel, as well as between the Baghdadi "lower classes," seemed an unspoken strategy for closing the gap between themselves and the British.

The depth of this continuing rift is reflected in a letter to the editors of the Bombay *Jewish Advocate* in 1945 entitled, "Subject: If Bene-Israels Are Black Jews, Who Is a Pure Jew and Who Is a White Jew?" After reviewing the history of intermarriage among Jewish populations and the host communities throughout time, the author, Bene Israel (Dr.) E. Moses, states:

> Ethnological, anthropological, linguistic and historical researches have proved that the so-called Aryans consist of four distinct races; the Semites do by no means form a racial unit and the Jews cannot be called a pure race. With such data, I solemnly ask who is a pure and white Jew and who a black Jew? Does not the mixed blood of foreigners run in the veins of Jews all over the world?

He continues: ". . . it is the Baghdadi Jews and White Jews of Cochin who are foremost in running down the Bene Israels and always trying to pass on a White Man's ticket." The editors comment that "the attitude of the past generation of the Baghdadi section of the Jewish community was intolerably wrong and un-Jewish. In fact (the irony of history) it was not much dissimilar to the present attitude which a section of the Continental community betrays toward the Iraqian section."[8]

BAGHDADI CHALLENGES TO BENE ISRAEL IDENTITY

The Baghdadis in Rangoon cited religious failings on the part of the Bene Israel: they refused to write the *get*, the document of divorce, in the traditional Aramaic; and they ignored the practices of *yibbum* (leverite marriage)—the marriage of a man to the widow of his deceased brother who has died childless—and *halitzah* (untying)—a ritual performed when the man refuses to marry the widow, and that frees her to marry another. The Bene Israel maintained that since few people could read Aramaic, it made more sense to write the *get* in the vernacular, and that the other two practices were unimportant to the definition of an Orthodox Jew. The Baghdadis offered to accept the Bene Israel into the "Jewish Community" if they would agree in writing to observe these practices; the Bene Israel declined, saying that they were already full Jews.[9]

Given the centrality of the synagogue in defining and maintaining Jewish identity in an alien world, to deny synagogue honors has deep implications, for it challenges a family's most basic connection with a worldwide community, as well as with a sustaining and essential identity. Starting in 1913, the Baghdadis moved to deny the Bene Israel full membership rights in Musmeah Yeshua: in that year they put in place synagogue rules prohibiting the Bene Israel from approaching the Torah during the seven regular *aliyot*. In 1926, the Bene Israel were barred from election to the synagogue's Board of Trustees, and barred again in 1929.[10]

In the 1930s there were only about sixty Bene Israel in Rangoon out of a Jewish population of about two thousand.[11] It would seem that given this small number, a conflict might have been avoided. But feelings ran deep. The conflict over Bene Israel rights may have contributed to tensions among the Baghdadis themselves, and led to a breakaway congregation, Beth El, in 1932. A singing procession led by stockbroker Arnold Aaron, who spearheaded the movement, carried a Torah from Musmeah Yeshua on 26th Street, across Dalhousie Street, to its new home on 31st Street in space donated on their premises by E. Solomon and Sons, at 31st and Dalhousie Streets.[12] Gabriel Solomon, who had led services at Musmeah Yeshua for twenty years, went with the new congregation, and Musmeah Yeshua brought Rabbi Yusaif from Baghdad to take his place. Beth El functioned well for ten years, until it was abandoned at the time of the Japanese invasion.

THE BENE ISRAEL GO TO COURT

In 1934, Bene Israel names were struck from the list of voters in Musmeah Yeshua. By then, however, they had taken the unprecedented step of suing the synagogue in British court to resolve, once and for all, the definition of Bene Israel Jewish identity and their rights, therefore, within the synagogue. Despite even more friction in Bombay, such an appeal to the British legal system had yet not occurred there. It may be that because the lead plaintiff, E. M. Ezekiel was himself a magistrate, the Bene Israel in Rangoon were more confident in challenging the synagogue's trustees.

Civil Regular Suit No. 85 of the High Court at Rangoon was initiated in 1932 and lasted until 1935. The plaintiffs, J. M. Ezekiel, and another Bene Israel, were represented by a well-known barrister, Sir Oscar de Glanville. Defendants C. S. Joseph and Aslan Benjamin, trustees of Musmeah Yeshua, were represented by Mr. N. N. Sen. Justice Leach and Justice Sen (brother of the lawyer) presided alternately over the course of the long trial. There was no jury. Yascha Malkhoo, a young proofreader for the *Rangoon Gazette*, attended the trial and took notes. He recalls that Mr. Ezekiel was the first to testify, asserting that the Bene Israel were being discriminated against and that their participation in the synagogue was being limited: they were not permitted to vote; they could not purchase synagogue honors and go up to the *bima*; they were prohibited from carrying the Sepher Torah during the seven rounds of the *haggafot* (processions) during Simhat Torah; and they were not permitted to lead or open the Torah. All of this, he said, because they would not observe the laws of *halitzah*, *yibbum* and the *get*. At this point, Sir Oscar de Granville intervened, saying that this does not mean they are not Jews. Mr. Ezekiel continued, pointing out that marriage between Baghdadis and Bene Israel was occurring, and that Bene Israel were being buried with Baghdadis in the Rangoon Jewish cemetery. Apparently, the religious objections posed by the defendants were ignored in these matters. The defendant, Charles Joseph, was asked to confirm these statements, and he did.

Two Baghdadi witnesses, A. J. Cohen and J. E. Joshua, testified in support of the Bene Israel. Another defendant, the Hazan Reverend Joseph took the stand. Asked to define *halitzah* for the Court, he read the relevant passages from the Torah, Deuteronomy (25: 5–9):

> When brothers dwell together, and one of them dies, and a son he does not have, the wife of the dead man is not to go outside (in marriage) to a strange man. Her

brother-in-law is to come to her and take her for himself as a wife, doing the brother-in-law's duty by her. Now it shall be that the firstborn that she bears will be established under the name of his dead brother, that his name not be blotted out from Israel.

But if the man does not wish to take his sister-in-law (in marriage), his sister-in-law is to go up to the gate, to the elders, and say: My brother-in-law refuses to establish for his brother a name in Israel; he will not consent to do a brother-in-law's duty by me!

Then the elders of his town are to call for him and are to speak to him, and if he stands (there) and says: I do not wish to take her, his sister-in-law is to approach him before the eyes of the elders.

She is to draw off his sandal from his foot and is to spit in his face, then she is to speak up and say: Thus shall be done to the man that does not build up the house of his brother![13]

Yascha Malkhoo recalls, "There was an awe of silence in the courtroom, and then Sir Oscar said, 'We don't live in the Medieval Age. The modern man today is educated and does not observe such nonsense.'"[14]

The defendants also challenged the Bene Israel's observance of the Sabbath. The Bene Israel replied that since many were government civil servants, they had no choice in the matter. As they had done before the case began, the trustees offered to allow the Bene Israel full synagogue rights in exchange for a written document promising that they would observe the disputed practices. Again, the Bene Israel declined; they were adamant at being recognized as fully Orthodox, fully Jewish, and refused to sign a document not required of other Jews. To agree to such a document would mean agreeing that their identity as Jews was suspect.

Both sides appealed to authorities in Iraq, Palestine and London. The High Court itself welcomed a decision from the London religious court, the Beth Din. Chief Ashkenazic Rabbi of the British Empire and the Beth Din J. H. Hertz supported the Baghdadis, saying the Bene Israel could be accorded full rights and be counted in a *minyan* if they would promise to observe the disputed practices. However, Dr. Moses Gaster, Chief Sephardic Rabbi of the British Empire, disagreed, and reiterated a stand taken twenty-five years earlier that the Bene Israel were already full Orthodox Jews.

In his judgment of April 9, 1935, Justice Leach said:

The evidence convinces me that there is no difference in the observance of these laws so far as the Bene Israel in the Province are concerned. . . . The two plaintiffs are supported by Mr. A. J. Cohen and Mr. J. E. Joshua, both of whom are unconnected with the Bene Israel. On the other hand there is no evidence worthy of the name in contradiction. Moreover, defendant 1, who is one of the most prominent Jews in Burma, made it quite clear that it is merely a matter of belief that the Bene Israel do not observe the laws referred to . . .

There will be a declaration that the plaintiffs and other Jews called Bene Israel are eligible for appointment as trustees of the Musmeah Yeshuah synagogue and are entitled to vote at elections of trustees. . . . Defendants are not entitled to exclude from the lists . . . a Jew merely because he is a Bene Israel. I consider that the costs of this case should come out of the (Synagogue) Trust Fund. Order accordingly.[15]

Almost immediately, on May 14, 1935, the decision was appealed in the High Court of Judicature at Rangoon. This time the appellant charged that whether or not the Bene Israel conformed with particular religious practices, the basic issue was the fact that the Bene Israel were not part of the Jewish community, that in fact they constituted a separate community. The appeal also stated that "the learned judge should have held that the question involved was a matter for the religious courts to decide and should have referred the matter to the Jewish religious courts in London or Palestine." And finally, it asserted that "For that the learned judge's judgment is otherwise contrary to facts and is bad in law." The Appellant was E. S. Cohen, 325 Tseekai Maung Tauley Street, Rangoon. Defendants were all those who took part in the previous case, on either side: J. M. Ezekiel, 41 Village Road, Gyogon, Insein; N. S. Ezekiel, 201 Rangoon-Insein Road, Gyogon, Insein; S. S. Aaron, 110 Lewis Street, Rangoon; C. S. Joseph, 61 Barr Street, Rangoon (Trustee); A. Benjamin, (Trustee), present whereabouts unknown, left Rangoon for good; E. S. E. Mordecai, 31 Prome Road (Trustee). The opinion was written by Chief Justice Arthur Page, who dismissed the appeal on January 8, 1936, stating that a new argument could not be raised for the first time in an appeal.[16]

The legal framework of the British Empire thus intruded into the private space of the synagogue concerning issues fundamental to Jewish identity in Burma, as well as the control of the Baghdadis over Jewish identification and practice.

The Rangoon rulings had reverberations throughout India, wherever Bene Israel faced off against Baghdadis. Their legal status as Jews was affirmed. The Rangoon decision was cited as a precedent in a court case the following year in Bombay over the use of trust funds established by Baghdadi Sir Sassoon J. David. At issue was whether Bene Israel could benefit from the provision for special beds set aside for Jews in the new wing of the J. J. Hospital, which were being financed by the trust funds. The chief trustee of the Fund, Sir Alwyn Ezra, claimed that the Bene Israel did not come under the category "Jews." The Government of India echoed the decision of the Government of Britain as expressed in the Rangoon decision, refusing to establish differences between Jews for political and legal purposes.[17] This, however, is not what happened: the Government did in fact classify the two groups separately.[18]

Legal decisions do not necessarily change privately held opinions. This issue, and discrimination, followed the Bene Israel to Israel. But in Burma, at least, the decision put the matter to rest, which was to be especially important when catastrophe struck.

NOTES

1. Roland, 42.
2. Roland, 20.
3. Philadelphia Jewish Exponent, April 26, 1974, 4–5.
4. *The Universal Jewish Encyclopedia*, 1940: 605.
5. This social strain is echoed in America in the rifts between the established German-born Jews and the refugees from Eastern Europe in the late nineteenth and early twentieth centuries, as well as the disdain of the American Sephardic elite for the refugees from the Ottoman Empire after World War I.
6. Joan G. Roland fully documents the friction between the Baghdadis and Bene Israel, especially in Bombay, in *The Jewish Communities of India: Identity in a Colonial Era*. Roland, 73.
7. Letter, January 19, 1992.
8. *Jewish Advocate*, Bombay, February 2, 1945.
9. In 1926, the son of one Bene Israel did write such an agreement, and was "admitted to the rights of a member of the Jewish Community." Civil First Appeal No. 78 of 1935, The High Court of Judicature at Rangoon, May 14, 1935.
10. It seemed for a while that things would go better for the Bene Israel in 1928 when A. J. Cohen became President of the Board of Trustees, but this good feeling soon evaporated when C. S. Joseph became president two years later.
11. Roland, 139, suggests that there were sixty Bene Israel among about thirteen hundred Jews in Rangoon at that time. The 1984 *Atlas of the World* sets the total number at approximately two thousand Jews, which is comparable to a 1939 estimate by the Institute of Jewish Studies/World Jewish Congress.
12. According to Yascha Malkhoo, members of the mosque across the street from the new prayer hall threw stones at the group as they approached. This is a rare instance of social hostility by Muslims at this time.
13. Everett Fox, ed., *The Five Books of Moses*, 1995: 967–69
14. Letter, November 11, 1996.
15. Cowen, 1971:177–79.
16. Appendix A.
17. Roland, 143.
18. Nathan Katz, personal communication, February 20, 2005.

Chapter Six

Desperate Passage to India: The War in Burma

The Golden Age of European—and Jewish—life in Burma came to a close with the advent of World War II. Events occurring thousands of miles away intruded into the comfortable cocoon of daily life in Burma. India, while strongly affected by the war, was never invaded; Burma's Jewish community was devastated and never recovered.

Even as bombs fell on Pearl Harbor, on December 7, 1941, life in Rangoon was continuing as usual. The British were, in fact, comforted by America's entry into the war, which was certain to help the Allied position in Europe. But it all seemed so far away, and they were confident that hostilities would never reach Burma. "For the Europeans," writes Alfred Draper,

> the club continued to be the hub of social life; cards were dropped with a meticulous regard to protocol; there was dancing, swimming, tennis, golf, bridge, polo, and one would never dream of not dressing for dinner. Race meetings continued to be attended by the Governor, Sir Reginald Dorman-Smith, at which the women wore beautiful dresses and wide-brimmed hats, yet still felt the need to carry a frilly parasol. Most of the men dressed as if it was Ascot Week.[1]

This "surfeit of optimism,"[2] this head-in-the-sand thinking, rested on another disastrously false premise: that the military equipment and training of the two thousand British troops in Burma were sufficient for the task, should that improbable day ever come.

Burma's struggle for independence from the British in the years prior to the war added another consideration for the frightened foreign populations in Burma. During the 1930s, anti-colonial movements had been gaining momentum in Burma as elsewhere in Southeast Asia, with demonstrations, strikes, riots, and dissident organizations. Young Burmese felt that their own economic and social development was arrested by the control of the British and the pervasive presence of foreign populations in Burma, especially the masses of Indian workers who were competing with them for jobs. While there were about two hundred thousand Chinese in the country in 1931,[3] they occupied a different, noncompetitive economic niche, as did the much smaller Jewish community, and so these groups were not the direct targets of the rioters' wrath. Nevertheless, anti-foreign sentiment was nourished by the Japanese, whose businesses, tourists, and scientific surveys throughout Southeast Asia became progressively more suspect as fronts for surveillance and espionage. Under the guidance of Colonel Suzuki Keiji, who had made contacts with dissidents at graduate schools in Tokyo, in 1940 the Japanese set up a secret office on Judah Ezekiel Street to gather intelligence. Colonel Suzuki was helped by a Japanese fifth column in Burma before the war: doctors, dentists, and photographers who took photographs of military installations and tracked troop movements to pass on to the popular Japanese counsel.[4] That year, the Japanese also contacted the leader of the Burmese opposition, Aung San, father of current Burmese opposition leader and democracy activist Aung San Suu Kyi, and offered assistance in raising a military force, the Burma Independence Army, to work with the Japanese in their subsequent invasion of Burma.[5] Although wary of Japan's own colonialist activities in China, the rebels saw Japan's assistance as the only feasible way of removing the British, and took hope in the Japanese slogans, "Asia for the Asiatics," and "We Buddhists." Thus two startlingly different views of the Japanese existed in Burma at the time. While to the British, Indians, Chinese, Jews, and other foreign populations, the Japanese were dangerous aggressors, to the Burmese they were potential liberators. The foundation of security in Burma for the nonnative populations rested, therefore, on very soft sand. Such was the British-focus of these populations that the reality of the political world around them all through the 1930s seems not to have penetrated their comfortable life, or was it that the fallibility of the British could not be envisioned?

Comforting illusions no longer sufficed with the bombing and strafing of Rangoon, which began on December 24, 1941, was repeated Christmas Day, and continued throughout the following weeks, until the ultimate fall of Rangoon on March 9, 1942. Rangoon was totally unprepared for the strikes, lacking shelters, an air defense system, enough fire fighters, or even a warning system. The city's wooden buildings burned easily, explosive bombs demolished stone buildings, the hospital was hit, as were the commercial and residential areas. Casualties were in the thousands.[6] Chaos reigned; looting was rampant, and gang fights broke out on the waterfront. While the general population panicked, British calm and assurance stayed steady, and Christmas dinners and New Year's celebrations were held as scheduled. Bank holidays were also observed as usual at this time of year—a considerable inconvenience for the terrified people who were trying to withdraw funds to take with them as they fled north or by ship to Calcutta.

British calm and apparent military might fed hopes that the British would stop the Japanese ground advance in the north and south, and that "fortress" Singapore would hold. For morale purposes, British troops were brought by sea from Calcutta and marched through the streets by day. What was not realized was that the troops were then sent under cover of darkness to bolster forces in Singapore, and that Rangoon's anti-aircraft guns were also removed to Singapore.[7] A systematic evacuation plan was never announced by the British nor was it until February 20 that an announcement was made that civilians should leave Burma.

Even so, the continual bombing and news of Japanese ground advances announced what the British didn't, and starting in December 1941, the panicked population began to flee the city—the Burmese to the countryside, the foreign populations to India. At the time, it was the largest migration in history. By fall 1942, approximately six hundred thousand people had fled to India by land and sea, some eighty thousand dying along the way.[8] In their panic and haste, they locked the doors of their homes as though going away for a weekend, not knowing that, for most, it would be forever. The docks were scenes of desperation. Boats crowded with British, Americans, Anglo-Indians, Jews, and similar "European" groups—Burmese natives were not allowed—made the 750 mile trip to Calcutta or the alternate thousand mile journey to Madras amidst bombs and Japanese submarines in ships that hugged the coast in darkness. The frightened people were allowed to bring only four days of cooked food and fifty pounds of baggage.[9] Among the precious possessions left behind in Jewish homes were testimonies of family and community history—photographs, documents, and material objects that connected the panicked refugees of 1941–1942 to those other Baghdadi migrants a century earlier. But others, reluctant to leave the only homes they had ever known, and accustomed to seeing the British as powerful militarily, took hope in British confidence that the Japanese successes would not be repeated in Singapore and Rangoon. As Solly Saul recalls,

> My father, of blessed memory, who had long been in the employ of British companies, was convinced that the Japanese would never get as far as Burma . . . my father was not at all anxious to evacuate to India. Nor is he to be blamed for this feeling. It was not easy, to say the least, for people to padlock their apartments, leave their life's possessions behind and set sail for Calcutta. Forthcoming events would prove that evacuating Burma when we could have by sea would have been the right thing to do.[10]

Christopher Bayly and Tim Harper note simply: "There were few parallels in history to this sudden and dramatic humiliation of an old and complacent supremacy—the British Empire in Asia—by an underrated and even despised enemy."[11]

All hope ended with the fall of Singapore on February 15, 1942. The fifty or sixty Jews remaining in Rangoon throughout February took refuge from the continual bombing in the Jewish School, which was some three miles from the center of Rangoon, huddling under improvised shelters made of concrete gutters, and from there went directly to the boats. Joe Abraham, who was still in Rangoon as a volunteer for Air Raid Precaution, was on the last chartered boat from Calcutta, the SS *Chilka*, along with his eight brothers and sisters, at the end of February 1942. They were among the three thousand deck passengers crowded aboard the ship, sleeping next to one another, cooking what they could on camp stoves or in galvanized buckets, thankful to be eluding the submarines that were tracking the ships in the Bay of Bengal. For six days instead of the usual three, the SS *Chilka* sailed on, keeping close to the coast and traveling at night in total darkness, until the ship was piloted up the Hooghly River and docked at the Outram Ghat in Calcutta. Boatmen, reaching up from their small vessels, offered free food to the hungry, weary passengers—*chapatis, kachowrees, bhaji*. On the dock, crowds of people searched the faces of the passengers as they disembarked, looking anxiously for a relative, a friend, and pressing fruit, pastry, and other foods into their hands. The last general passenger ship, the *Hong Pang*, had left the day before.[12]

Perhaps because their home was destroyed in the December bombings, the Zaccai family had quickly moved north toward apparent safety. In January 1942, they traveled by boat to Mandalay, a city which still seemed in denial that the Japanese would ever reach that far. Life was continuing as usual, the British seemingly oblivious to the panic farther south, and the city had enjoyed a brief prosperity as Chinese and British soldiers and richer refugees filled the city. Like Joe Abraham, Dick Zaccai had also remained behind in Rangoon as part of the Air Prevention team. When, in the latter part of February, the British decided to abandon the city, he joined the dense procession north to join his family in Mandalay, a six-day trip by car. They went immediately to the airfield at Shwebo, about fifty miles northwest of Mandalay, where workers were crowding as many of the wounded and refugees as they could into planes to Chittagong; from there the trip to Calcutta continued by train. With space on the C47 American Army transport plane at a premium, the Zaccais were told that the younger people, Dick and his sister Annie, would have to walk to India. Fearing with reason that they would be lost, Samuel Zaccai refused to be separated from his children, and in the end the family traveled to safety together.[13]

Those who stayed behind in Rangoon until the last moment witnessed the conflagration that accompanied the final retreat of the British. As they departed, the British destroyed or set fire to anything that might aid the Japanese: the docks, the telegraph and telephone offices, and especially the oil storage tanks. The scorched earth policy meant that the oil fields in the north also went up in flames.

OVER THE TAUNGUP PASS

Thousands of refugees escaped to India through the Taungup Pass to Akyab on the Bay of Bengal. Chaos reigned in the city as British officials fled and hospitals were left without staff even as refugees poured into Akyab and other cities on the coast. Between February 9 and March 25, approximately seventy-four thousand people left Akyab for India, but at least five thousand others died of cholera or exhaustion crossing the high mountain pass. Abraham Shalom Judah made this trek, first taking a train from Rangoon to Prome.

> Our home with all its contents was left standing as it was. All that I took with me were a couple of shirts, an additional pair of trousers, some underwear and a few tins of sardines, cheddar cheese, etc. At Prome I was told that many thousands were fleeing over the Arakan Yomas to India, and that thousands of people were dying of cholera en route. (A doctor in Prome) advised me that the inoculation he gave me would not prevent the disease but that the attack would be of a lighter nature. He also gave me crystals of potash of permanganate to put into boiling water and drink whilst on the way to Padaung. At Padaung I met two Anglo-Indian boys of my age and we decided to keep together during the trek. We jointly hired a bullock cart so as we could take turns sleeping in the cart, one at a time whilst the other two walked. We pooled our provisions, and set over the Arakan Yomas until we reached Taungup on the coast. Over the Arakan Yomas, we could buy from the various mountain villages small quantities of rice which we cooked by the wayside and ate it with our scanty provisions, and latterly just with salt, or saltfish which we sometimes obtained. Many people died. Corpses were littered all along the wayside and cholera took a heavy toll. I remember on one occasion standing on a peak, and looking at the unending chain of humanity winding its way along the sides of the mountain, and thinking what an epic Cecil B. DeMille could have created from this scene. One just walked and followed those in front of you. No one had a map and no one knew if we were on the right track. Before sunrise it would be bitterly cold and our clothing would be drenched with dew. It was heavenly to feel the warmth of the sun. From Taungup we got a ferry which took us on to Akyab and from there yet another ferry to Chittagong. From there, I traveled by train to Calcutta where I joined my sisters and their children, who had left Rangoon earlier by boat.[14]

MANDALAY

"If Maymyo was Burma's Shangri-la, then Mandalay was its Hades."[15] Even before the fall of Rangoon on March 8, the disheveled second city of Burma became the destination of hundreds of thousands of refugees from the south. In desperation, they convened on the city, traveling by foot, boat and, rarely, by car, overwhelming Mandalay's resources. They soon found themselves in a nightmare of filth and cholera, with diminishing supplies of food and water. There was no early warning system, nor were there anti-aircraft guns to counter the repeated bombings. The wooden city burned freely. Corpses lay in the streets. Ramah Agasee, now of London, recalls a terrifying time in Mandalay when

> the Japanese lobbed incendiaries almost all night in a ring around us. That ring of fire seemed to be closing in on us and we stayed up all night watching it coming closer. In the morning, the authorities blasted a way out and we were all taken by transport to a tiny Burmese village where we camped in a forest opening completely sheltered by trees. We were eventually evacuated by an American volunteer group from Myitkyina (an airfield in the far north) to Assam.

Ezra and Mozelle Saul, their son Reuben, daughter Rachel, and her husband fled by boat to India in January. David Saul's son Maurice and Ezra's son Mordy (Mordecai) stayed behind to run the factories and save the business, if possible—all in the vain hope that the Japanese would not reach Mandalay. Abraham Jacob also remained in Mandalay to guard his crockery business, but sent his family ahead to India.

The refugees who streamed north had abandoned hope of escaping by boat to India and were trying to outpace the Japanese in their rapid advance upcountry.[16] They hoped for flights to India from the airfields near Mandalay, but this route became equally unlikely as the planes were overwhelmed with wounded as well as by the thousands of people clamoring for space on the precious flights. Once the southern Taungup Pass was blocked by the advancing Japanese, and securing flights became almost impossible, the Tamu Pass on the border between Burma and Assam, four hundred miles north of Mandalay, seemed the only remaining route to safety.

THE TREK

There was no way to anticipate what the arduous month-long trek across the poorly-mapped Indo-Burmese frontier would entail, but there appeared to be no other option for those trapped in Mandalay. By the second week in March, thousands prepared to walk through the forbidding terrain. "The overland retreat to India through the jungle-covered mountains of Burma was the longest and most humiliating defeat in the annals of British military history.... The screams of starving children, the groans of the sick, wounded and old; the pleas of hundreds of wounded soldiers we had to leave behind on jungle roads haunt me in my dreams," recalls Gurkha Manahadur Rai.[17]

Those setting out in March walked through the worst weeks of the trek, during the early monsoon of 1942, exhausted and depleted of energy and resources. With the Japanese Army about twenty miles from Mandalay on March 15, Mordy and Maurice Saul hastily packed two blankets, some clothing and a piano accordion, and traveled by car until the gas ran out. The music of the accordion provided some relief and entertainment at the end of the difficult days, days in which Maurice fell ill with a septic leg infection and fever, and Mordy developed malaria. Their cousins, the children of Kelly Solomon, also took their musical instruments with them on the trek, which was to prove fortunate: occasionally they came upon English tea plantations in the hills of Assam and in other isolated spots where, in return for making music for the planters in residence, they were given food and allowed to sleep on the bungalow verandah.

Albert Judah of London, who also started the trek in March, has given one of the clearest accounts of this terrible journey.[18] As the war approached, he left Bassein, where he was a clerk in the store of Raphael and Sons, and arrived in Rangoon on February 15 to find the city half deserted, shops locked, and people hastily burying their valuables in the hope that they would retrieve them after a brief stay abroad. As the Japanese army advanced, and the ports closed, the railways offered the only remaining escape route. Along with thousands of other panicked residents of Rangoon, Mr. Judah, his sister Lulu Saul and her children Seemah, Solly, and twins Charlie and Simon, and an elderly aunt, fled to temporary safety with relatives in Mandalay. On March 8, as monsoon season approached, they joined the desperate, sorry procession of British, Anglo-Indian, Chinese, Jewish and Indian evacuees who trekked by foot, boat, sampan, mule and elephant, through mud, monsoon, and intense heat, across high mountains and through jungle and swamp. The "route" started by boat or by foot along the Chindwin River, but the river soon grew shallow and everyone had to walk.

Feeding stations were organized by the British, and drinking water was a rare commodity: a British officer, armed with a gun, guarded the tank; the ration was a cup of the highly chlorinated, foul tasting precious liquid a day. Food was a bowl of rice with lentils mixed with chilies, and might include small stones, mud and grit. Health care was nonexistent; the refugees were afflicted by malaria, dysentery, diarrhea, cholera, *kala azar*,[19] and voracious leeches, which incessantly crept into mouths, ears, nostrils and other body orifices. Some of the infirm, sick or aged were carried in a *dhoolie* (a wooden cart hung from bamboo poles carried by two or four men) or rode on elephants, but everyone else—young and old, pregnant, malarial, feverish—walked six to eight miles each day, starting early in the morning and stopping by noon because of the heat. Camps had been quickly improvised; beds were simply bamboo slats, toilet facilities were absent, and washing was possible only if near the river.

After Tamu the way was even more arduous, following footpaths or mule tracks over the steep divide to Palel. Those unable to continue were simply left behind. The roads were lined with dead bodies, including those of the family of Ernest Ezekiel and Hannah Sassoon; the parents and seven children began the journey but only two children, Rosie and Joseph, survived. Some groups were set upon by bandits. Bitten by mosquitoes and sand flies, stepping on swollen feet, subsisting on little more than rice, lentils and salt, some two hundred thousand[20] struggled across the Tamu Pass and then on to Imphal and Assam. "Of all the memories of the trek, the most harrowing are of the dead bodies, which were collected every day at the camps and of the dead bodies floating in the Chindwin," recalls Albert Judah.[21] It was four weeks, on April 5, before he and his family reached Palel in Assam, after trekking for five days over the steep mountains. There they were given some medical attention, washed with hot water, and served at tables with clean linen. With little more than wormy rice to eat during the last days of the trek, "We fell upon them like savages, like animals," recalls Seemah Saul Betz, "grabbing food, shoving it in our mouths."[22]

Alfred Draper describes the scene as the once-proud British troops, and the refugees, struggled to India:

> The long columns of troops that writhed along the dusty track like a snake with a broken spine had lost all sense of time. Days and nights merged into one nightmarish blur; one foot followed another, propelled by a burning determination to survive. Bearded, emaciated, wide-eyed with fever and covered with festering sores, they were totally oblivious of the terrain. Many were only kept upright by improvised crutches or bamboo poles and those fortunate enough to have clothes were infested with lice. Occasionally an officer or N.C.O. croaked out an obscenity followed by an order to keep going whenever anyone showed the slightest inclination to sit or lie down for a short rest; there was a grave danger they would not rise again.... But for the fact that so many carried weapons they were barely distinguishable from the thousands of refugees who walked with them.

At Imphal, the desperate refugees were met by the Burma Refugee Organization set up by the government of Bengal. They were served a cooked breakfast, and offered clothing, shoes and various other items to make them more comfortable before they boarded the train for Calcutta, holding bread and eggs for the journey.

Arrival in Calcutta for many, including Albert Judah, meant immediate transfer to hospitals for treatment of malaria and other illnesses. Seemah Saul Betz spent a year in a Calcutta hospital recovering from typhoid. A Burmese Government report estimated that ten thousand people died on the trek.[23] "Details of the trip have almost faded from my memory, but the names of the towns along the route have not—Kaleva, Tamu, Kohina and Imphal—these names are forever embedded in my memory," recalls Seemah's brother, Solly Saul.

Youthful memories are often humorous ones also. Within this terrible time, Albert Judah remembers one thing positive: he tasted elephant's milk ("It's sweet!").[24] And his nephew, Solly Saul, recalls how his twin brothers Simon and Charlie confused those in charge of food, thinking they had already given the precious allotment to the boy before them.[25] More sobering is the tale of a Jewish child who fell behind on the trek and was rescued and adopted by a tribal family; reclaimed after the war by a surviving relative, she came with them in great despair, in pain at losing yet another family.

The depth of piety and tradition binding the Jews of Southeast Asia is reflected in the simple statement by exhausted, malarial Albert Judah, who notes that "We reached Calcutta on the 8th of April, 1942, where we could then really observe the religion. The 8th of April happened to be the seventh day of Passover, and that is when I recited my Seder night."[26] An even more dramatic expression of the meaning of Jewish tradition to the Baghdadis is in the following recollection, as explained by Mavis Hyman in *Jews of the Raj*:

> Azeeza Cohen was the head of a family of eight on the trek, with a baby one month old and two small children. . . . While they were walking in the mountains, less than a week before the journey's end, they "saw Indian soldiers making *chappatis* and tea, which they very kindly gave to us. However, as it was Passover, my mother refused to eat *chappatis*." It was very rare to find food on the trek, and when it was available the cost was high. To refuse an offer, when hunger and thirst had been endured for three weeks of trekking was remarkable in itself. But bread had not been part of their diet since they left Mandalay, so it was a special treat. To refuse bread when the aroma was actually rising from the cooking required nothing less than deep faith and an iron will. So great was the faith of the people of this generation, and so important the values they attached to religious beliefs, that even in extremity they did not let their standards fall.[27]

Solly Saul recalls his amazement on reaching Calcutta to be greeted by his father, whom he had left behind in Mandalay. While Solly and his relatives were struggling across the mountains, an airlift had brought some of those remaining in Mandalay to India. By April 7, 1942, Mandalay was totally devastated; the railway, the hospital and the Bank of India were in ruins. Some seventy thousand refugees remained in the area, and the Governor of Burma sent a plea to the Secretary of State for Burma to request American airplanes for an immediate airlift to India for those physically unable to make the long trek or who might be most endangered by the Japanese presence.[28] Flights were organized from Magwe (150 miles southwest of Mandalay) and Shwebo. Abraham Jacob was one of the fortunate ones to secure a seat on the planes, arriving in Calcutta on April 17. His wife Sarah and three of their five children had left for India via the overland trek on March 8, while he remained in Mandalay. Sadly, once in Calcutta, he learned that his pregnant wife had died of malaria two days before.[29]

After heavy bombing by the Japanese, the airfield at Myitkyina was closed on May 6. Refugees unable to get flights but who had reached Myitkyina, "were told they'd have to walk through the Hukong Valley, the hardest part of the route, and weak with hunger and illness, they simply could not. So they sat there and died, unrecorded. A party of Allied troops, going through two years later, found the bodies piled in jeeps and trucks. No one knows who they were. Whether any . . . Jewish refugees would have been among them, there's no way of knowing," recalls Yoma Ullman, who was part of the evacuation organized by the Burmah Oil Company.[30]

The evacuation brought unforeseen events to all the arrivals in Calcutta, but none as improbable as that of Helen Abraham, who met her father for the first time after completing the overland trek. Her parents had been separated while she was a baby and her father had moved to Australia. By sheer coincidence, he arrived in Calcutta about the same time as the refugees. Father and daughter kept in touch until his death in 1957.

COMMUNITY ASSISTANCE

Approximately fifteen hundred Jews reached Calcutta; the exact number is elusive, since many were immediately taken in by relatives and never appeared on the roles of the Jewish Refugee Relief Association at 3 Theatre Road. The Jewish refugees were met at the boats from Rangoon and the trains from Assam by members of the Burmese Refugee Committee and by a representative of the Calcutta Baghdadi community, who greeted them as one does with extended family, with food and offers of clothing, cash and other assistance. Except for this welcoming party, there was no formal assistance from the government or any other organization, and the refugees had to fend for themselves.[31] Despite the obvious hardships of refugee status, the Jews were fortunate, for thousands of other refugees, without the ties of an international "family" network as existed for the Baghdadis, huddled on the streets of Calcutta, hungry, destitute, disease-ridden.

The Calcutta Jewish community's resources were severely strained by the rapid influx of so many suddenly impoverished Jews from Burma, as well as of European Jews who were fleeing the war. The Jews from Burma found immediate refuge in the Jewish Girls School or in other locations until more permanent arrangements could be made. Fearing a Japanese advance into India, many Jewish refugees as well as Calcutta residents preferred to move to the mountains or to destinations farther west, especially to other Baghdadi communities in Bombay or Poona. The situation was exacerbated in December 1942 with the bombing of Calcutta. Fortunately, the raids did not continue, and funds raised in cooperation with the Calcutta Jewish Women's League could be devoted to the relief of indigent evacuees.

Calcutta during the war years offered many advantages to the refugees from Burma. Because many people left the city for safer havens, housing was easy to find. Calcutta was a center for production of war materials which would ship through its excellent port, as well as the site of American and British military bases, which made it an appealing target for the Japanese. At the same time, this meant that employment opportunities for the English-speaking Jews from Burma were plentiful; some found jobs with the British and American military and others with the service industries. The B. N. Elias & Company employed many refugees and also provided financial support for refugee resettlement.[32] And community life was familiar and comfortable, even during these troubled times.

With the exuberance of youth, Solly Saul—fresh from the trek from Burma to India—remembers his days in Calcutta as an exciting new adventure. He found himself in his grandparents' home, surrounded by relatives. School, home and synagogue were central to their daily lives—just as they had been in Rangoon. Wearing British schoolboy caps, the new boys from Burma easily adjusted to the Elias Meyer School. The curriculum was similar to that in Rangoon, except that now they also had to learn Urdu. What was different was that the larger Calcutta Jewish population could afford to support separate schools for boys and girls. While domestic life was reassuring, the war raged all around them: anti-aircraft balloons dotted the sky over the Howrah Bridge and the Hoogly River, sirens pierced the air, blackouts were frequent, essentials were rationed, and British and American soldiers, and air raid shelters, were everywhere.

An unexpected by-product of the Allied military presence in Calcutta was that Jewish soldiers provided knowledge and support for the Habonim (The Builders) Zionist movement, teaching these youth in India songs of the nation-to-be. Although Habonim had been established several years before in Calcutta, political Zionism was a new idea for the Jews from Burma. For them, as for Jews elsewhere, Israel had always been an ideal "promised land," but one to be realized only "when the Messiah comes." Now return to Israel was encountered as an attractive and active possibility, a concept and a pragmatic plan that was to become especially important for the refugees from Burma when that country no longer offered them a future.

The wartime experience of refugee Eriz Jacob and his wife provides a snapshot of how another family coped with the sudden disaster of refugee status. A graduate of the University of Rangoon, and on the Physics Faculty at the University at the time of his hurried departure, Mr. Jacob and his wife arrived in India in December 1941 with educational advantages but few possessions: "Our exit from Burma was somewhat like the Exodus from Egypt. The miracle . . . was that we could escape with our lives."[33] He found good employment at the Government of India's Survey Stores Office in Dehra Dun, in the foothills of the Himalayas north of Delhi, where the Saul family from Mandalay also settled temporarily. Because of its large map printing activity, the Survey Office was important to the war effort. It was at Dehra Dun that maps of Japan needed by the American forces, based on pre-war surveys by the British, were produced. While in Dehra Dun, the Jacob family hosted Jewish members of the British and American military for Sabbath and holiday meals, and for prayers. After the war, soldiers from both militaries offered to help the family resettle in their home countries. They chose the States, the soldiers kept their promise to procure visas and sponsorship, and the family arrived in Philadelphia in February 1948.

For Solly Saul and his family, it was marriage that led to resettlement in America (figure 6.1). Both Solly's mother and sister Seemah worked at the American Army Depot outside of Calcutta, where Seemah met her future husband. A few years later, the rest of the family followed Seemah to America.

THE WAR YEARS IN BURMA

While others fled to India, a small group of Jews remained in Burma throughout the war. Some were intermarried with Burmese, who could not qualify for space on the European-only ships. Some lived too far from Rangoon's port to escape in time, others stayed behind with elderly relatives in Bassein, and still others stayed in Rangoon to assure the safety of the synagogue. And some returned to Burma to fight the Japanese occupation.

Those who remained in Burma during the war years were enmeshed in the Burmese nationalism that accompanied the Japanese advance. Despite the fact that they had been born in Burma, to the Burmese nationalists the isolated Baghdadis were "Europeans" and therefore allies of the British. What reason could they have for being in Burma other than as spies for the other side? Ac-

Desperate Passage to India: The War in Burma 91

Figure 6.1. Trek Survivors Seemah (Betz), Solly, Charlie, and Simon Saul. Courtesy of Solly Saul.

cusations of spying took their toll on the families but only once had fatal consequences.

For the Jews in Rangoon during the war, their prime and sacred mission was to protect Musmeah Yeshua, the emblem of their religious devotion as well as of the Jewish community in Burma. Although, unlike their German allies, the Japanese demonstrated no singular antipathy to Jews, they did exacerbate tensions between the races during this period, resulting in hostility among Indians, Japanese, Chinese, and Burmese, and increased hostilities between the Burmese and hill tribes. The "formation of the Burma Independence Army was ostensibly part of a Japanese policy to conduct a *seisen* or holy war to liberate the one hundred thirty millions of tropical peoples (from) the colonial policy of the white peoples."[34] Ironically, the Baghdadis were finally accorded the "white" status denied them by the British and it was for this reason, not for being Jewish, that they were in danger.

News of the war was sparse. After December 1942, only Japanese-controlled radio was permitted, with dire persecution for violations. Radios were collected and adjusted to receive only allowed stations. To learn news from the Allies, one had to have a clandestine radio run on batteries. Information received this way apparently caused the death of the synagogue's caretaker, Elias Shamash, the only Jew to die during the war in Burma. A local betel-seller accused him of making pro-British statements, and the Japanese arrested him and tortured him to death by tying him by the ankles, hanging him upside down from a tree, and whipping him until he died. Isaac Samuels received the body for burial. Isaac Samuels and some of the other Jews were also imprisoned and tortured, surviving for a month on little more than weak tea.

The synagogue was a substantial building whose walls had been reinforced following an earthquake in 1932. Because of this, it withstood the bombing that shook Rangoon and destroyed the surrounding area. Looting and fires had erupted throughout the city during the interval between the British and European evacuation and the arrival of Japanese troops, but the synagogue was spared because the Jews raced to the roof and threw water on the embers that endangered the building. The synagogue might be of great interest to the Japanese, however, should they realize that the valuable silver-encased Sifrei Torah were hidden inside. With that danger in mind, Isaac Samuels and the others erected a few commercial shacks in the courtyard facing the street that obscured the synagogue and camouflaged the entrance. For six months, the synagogue went unnoticed by the Japanese, until one day a Japanese officer drove by, stopped his staff car, and demanded that the doors of the synagogue be unlocked. Fearful, the Jews stood by while the Japanese officer approached the *hekhal*, the small room where the Torah scrolls were hidden. Abruptly, surprisingly, the officer turned back without opening the door, and ordered the building to be locked and an "enemy property" sign placed on the entrance. And so it stayed until the liberation of Rangoon. As war ebbed, and the Japanese army began to retreat from Rangoon, looters again tried to force their way into the synagogue. They were held back by Jewish protectors with rifles.

Not so fortunate were the historical and financial documents belonging to the synagogue, which were stored for safe-keeping in the Hong Kong and Shanghai Bank at Barr and Merchant Streets. The bank was bombed during the war, and the documents lost. Fortunately, the personal records, the community registries, had been retained at the synagogue.

To the northeast of Rangoon, optometrist Isaac Sassoon, his Karen wife Naw Erra, and their children remained in Pegu. A crisis erupted when the Japanese mistook Isaac's *tefillen*, or phylacteries—the little boxes worn on the forehead and arm by Orthodox Jews for morning prayers—for radio transmitters, and came to arrest him as a spy. Only effective pleading by Naw Erra saved him, and the family survived the war without further incident. At the same time, Japanese soldiers courted the children, giving them candy, engaging them in sports, singing songs. Isaac's daughter Sarah still remembers the

Japanese songs the soldiers taught her as a child. After the war, in 1949, Sarah, her mother, and brothers converted to Judaism in Musmeah Yeshua and the family left Burma for Israel, where her brother died serving in the army during the Suez War.

In Bassein, the Raphael family decided to remain in their home rather than leave behind the elderly grandmother who could not make the difficult trip. Eight members of the family waited out the war in their home and then in the jungle near Bassein, recalls Margaret Raphael Glicksohn: "My aunt Sarah, Uncle Raphael, my father, my Uncle Jacob (who died later during the war), my cousin Abraham, myself, my mother, and our *shochet*, his wife, and grandson. We always stayed together."

"As Jews, the Japanese did not harm us except when the leaders of the town were taken for questioning. My uncle was taken with them, and held for months. He came home a different person, refused to talk and shut himself in a room for days." A dangerous situation arose when some of the local people, jealous of the Raphaels' wealth, told the Japanese that they were spies. When the Japanese came to confiscate their property, the Raphaels asked for a week of grace, and in that week appealed to a person they knew in Rangoon who was administering the country along with the Japanese. The order was rescinded. Margaret's year-by-year account suggests the experience of the Raphael family, cut off from community, living with little news and many bombs, and counting the years by how Passover was spent. She notes wisely, "Life was not easy for us in the jungle, but we survived, and that is what was important."

1942 Looting started. Jail open. Panic. No law and order in Bassein. *April*: Spent Pesach in a small village. Bombing, people were scared. *May*: Before the monsoons break, returned to Bassein. Law and order. Japanese enter Bassein. *August*: Japanese confiscate our property. *October*: Uncle Jack went to Rangoon, which took three days going, and three days coming by boat. *December*: Uncle Jack was taken away for questioning, and put in confinement camps by the Japanese.

1943 *January*: Uncle Jack was released. He broke down. *February–October*: We were busy doing the catering in our halls for Japanese and Burmese functions. Spent Pesach at home. *November*: Heard Wingate landed in Upper Burma. The bombing by the British and Americans became stronger.

1944 We moved to outskirts of the town. We spent Pesach there in the huts that we built. Uncle Jack took very ill. Bombing was going on everyday and life became terrible so we made arrangements to go deep into the jungle. *October*: Uncle Jack died. *November*: We left for the jungle. For the first time we listened to the radio which was run on battery. We heard the news from BBC and also the war songs like "Lili Marlene," "Yours," "Bless Them All," "There'll Always Be an England," etc. We treated the sick people from the jungle. In return they brought for us eggs, vegetables, and fresh fruit.

1945 *April*: We spent Pesach in the jungle and the bombing that night was very severe. We kept on saying (the traditional Passover question), "Why is this night different from all other nights?" *May*: Returned home. Rangoon taken, Japanese on the run. We heard V Day on radio. *June*: 14th Army troops enter Bassein in a convey system from India. A concert was held in honor of them with me taking the part of Britannia. *July*: A supply of food dropped from the air. For the first time we received letters through the Red Cross from friends and relatives from India. *August*: Nagasaki bombed, then Hiroshima atom bombed. Peace. The Japanese surrendered.

Isolated in the jungle near Mawbin, the Hayeem family thought they were the only Jews remaining in Burma during the war. As the Japanese advanced, the family fled from Rangoon with five children under six, two of whom died during these difficult years due to lack of medical attention and medication, and an inadequate diet of rice and occasional fish. Suspecting that they might be spies, the Japanese searched the Hayeems' house during the middle of the night but left them alone after nothing was found. After the war, the family returned to Rangoon but not as quickly to health, nor was it easy to recover the five years of lost education for the children.

Saw Benson—formerly Moses Ben-Zion Koder—also remained in Burma during the war. The descendent on his father's side of the prominent Koder family of Cochin, and on his mother's side from the Sephardic Leynado family, he was orphaned as a child and sent to a convent school in Calcutta, where he converted to Christianity at the age of fourteen. On return to Burma, Benson became a clerk in the store of B. Meyer and Co., and in 1939, he married a Karen woman, Naw Chit Khin. Benson was ever grateful to the Karen, who saved his life during the war, and was forever committed to the Christian Karen tribe's struggles against the Japanese occupation and afterward for independence from the Burmese majority. For this he was to suffer.

Two close friends returned to Burma during the war as military officers. Captain Saul Ezra Saul of Mandalay and now with the Royal Artillery Regiment had retreated with the British from Burma in January 1942. He came back to the land he knew so well as commander of a Gurkha regiment of the Chindits—the British, Indian, Gurkha and Burmese soldiers led by General Orde Wingate who fought in the treacherous highlands of northern Burma. Commander Ezra Solomon, Burma Division, British Royal Navy, who had trekked to India in 1942, was in charge of a gunboat in Lower Burma.

POLISH JEWS IN BURMA AND INDIA

Ironically, just before hostilities began in Burma, thirty-two Jewish refugees from Poland had been resettled by the Joint Distribution Committee, very unhappily, in Rangoon.[35] After a long trip through Lithuania and Siberia, they first went to Shanghai or Kobe, but these areas were overwhelmed by the massive movements of refugees from the war in Europe and requested help in directing refugees to safe locations elsewhere. In Rangoon, many came down with tropical fever or influenza, and could not adjust either to the weather or the living conditions. Unable to find jobs, sick, and disoriented by Burmese society, they immediately petitioned the American Jewish Joint Distribution Committee and the Hebrew Immigrant Aid Society for assistance in moving from Burma to a place where they would be more physically comfortable and could use their professional skills. Their first choices were Australia or Palestine. In a letter, dated October 31, 1941, written to the American Jewish Joint Distribution Committee, Cracow lawyer D. Bernstein Szymon explains the situation:

> After two years of wandering in the hardest conditions, bereft from our native country, homes, families and properties we were directed to Burma. We hoped to get here jobs and positions and to establish ourselves in this country. Thus we expected to become again useful members of the society not compelled to profit by the beneficence of others.
>
> Unfortunately our hopes failed. In a period of 3 months few persons only of our party could find jobs, whilst most of us cannot make their living. The prospects for an improvement of this situation are quite adverse as there are no possibilities to obtain further positions for the unemployed part of our group. A great many of us remain without any means to meet such indispensable expenses as shoes' repairing, laundry, soap, cigarettes, etc. . . . Besides coming from the North we can hardly get accustomed to the tropical climate prevailing over this country, which is distinctly proved by the sick list of the group, 3–6 persons falling ill daily . . .

The lack of an organized Jewish relief organization in Rangoon surprised N. Berman, who says in his letter to HIAS, dated September 26, 1941:

> As we wrote you before, quite apart from the fact that the Polish refugees represent an element unsuitable for the country, there is no Jewish community, no social workers, no one to whom the refugees could apply, which naturally tells on the situation of the refugees. The majority of the Jews living there are in bad financial circumstances themselves and the refugees cannot expect any help from them, while the richer Jews—capitalists, industrialists—are assimilated and take hardly any interest, if at all, in them.[36]

The Polish refugees fled to Calcutta with the other Jews of Burma and were assisted by the Calcutta Jewish community. In Calcutta, they continued their requests to the American Jewish Joint Distribution Committee for assistance in traveling further, citing continuing illnesses and inability to find jobs in India. They ultimately received visas and travel funds for Santo Domingo, Bolivia, or Australia.

NOTES

1. Alfred Draper, *Dawns Like Thunder: The Retreat from Burma*, 1–2.
2. Draper, 2.
3. Bayly and Harper, *Forgotten Armies*, 95.
4. Draper, 23.
5. Aung San became Minister of Defense in Ba Maw's puppet government (1943–45). Disillusioned with Japanese promises should they win the war, and unhappy about their treatment of the Burmese forces, he switched allegiance to the Allies in March 1945.
6. Estimates for the first bombing are 2,750 dead and 1,700 wounded. Hyman, 160. There was one Jewish casualty, Shlomo Solomon.
7. Muriel Sue DeGaa Uphill, *An American in Burma*, 194.
8. Bayly and Harper, 167.
9. Mavis Hyman, *Jews of the Raj*, 159 (Governor General to Secretary of State for India.) Deciphered telegram 14:1:42. POL 361. IOR, File L/P&J/8/436. Oriental & India Office Collections (OIOC). The British Library, London.
10. Solly Saul, *Sephardi Bulletin*, New South Wales Association of Sephardim, March 1995, 14.
11. Bayly and Harper, xxiv.
12. Hyman, 166–67.
13. Bayly and Harper, 175.
14. Personal communication.
15. Draper, 215.
16. In four months, from mid-December 1941 through mid-May 1942, the Japanese advanced 1,000 miles.
17. Manahadur Rai (M. Gyi), "'Gorkhali ayo!' Gurkha Soldiers in the Battle for Imphal, 1944," *Command*, 1992, Vol. 16.
18. Hyman, 159–77.
19. A potentially deadly disease transmitted by sand flies that affects the spleen and distends the abdomen.
20. Estimates of the number of refugees vary widely, from 100,000 to 200,000. Hyman puts the number at 200,000, based on Extracts from Report by the Administrator General on the Evacuation of Refugees from Burma to India (Assam), January–July 1942. Section I.IOR, File L/P&J/8/439 (OIOIC). The British Library, London.

21. Hyman, 164.
22. Personal communication.
23. *Burma Today*, January 1945, Government of Burma, Simla, as quoted in Andrus, *Burmese Economic Life*, 35. This supports the British estimate, as quoted by Hyman, 162/245.
24. Personal communication.
25. Personal communication.
26. Personal communication, July 1993. It is a duty of every Jew to take part in a Seder ritual on Passover; Albert Judah means that he recited the haggadah and fulfilled the requirements.
27. Hyman, 133.
28. Hyman, 169, quoting IOR. File L/P&J/8/436 Burma 11928 (OIOC). The British Library, London.
29. Hyman, 170.
30. Personal correspondence, July 6, 2003.
31. As difficult as it was for other refugees, the exhausted and emaciated British soldiers faced a different and surreal situation: a British military in India still living the proper social life of parties and fine clothing of pre-war Burma, and who looked askance at the "disheveled" new arrivals. Draper reports that "Earlier in the war the British Army had evacuated from Dunkirk and when the weary men reached England they were greeted like returning heroes and given every available comfort by a grateful people. The Burma Army looked forward to a similar reception; instead they were treated as something of a nuisance and subjected to a great deal of sarcasm and bullying from some commanders and their staff." *Dawns Like Thunder*, 259.
32. Hyman, 169.
33. Paper given at Temple B'nai Hayim, Los Angeles, on Friday, May 24, 1985.
34. Andrew Selth, *Race and Resistance in Burma, 1942–1945*, 494–95, 497.
35. The number quoted varies from 32 to 50. Archives of the American Jewish Joint Distribution Committee 1933/1944; File #440.
36. AJJDC Archives, File #440.

Chapter Seven

Return to Burma

Hoping to retrieve the happy life they knew in Burma, three to four hundred Jews returned to Rangoon and Mandalay after the war,[1] joining the few who had lived out these years in Bassein, Pegu, Mawbin or Rangoon. They eagerly anticipated seeing beloved *ayahs* and friends left behind, and envisioned the peace and warmth they remembered after so many turbulent years. Some with limited finances or willing to undergo another relocation returned with the hope that postwar Burma would offer them financial security. What they found was devastation, both economic and material.[2] The once-stately colonial city of Rangoon was gone, demolished by bombs, fire and theft, and deep in filth and garbage. Dalhousie Street, long the center of Jewish commercial life, was in ruins. Homes were occupied by others and usually looted, the memory-saturated possessions of Baghdadi lifetimes gone forever. Buildings were stripped of wooden doors, wiring, metal, panes of glass, and even doorknobs, and there was no electricity or running water. The lake area was a shambles. There was no transportation of any kind. The Jewish school was severely damaged.

Yet amid the burned-out buildings of central Rangoon, the synagogue still stood, unharmed, its Sifrei Torah undamaged and ready to serve the shattered community. The beautiful synagogue was a symbol of hope for the returning population, and its reopening in 1945 was celebrated on Shavuot with Jewish American and British soldiers in Burma, under the guidance of Senior British Chaplain Rabbi Morris Jaffe. A seminar for Jewish soldiers and community members was also held that year in Rangoon.[3] In a later discussion in Bombay, Rabbi Jaffe remarked that he was surprised to find two families living in separate shacks in the synagogue compound. In spite of the ordeal they had gone through, they were still not on speaking terms.[4]

These were very difficult times. It was hard to make a living in Burma after the war. Many Jews who returned from Calcutta with such fond memories and cautious hopes soon found the obstacles of a destroyed economy and lost homes too much to overcome. Some were able to reestablish businesses, but more entered the service sector, working for the railroads, customs and other government offices, as wireless operators, clerks, or as salesmen, manufacturers' representatives, or in another capacity as employees of American or European firms. Many of the returnees were destitute, and the fledgling community, struggling to reconstitute itself, had few funds to support them. The most needy were resettled at the site of the Jewish school at 22 Sandwith Road and given a small allowance from community funds to tide them over, funds which sorely tested the resources of the community.

Over all loomed the question of the future of minority communities now that the British protectorate was gone. Burma became an independent sovereign republic on January 4, 1948. Unlike India, Pakistan and Ceylon, at similar crossroads, Burma declined membership in the British Commonwealth,[5] thus closing the British "umbrella" that had seemed to shelter the Jews and other minorities in Burma. There was a strong movement to declare Buddhism a state religion, and in so doing draw a more clearly articulated line between Burmans and minorities. Writing in *Religion and Politics in Burma*, Donald Eugene Smith says,

> In Burma, Buddhist Burmese communalism coalesced easily with nationalism. There was little support for the concept of a nation composed of diverse ethnic groups, speaking different languages, and professing different religions. In contrast, Indian nationalism by definition had to mean something more inclusive than Hindu or Muslim communalism. Undoubtedly, the nationalist theme of the glory of India's ancient culture was closely associated with Hinduism, but this could not be emphasized to the exclusion of the thousand years of Indian Muslim culture. The Muslims were a large minority (25 percent), mostly of the same racial stock as the Hindus and speaking the same languages. . . . In Burma, on the other hand, many of the non-Buddhists were aliens, and this fact tended to reinforce the traditional notions of the Burmese national identity. Buddhism was a Burmese national symbol. The Buddha was an important figure in the national heritage, and many Burmese villagers refused (and still refuse) to believe that he was an Indian.[6]

A deliberate process of "Burmanization" followed. At the time of the transfer of power from the British to an independent Burma, the British had advised the foreign business community that it would be in their best financial interests to leave the country, but many ignored that advice out of reluctance to relocate or false optimism. Burmese citizenship was now advocated for all residents, and all citizens were to adopt Burmese names. The English names of many thoroughfares in central Rangoon were replaced by Burmese names: Dalhousie Street, named after a British Governor-General of India, became Maha Bandoola Street to honor a great Burmese military commander of the nineteenth century; Phayre Street, named for a Chief Commissioner of British Burma, became Pansodan Street, and Judah Ezekiel Street, Thein Byu Street. Barr and Lewis Streets had been home to many Jews before the war; now they were called, respectively, Bandoola Gardens Street and Sek Khan Tha. Montgomery Street became Bogyoke Aung San Street; Sparks Street, Bo Aung Kyan Street; Windsor Road, Shin Saw Pu Road; and the Scott Market, a landmark in the commercial center of prewar Burma, is now the Bogyoke Aung San Market.

Section 23 of the new Constitution of the State of Burma, entitled Economic Rights, begins: "(1) Subject to the provisions of this section, the State guarantees the rights of private property and of private initiative in the economic sphere." Ominously, it continues: "(4) Private property may be limited or expropriated if the public interest so requires but only in accordance with law which shall prescribe in which cases and to what extent the owner shall be compensated," and "(5) Subject to the conditions set out in the last preceding subsection, the individual branches of national economy or single enterprises may be nationalized or acquired by the State by law if the public interest so requires."

Burmese entrepreneurs were encouraged to enter areas of business formerly dominated by Indian, British and Jewish merchants. While for the Burmese this was a period of optimism, the chaotic, altered economic and political situation in Burma had the opposite effect on many of the Jewish returnees. For them, the upheaval accompanying Burmese independence delayed or seemed to preclude social and economic recovery.

Writing in 1949, Nissim Meyer expresses the dilemma faced by the Jews who returned to Burma:

> The future of the Jews in Burma is very uncertain. Burma became an Independent Sovereign Republic on January 4, 1948 . . . there is no anti-Semitism in Burma. In fact, the Burmese people and Government have great sympathy for Jewish sufferings during the last war. The Burmese Jew now stands at the crossroads. Will he become a Burmese national or remain a British subject? The Burmese Government has given its people two years in which to make their choice. The present political unrest and turmoil in the country together with the leanings of all responsible Burmese leaders to the Left will make it very difficult for business enterprise in the country. The economy of the country is purely agricultural based on the growing and export of rice. All industrial and business enterprises are to be State-run. Whether in this context the small businesses will

suffer, the next few months will show. As it is, the growing Government restrictions on export and import are hitting them badly. It will be a hard choice, as almost the whole of the Jewish community have a great affection for the country and its people. Again to trek to other lands and start afresh would be a bitter blow to them.[7]

Adding urgency to the situation was the notification by the Union of Burma that everyone who was not a Burman must register by the end of June 1949. Echoing Nissim Meyer's concerns, the synagogue's President of the Board of Trustees Charles Manasseh asks,

If they register, the point now raised is whether in the event of Burmanisation what will be the position of those who had registered as foreigners. Will they be forced to leave the country in the event of their not choosing to become Burma citizens? Will they be allowed to carry on business as heretofore? These are some of the questions perplexing the minds of those who wish to remain behind till their affairs are wound up. It is problematic if the indigenous races will be given a free hand in business as it is made clear from posters and slogans 'BURMA FOR BURMANS.'[8]

Reluctantly, many returnees reassessed their decision to come back to Burma. In a letter to the Immigration Department of the Jewish Agency, Charles Manasseh says:

Owing to insurgent activities all over the country and the chaotic conditions prevailing, brought about the armed insurrection by dissident elements against the present Government, living conditions are not too comfortable. Businesses have been stagnant owing to restrictive measures imposed by the Government of the Union of Burma. Blackmarketeering is rampant and the cost of living has gone up by leaps and bounds. Law and order are the things of the past. Armed robbery is the order of the day and everyday brings fear in the hearts of the people not knowing what the day will bring in its wake. There is no sign yet to give an inkling as to when conditions will return to normal. What with communist threats from the north (China) and internal faction, I am inclined to think that the sooner the people are evacuated to Israel the happier will be their lot. Delay in sending aid may bring about added dangers to their well being and safety.[9]

Israel appeared as the best and perhaps the most expedient alternative to Rangoon, a destination in keeping with the Baghdadis' traditional religious orientation. Nissim Meyer had presided over a quiet celebration in the synagogue to mark the Declaration of the State of Israel, on May 22, 1948. Starting in 1949, Jews from Burma as well as India sought visas to immigrate to Israel.[10] To Charles Manasseh, the most pressing situation was that of 143 individuals in forty-five families, most of whom lacked even the funds to immigrate to Israel. In early 1949, he asked the World Jewish Congress for assistance with visas and travel funds, and included two lists of potential emigrants according to urgency: an A list of the forty-five families and a B list of an additional 178 potential emigrants.[11] He also requested assistance in transporting many of Musmeah Yeshua's Torah scrolls to Israel.[12] In May, he noted that the A list now included forty-two families, as three had found a way to leave for Israel.

The lack of good higher education in Burma, and the uncertainty about the future, also influenced the decision to emigrate. The University of Rangoon had opened with a reduced staff in August 1946, but strikes from January to March 1947 seriously impeded academic work, and immediate improvement in the situation seemed doubtful. In January 1949, E. N. Abraham cited his son's education in his appeal to the World Jewish Congress for assistance in emigrating to London or New York:

> The education here in schools and at the Universities is extremely below the prewar standard. In the Medical College there is not one European professor as there used to be in prewar days. Most of the professors and lecturers are students who passed out from the same College and have no foreign degrees at all . . . to admit (my son) in the college here is a waste of time and money and the qualifications he will receive will not be worth the trouble.

Mr. Abraham notes that he has a profession and is earning a decent wage, and further writes that "Some quarters are of the opinion that foreigners will be asked to leave the country in time to come. If such will be the case, we will find ourselves stranded not knowing where to go. India may not have us, if she goes out of the Commonwealth."[13]

As in other *rites de passage*, new social identities were to be reinforced by new names. The new independent Burma now insisted that its citizens take Burmese names. Similarly, Jews who declined to become citizens of Burma and chose another nation instead sometimes announced their new national identity by changing their names. Thus, on going to Sydney in 1948, Solomon Gabriel Solomon became Stephen Gilbert Solomon. Perhaps in anticipation of such a future, names for newborns now included Shirley, Yvonne, Ingrid, Diana, Sandra, Kate, Rosie, Edwin and Sherwan.

CITIZENSHIP

Complicating emigration was the question of British citizenship. Simple understandings of citizenship which had comforted the Jews of Burma before the war turned out to have uncomfortable qualifications when put to the test.

British citizenship was automatic if it could be proven that the person's grandparents or parents had been born in England—but this, of course, was rarely the case for the Jews of Burma. More commonly, some Jews had been naturalized while in Burma, and therefore held British passports. As the children of naturalized citizens, their sons and daughters had derivative British citizenship. However, after the war derivative citizenship was not sufficient for immigration into the United Kingdom. It took an Act of Parliament to affirm their citizenship, and even then there was a delay in receiving permission to enter Britain. Until this happened, these derivative citizens were stateless.

Others had not considered it necessary to worry about their legal status, since it seemed to them that Jews, as well as other groups living under the British, were considered British by birth. This was not what they found after the British relinquished sovereignty to the Burmese. The British ambassador refused to recognize such individuals as British citizens, and therefore they found themselves stateless. If it could be proven that one's parents or grandparents were born outside of Burma, a temporary passport would be issued, valid only for the named destination. If, as was often the case, the person had no proof of place of birth, he or she could not secure a passport. This is where the detailed birth records of Musmeah Yeshua were helpful, for they documented the full name as well as the parentage of the applicant.

In 1936, Albert Judah could not foresee how useful his decision to become a naturalized British citizen would be in the complicated days after the war. On July 6, in Bassein, he took the following oath: "I, Mr. Albert Judah, Clerk, Messrs. A. Raphael & Sons, No. 9, Merchant Street, Bassein, do hereby swear that I will be faithful and bear true allegiance to His Majesty the King, Emperor of India, His Heirs and Successors." His citizenship was not valid in Calcutta, but it was in London, and his way was further eased because Jews from Burma had a larger quota for immigration than their cousins in Calcutta.

By the 1950s, it seemed the cosmopolitan atmosphere of prewar Rangoon might be reestablished after all, at least as represented in the English-language newspapers. One could buy Hayward's Fine Brandy at Charles Joseph and Co, Ltd, 95–97 36th Street; vitamin Tonic Okasa at Benjamin and Co, 272 Mogul Street; Varlo Malted Milk a few doors away at the shop of Aaron J. A. David, 364 Mogul Street; or a typewriter on the still-named Judah Ezekiel Street. Rangoon's *Burmese Review* carried cultural and political news from all over the world, but relatively little domestic news: articles by Arnold Toynbee, Bertrand Russell, George Bernard Shaw, Jane Jacobs; profiles of Gandhi, John Foster Dulles, Eleanor Roosevelt, and Esther Williams; articles on town planning in America, the Pierpoint Morgan Library in New York, and Romanian Folk Art. International news—from political events to society happenings and fashion—filled the pages, so that in far-off Burma one could still be in the mainstream of world events. Benny Goodman and his band played in Aung San Stadium in late December 1956 and early January 1957, with Prime Minister U Nu in attendance, and the movie theaters—the Globe, Royal, Grand, Carlton, Excelsior, and Palladium—showed the same films as in London and New York. In 1956, the first Miss Burma contest was held.

However, beneath this veneer of international sophistication lay the irrefutable prospect of a sour economic and political future, and many of those who had returned and even had secured positions with foreign companies redoubled their efforts to emigrate.

WORLD JEWISH CONGRESS

In October 1947, and throughout subsequent years, the World Jewish Congress invited the Jews of Burma to affiliate with it, citing the prior affiliation of the communities in Bombay, Calcutta, and Shanghai. In a letter to the community, the World Jewish Congress stressed that it would have greater leverage in dealing with the postwar problems of Jews worldwide if it could demonstrate that the organization speaks for the broadest range of Jewish settlement.[14] By 1949, the Cochin community had also joined the WJC. Finally, on March 24, 1949, the Burmese community became the sixty-fourth country to affiliate with the World Jewish Congress.[15] Affiliation was formalized on February 16, 1950.

Apparently, however, the needs of the Jewish community in Burma, which prompted the affiliation, and the needs of the World Jewish Congress at the time, were at cross purposes, or were limited by resources and priorities of the time. The Rangoon community wanted wider recognition and economic support for its plight, a local representative acknowledged by the World Jewish Congress (and later, by Israel), and assistance in emigration, including a request to the British Embassy to issue passports for those who wished to settle elsewhere.[16] While somewhat sympathetic to these needs, the WJC seemed to be unaware of the situation in Burma, and their first priorities were the establishment of a quasi-political presence in the postwar world, and the reconstruction of lives in Europe following the Holocaust and the founding of the State of Israel.

Starting in 1949, Charles Manasseh repeatedly asked the World Jewish Congress to designate him their representative in Burma, citing the need of an "official" Jewish advocate in Burma. While relations between the Government of Burma and the small Jewish community were cordial, he noted that other minority groups, such as the Chinese, Christians, British, and Indians had such outside leverage to protect their communities. A visitor to Burma in

1949 confirmed Manasseh's perspective, writing that "the Jews in Rangoon are not at any greater disadvantage than other foreign nationalities and races. . . . The only difference is that the Jews have no home government to protect them as do the others." He adds, "The question in Burma seems to be a question of anti-whites and anti-foreigners. There is no question of anti-semitism."[17] The new Legation of Israel, cautiously establishing diplomatic relations between these new nations, could not or would not get involved in Burma's internal political situation.

In response, the World Jewish Congress pressed for a census, reports, and biographical data that would familiarize them with the domestic situation, as well as attendance at international meetings in Europe to enhance the WJC's roster of nations and international reach. Given the precarious financial state and passport problems of the Jews in Burma, attendance at international meetings, no matter how desirable, appears an unlikely request. The Congress did take note of the fact that there was no Jewish school now operating, and promised help in securing rabbinical and educational resources, as well as a local representative for Jewish interests.[18]

When, in 1950, the WJC seemed open to the idea of such a representative, Charles Manasseh had resigned his position to devote more time to his business. By 1950 also, about 150 Jews had already left Burma for Israel, India, the United Kingdom, and the United States.[19] The Jews in Burma were now voting with their feet and leaving the country for better prospects. Nevertheless, a very optimistic memo that circulated through the World Jewish Congress's executive circle in May, 1950, saw a brighter future for the approximately three hundred Jews remaining in Burma. It cited the prospect of diplomatic and trade relations between Israel and Burma, which might benefit Rangoon's Jewish businessmen. If, however, prosperity did not come, emigration to Israel would be helped by Israel's diplomatic presence in Rangoon. Landing permits in Rangoon for international airlines would help in the case of emigration to Israel and an Israeli diplomatic presence would help Jews transfer their assets to Israel on emigration. In addition, the memo suggested that Israel could buy Burmese materials which could be paid for by Jewish funds for those leaving for Israel.[20]

A SHATTERED, SHUTTERED COMMUNITY

The unsettled status, marginal incomes, and limited finances plagued the returnees even as they tried to reestablish the social and religious life of the community. Before the war, Jewish shops were closed for the eight days of Passover and Sukkot, for Shabbat, and all holidays. After the war, businesses were closed only on Shabbat and two days of Passover, and those who worked for non-Jewish businesses often had to work on Saturday as well. Where once there was a vibrant Jewish school and a religious practice in the Iraqi traditional mode, now there was no one to teach Hebrew, nor was there a *mohel* to perform circumcisions, a *shochet* to prepare kosher meats, or a ritual leader to assure the correctness of the traditional religious service. Given their constrained finances, the community sought a religiously trained person to assume the multiple functions of cantor, Hebrew teacher, *shochet* and *mohel*. For ritual occasions, someone now had to be brought from Calcutta. The following description of a ritual circumcision in the mid-1950s illustrates the drastically changed circumstances of this formerly traditional community:

> It was on the occasion of the *Brit* and *Pidyon HaBen* of a new Jew that we first encountered the remaining Jews of Burma. The occasion was celebrated in traditionally Sephardi-Burmese Jewish style. The baby was eight months old,[21] a not surprising fact, since his parents lived in the interior, and travel was difficult. The Raphaels, the Solomons, the Josephs and the Davids—all the Burmese Jewish families—were there, including visiting aunts, cousins, uncles and in-laws from Calcutta. Burmese dignitaries were there too, and the whole Israeli contingent. Despite the delicious curry, the presence of the *mohel*, the Burmese in their colorful national dress and the Indian aunts in their gold-bordered saris, it was a party not without a touch of nostalgia for the glorious occasions of the past.[22]

Nostalgia for the glorious past as well as lingering loyalty prompted the notice in the *New Times* of Burma on February 14, 1952, announcing a special prayer to be held at "Musmeah Yeshua Synagogue on 15th February at 5 p.m. for His Late Majesty King George the VI," who had died in his sleep in London a week before.

With the former Jewish school now dilapidated and abandoned, Jewish families had no option but to send all children to the international missionary schools. The Israeli Ambassador's wife, Mrs. David Hacohen, taught a small Hebrew class on Sunday morning, and a *hazan* taught Torah. In compliance with requests from the World Jewish Congress, a commemoration of the Warsaw Ghetto uprising was held each April. An Israeli Club held dances, a sport club convened, and a fund for Israel, the Keren Hayesod United Israel Campaign, was established, but these activities did not replace the tradition, religious orthodoxy and common experience that had bound the community for so many years. In early 1955 forty-five Sifrei Torah encased in gold and silver *tiks* and 143 *parochets* were sent to Israel on the SS *Ethrog*, carefully disguised in mundane metal cases, since by that time Burma prohibited the export of such valuable objects. The community was now estimated to number about 150 people (figure 7.1).

Figure 7.1. Inside the Synagogue, 1959. Courtesy of Margaret Raphael Glicksohn.

And then, in November 1956, another blow was dealt the small Jewish presence in Burma. Events in the Middle East had finally reached far-off Burma in an ugly way. On November 9, at the time of the Suez War, anti-British, anti-French and anti-Israel demonstrations were organized by the pro-Egypt, mostly Muslim, Suez Committee. Shouting hostile slogans, a procession of three to four thousand people marched through downtown Rangoon. Finding the British, French and Israeli Embassies well guarded, they continued on to the more vulnerable site of the synagogue, breaking doors and windows, and destroying books and furniture. The shops of Aaron J. A. David and E. S. Mayer & Gandhi were stoned and pasted with anti-Israel posters. Another group of protesters headed toward the primary Jewish residential area and the former Jewish school, with the intention of setting it on fire. By then, fortunately, the police were in force and turned the crowd away.[23] Although there were no casualties—the shops were closed for the day—for the first time in Burma, Jews feared for their lives *as Jews*. The Legation of Israel discussed the situation with the Burmese government, asking for more protection for the community, and things quieted down in a few days. Nevertheless, the political realities added another reason for emigration.

The diminishing numbers exacerbated the problems for the Jews remaining in Burma. Trust funds were depleted because of expenditures for synagogue maintenance and contributions to the United Jewish Appeal, and the trustees looked to the World Jewish Congress for assistance in creating a library and restoring the school.[24] In turn, during the 1950s and 1960s, the trustees received numerous appeals for assistance, for school fees, for housing, for passage abroad, and for money to live on. Until the property was sold in 1961, temporary accommodations were available on the top floors of the Jewish school for people awaiting emigration or who had no other place to live. In Moulmein, the cemetery was in need of urgent repairs, and villagers were already removing bricks from broken graves.[25] The trustees were also receiving requests to help validate emigration papers by providing birth certificates, a request they could not always honor. Not all births, especially in the small towns throughout Burma, had been recorded in the Musmeah

Yeshua's Registry, and without such information a valid birth certificate could not be issued.

The synagogue remained the focal point of Jewish pride and the location of social assembly, but lifestyles were changing, and the force of tradition and social consensus no longer held individual Jews to the absolute standards set in Iraq. In addition, the contentious nature of relationships within the small community hardly helped the situation.

With marriageable partners fewer within the Jewish community, intermarriage increased; with economic difficulties, business partnerships with people who were not Jewish—and therefore not bound by Jewish law—also increased. Problems multiplied. Jews were interacting with the non-Jewish community, books and Torah scrolls were deteriorating, and the ritual status of intermarried Jews and of Jews who violated Jewish law was unclear. The result was dissension within the community and questions about ritual status within the synagogue. With no ritual authority on site, common understandings in Judaism needed to be restated by the Beth Din. After the war, the trustees appealed to the Beth Din Rabbinical Court in London, rather than in Iraq, for such rulings. The following letter, addressed to The Court of the Chief Rabbi, Adler House, Adler Street, London, on June 18, 1957, asks opinions on these important questions—questions unthinkable twenty years earlier:

1. Any Jew having a gentile partner whose business premises are open publicly on the Feast of Passover, Feast of Weeks, Feast of Tabernacles and New Years Day, does our law allow . . . any Jew having a partner (junior) to have the shop open for business on such Religious Holidays as stated? Can this type of Jew hold office as a Trustee of a Synagogue?
2. Any Jew having a gentile partner, can this partner of a different caste . . . have an idol picture with a light burning in the business premises when in the same premises a Maezooza is at the shop door (?) . . . does our law stretch any point that this is allowed? Can the idol picture be there considering this partner is a non-Jew? Can this type of Jew become a Trustee of the Synagogue and hold office as a Trustee?[26]

At a time when decreasing numbers might make it difficult even to assemble a *minyan*, questions of ritual appropriateness became increasingly troublesome. A significant problem was that there was no one to repair damaged Torah scrolls. Strict rules and training guide the scribe who writes and repairs a Torah; it cannot be done by someone who is unqualified. Like the Author of the text, each of the words is holy and must be perfectly transcribed. Therefore, when words become defective, the Torah is ritually impure, *pasool*. Relaxation or disregard of orthodox tradition presented many other difficult issues, given the need for a full *minyan* for congregational prayer. On February

12, 1961, J. S. Meyer, the Secretary of Musmeah Yeshua, wrote again to the London Beth Din for guidance. The reply advises that:

1. It is improper for a Jew to enter Pagodas if they contain either idols or any symbols of worship.
2. a) A Sepher Torah "if you know one word to be Pasool" is not to be used for the Reading of the Law on Sabbaths, Festivals, Fast Days, Rosh Chodesh, Monday or Thursdays. If, however, there is no other Sepher Torah available, it would be permitted to read from it if the "Pasool" word is not in the Books of the Five Books of the Torah from which the Pareshah has to be read; for instance, if the Pasool word is a Parashah in the Book of Exodus only, you may read a portion from any of the other four Books. When, however, a portion has to be read from the Book which contains the Pasool word and there is no other Sepher Torah available, the portion may be read from it as one would read from a Chumash without calling up for aliyot and without Beracha before and after the reading.
3. If a Jew who has married out of the Faith demands to be called to the Sepher Torah, he may be called to the Sepher or given a Mitzvah only on the day of, or on the Sabbath before, his Yahrzeit. Where there is no alternative, he may be counted for Minyan.
4. One who does not know how to respond Amen or respond Kadeesh or repeat Kaedoosha may be counted for a Minyan; he may be called to the Sepher if one who is standing by prompts him with the Beracha.
5. A Jew who smokes on Sabbath and eats Asoor ("forbidden," i.e., non-kosher food), if such violation is willful and deliberate that he could be called a (word missing) he may not be counted for Minyan and should not be called to the Sepher. If, however, such violation arose out of his ignorance of Jewish observance he may be counted for Minyan and called to the Sepher Torah.
6. Where there are two or three Cohanim one is to be called up first, the other Cohen may be called up for Acharon, i.e., a portion of no less than three verses is left after the seven regular Aliyot, and the third may be called up for Maftir.[27]

Later that same year, the trustees wrote again to London on a variety of other religious matters that reveal how difficult it was to reconcile traditional practice with current conditions in Burma. They asked whether a boy prior to his Bar Mitzvah might be counted for the *minyan*; if a Pasool Torah could be used on the Day of Atonement; how to observe Rosh Hashanah now that no one was left in Burma who could sound the *shofar* for the Tekiyot ceremony; whether a *kohen* who was intermarried could be called to the Torah as a *kohen*; about the distribution of charitable funds; if they could use local flour to make matzah; and if there were rulings about proper dress for synagogue attendance. The reply came on August 10, 1961, 28th Ab 5721:

1. A boy a few months prior to his Bar Mitzvah (only in the event of there being extreme difficulty in obtaining a Minyan) may if he holds a Chumash in his hands be permitted to be counted in the Minyan. This dispensation is only permitted in cases where there would otherwise be no Minyan, *and only when the other nine persons are adults.* He cannot be called to the Sefer until Bar Mitzvah.
2. If it is your custom to take out all the Sefarim from the Holy Ark on Kippur night, the Pasool Sefer is permitted to be taken out. Every effort, however, must be taken to have the Pasool Sefer repaired by a competent Sofer as soon as possible and without delay.
3. [You ask] if there is no Tkaiya to sound the Shofar. On Rosh Hashanah what is there to be done? ... one of your laymen, a Shomer Shabbat, should try his utmost to practice the sounding of the Tekiyot.... If such a thing is not possible and you cannot bring in a Baal Tekiya from outside your Community, you will have to have the full Service, but unfortunately without Tekiyat Shofar ...
4. Where there are ten men, that is a Minyan, a Sefer should be taken out for the Reading of the Law even though there be among the men one who has a non-Jewish wife. If he is a "Cohen" he may *not* be called up as a "Cohen." Even if he is a "Levi" or "Yisrael" he may be called up *only on the occasion of Yarhzeit.*
5. Charity from your Synagogue funds may be given to any Jewess if she is destitute and in need.[28]
6. Flour from the market is not permitted for Matza for Pesach. Even wheat has to be specially selected and treated in a particular manner in milling to be kosher for Passover. We can see no other way for you but to import Matza bearing the Hechsher (kosher certification) of a recognized orthodox Rabbinate either from this country, or from Israel.
7. It is proper to be dressed correctly in Synagogue, particularly when being called to the Sefer, and every effort should be made to maintain such standards. In cases of difficulty, it is not improper for you to continue your present practice.[29]

Death presented yet another set of problems. On January 7, 1963, the community asked for rulings about how to handle an accidental death (answer: *Tahara*, purification, should be performed, but not on a part of the body where there is blood) and the proper disposal of an old *arone*, or bier ("it is to be broken up and buried in the cemetery"). Apparently in response to a question relating to relatives of the deceased, the Beth Din reiterates that a man with a non-Jewish wife is not to be called to the Torah: "It is preferable that the brother and the father and son be called up following each other rather than invite this man to the Sepher." The community even needed to be reminded about essential laws of traditional Judaism:

> There is no difference between pork and beef from an animal not ritually slaughtered. All is Trefah and forbidden in Jewish law.
>
> This married Jewish woman who lives with another man is not permitted to return to her husband. If she has a child from the non-Jew, the child is considered a Jew.
>
> No person is permitted, even if he knows the Law, to act as a Shochet without a certificate of qualification—Semakah—from a Rabbinate. Therefore, even if he has a certificate for "Of," he is not permitted to do shechita for Bayhayma.

And, yes, the Beth Din concurred, a *parochet* may be taken from the synagogue, with the permission of synagogue authorities, and sent to any synagogue in Israel.[30] Many *parochets* donated years before in honor of family members were carried to a new life in Israel, and others line the walls of synagogues in London, Sydney and Los Angeles.

Despite the many difficulties involved, it would appear that some people did keep to traditional practice, and found the loosening of the law highly objectionable. Perhaps this accounts for the letter from the trustees of the synagogue to Solomon E. Joseph, who had been outraged that a sale of synagogue honors for the New Year was to be held on the Sabbath. The trustees "kindly" ask that he explain the following words uttered at the synagogue: (a) It is Hitlerism; (b) Topsy Turvy; (c) To whom will you sell—to the walls. They ask him to send his objection in writing and take full responsibility for the canceling of the sales, and its consequences.[31]

SYNAGOGUE MANAGEMENT

Few Jews in Burma meant fewer people who might manage the affairs of the synagogue. The formal management of religious institutions was a civil matter, and the number of trustees as well as their qualifications had to be registered and approved by the civil government. In 1937, in High Court of Rangoon, the number of trustees of Musmeah Yeshua had been set at five,[32] but in the early 1950s, with fewer people to assume leadership, the synagogue requested clarification about the eligibility of potential trustees. The present Scheme said that only males, ordinarily resident in Rangoon, were eligible to be trustees. But what, the membership asked, did the term "ordinarily resident" mean? Could a person who stays in Rangoon for most of the year, but whose family resides elsewhere, be considered "ordinarily resident?" Could a person who travels, and lives for intermittent periods in Rangoon, be a trustee? Could someone from the outskirts of Rangoon be included? Could someone not eligible himself to be a trustee or to vote propose or second a candidate?

The Court, in 1952, stayed strictly constructionist. "Ordinarily resident" meant that one's permanent home had to be Rangoon, and while someone could take a "short break" from Rangoon, he must be in Rangoon most of the calendar year. And no, if someone is not himself eligible to be a trustee, he "will not be competent to propose a candidate or second one." Similarly, the Court insisted that all trustees must live within ten miles of Rangoon.[33]

Even before the Court's ruling that the number of trustees could be reduced to three, the synagogue did just that, in 1950. The new trustees were now in place for what was to unfold as an acrimonious few years. They included: E. S. Meyer, President, Managing Partner, Messrs. Meyer & Gandhi, 291 Sparks Street; J. S. Meyer, Treasurer, Proprietor, British Trading Co., 268 Phayre Street; and S. Jacob (Secretary), Vulcan Trading Co., Ltd. By 1953, S. Jacob had resigned his post, and E. S. Meyer was complaining about the apathy of most of the members and about "three members of the community who are always objecting for reasons of their own, and not to the wish of the majority."[34]

The Legation of Israel tried to stay out of the internal matters of the synagogue. However, with dwindling numbers, each Jew in Burma was important to the functioning of the community. Israeli representatives were "ordinarily resident" in Burma according to the terms set out in 1937 and therefore the position of the Legation needed to be stated clearly in writing. In a letter dated August 6, 1956, to Solomon Joseph and E. S. Meyer, Minister of Israel Y. Shimoni wrote that "the inclusion of our names would be correct and called for, in accordance with a ruling on a similar question given in the past by a Court of Law—but, if there are any objections or doubts as to the correctness of this procedure, it is entirely up to the Board of Trustees to clarify this matter. I should not like to, and in fact I cannot, interfere in these internal matters of the local Community."[35]

This did not apparently settle the matter, for in February, 1957, members of the Legation, as well as British and American Jews resident in Rangoon, were asked to appear before the High Court of Burma to establish whether they had been in the country for at least one year. The Legation declined the invitation, declaring that "as members of the Diplomatic Corps and as foreigners, it would not be proper for us to appear before the Registrar to support a claim which is not our personal claim but a matter of principle concerning the Board of Trustees of the Jewish synagogue." The Legation suggested that if the data was essential, the Court might consult immigration records or request submission of passports.[36]

The Legation had good "diplomatic" reasons for wanting to stay out of internal matters relating to the synagogue. Disputes among trustees were now being appealed both to the Civil Court as well as to the Beth Din, resulting in additional conflicts between secular and religious rulings. In a sharply worded letter in August, 1956 to trustee J. S. Meyer, lawyer N. R. Burjorjee calls the Beth Din's ruling on the number of people eligible to vote in a synagogue election "ridiculous" and warns him not to institute any proceedings to hold elections, on threat on civil or criminal action. After the September festival period, Mr. Burjorjee's clients, Solomon Joseph, Shalom R. Sassoon, and Chummy Moses, were authorized to hold elections.[37]

In 1958, the trustees were back in court. S. E. Joseph sued the other trustees, E. S. Mayer, E. E. Shamash, I. Joseph, and Isaac David, over whether they had the right to pay a large sum as advocate's fees. The case was dismissed and the plaintiff was ordered to pay Court costs.[38]

Even more, matters of religious orthodoxy also became entwined with civil, and even criminal, issues. By 1959, there were only 152 Jews remaining in Burma, most in Rangoon, a few in Bassein, Mandalay and Maymyo. Nevertheless, in that year J. S. Meyer sued E. S. Meyer and four other defendants in criminal court to restrain them from holding a synagogue election.[39] In his defense, E. S. Meyer says the accusations against him of pocketing business profits earned in association with non-Jews, instead of giving the money to charity, are motivated by the plaintiff's other objections to the religious qualifications of three of the trustees:

> ... I would not consider it a misdeed if a Jew pockets his profit earned by a non-Jewish partner opening a shop on a holiday. The reason is that the Jews have now-a-days various interests either as partners, Directors or as shareholders. I do not consider that a sin. In my conscious I do not feel that I should enjoy such profit. So I say I give such money in charity ... not because I consider such conduct a sin ... I can prove that I gave such money in charity. I do not intend to prove this fact. It is not true that I ... pocketed it ...
>
> I can prove that (the accusations against me are motivated by) malice. I now produce a letter, dated 22.12.52, written to the Chief Rabbi, London, asking him whether a certain Jew who marries a gentile and has illegitimate children can be a Trustee. . . . I also produce now the copy of the reply to the said letter, dated 6-1-53 from the Chief Rabbi. . . . According to it, in the opinion of the Chief Rabbi it is not permissible for the persons referred to in the letter to hold the position of Trustees. The names of Trustees put in for election were (1) Shalom R. Sassoon. He had a shop which he opened on Saturday. (2) C. S. Moses. He married a Christian girl in the Church. He smokes on Saturdays. He was proposed and seconded to stand for election as a Trustee. . . . (3) Mr. M. Daniel. He is a Bene Israel Jew. The Beth Din had not accepted such a Jew as Jews. The said candidates were put up along with the accused for election as Trustees. This shows that the . . . objection to my candidature (is not) bone fide.[40]

1960s

By the 1960s, however, the strict rules of governance were increasingly hard to follow, and personal animosities compounded the problems. On March 13, 1961, an amendment was approved formally reducing the number of trustees to three.[41] When a month later, two of the three trustees—Solomon Sassoon and Maurice Dawood—resigned, the synagogue again needed clarification from the court. Jacob Saul Isaac Meyer was left as the only trustee. He had put up notices for new elections in May and again in June, with no response. He then informed the community that he would act as the sole trustee—a Catch-22 situation. Under the Government-sanctioned Scheme, two trustees were required to withdraw funds on deposit at the Merchantile Bank; therefore, while the remaining trustee could deposit funds, he could not withdraw funds needed to run the synagogue. The bank denied his attempt to open an alternate account for synagogue funds.

At this point, Solomon Sassoon petitioned the Court. He objected to Jacob Meyer serving as the sole trustee, and asked the Court to supervise elections for three, not two, new trustees. At this, the Court seemingly threw up its hands, saying there is nothing in the original management Scheme for the synagogue saying that if two trustees resigned, all three should be replaced, and said also that Mr. Meyer had done the best he could. Mr. Meyer was directed to hold new elections on December 16, 1962, with fair oversight, and that "it lies within the ability of the community to end this deadlock. They ought to come forward and participate in the election for the two trustees."[42] And so, the notice below was posted. It indicates the families remaining in Rangoon at the time, dual names held by some members, and also lists Embassy staff as qualified to vote.

Notice

The Jewish Community are hereby informed that in accordance with the Order of the Chief Court at Rangoon passed in Civil Miscellaneous Application No. 288 of 1962, a General meeting will be held on Sunday the 16th of December, 1962, at the Musmeah Yeshua Synagogue, No. 85, 26th Street in the city of Rangoon, between the hours of 9 a.m. to 11 a.m., for the purpose of electing two trustees.

The candidates are as follows:

1. Mr. Isaac David
2. Mr. Solomon Ezekiel Joseph
3. Mr. Ephraim Salim Meyer

The following is a list of voters:

1. Mr. Daniels, A. Elias
2. Mr. Daniels, E. Elias
3. Mr. Daniels, Manasseh
4. Mr. David, Elias J. A.
5. Mr. David, Isaac A. J. A.
6. Mr. Ezekiel, S.
7. Mr. Joseph, Isaac J.
8. Mr. Joseph, Hai J. I.
9. Mr. Joseph, Moses E.
10. Mr. Joseph, Solomon E.
11. Mr. Joseph, Ezekiel I.
12. Mr. Joseph, S.
13. Mr. Jacob, Moses
14. Mr. Chummy Moses (British Embassy)
15. Mr. Moses, David (Teja Singh)
16. Mr. Meyer, Jacob S.
17. Mr. Moses, D. (Geoffrey Manners)
18. Mr. Meyer, E. S.
19. Mr. Raphael, R. A.
20. Mr. Raphael, A. F. J.
21. Mr. Raphael, Abraham
22. Mr. Samuels, Isaac
23. Mr. Daniel, Samson
24. Mr. David, Jackie Elias
25. Mr. Ezekiel, M.
26. Mr. Jeremiah Daniels
27. H. E. Eliashiv Ben-Horin
28. Mr. Michael Elizur

J. S. Meyer
Trustee
Musmeah Yeshua Synagogue

Elected: Isaac David, President; J. S. Meyer, Treasurer; S. E. Joseph, Secretary.

Even prior to this management dispute, the future of the synagogue itself was a matter of general concern, prompted by the diminishing community and the consequent loss of financial resources for the building. During a general meeting held in October, 1960, the community passed a resolution that sale of the synagogue might be considered. This matter was raised with the Court during the petition discussed above, but the Court declined to discuss it, saying that the meeting occurred before the two trustees resigned and it could not be considered until the matter of trustees was resolved. In 1962, a letter was sent to the London Beth Din, asking if it would be possible to sell the site to gentiles and use the money to buy a smaller site. The letter cites immigration to Israel and financial difficulties as the reason for the request.[43]

Again, the Legation of Israel had reason to be wary of entanglements with the trustees. In December 1962 the President of the Rangoon Bar Association received a letter from the lawyer for J. S. Meyer saying that Michael Elizur, Counsellor, Embassy of Israel, was unfit for his post because in correspondence during a court matter he "referred to the advice received by Mr. J. S. Meyer as 'bad advice (legal and otherwise).'" According to the lawyer, this statement rendered the letter defamatory. The letter asks for an urgent meeting of the Rangoon Bar Association to discuss the matter, since no redress could be taken against Mr. Elizur because of his diplomatic immunity. Mr. Meyer thought it unwise to approach the Foreign Office about the affront, since it "might embarrass the two Governments concerned. However, in my opinion, Mr. Elizur is not a fit person to represent his country in any capacity."[44]

As if there were not already enough reasons for dissension, a new issue was raised: allowing women to serve as synagogue trustees. This never happened.

A PARALLEL UNIVERSE

While these problems and internal arguments consumed the community, one former member pursued his own path. Throughout the years following the war, Saw Benson continued the fight for Karen autonomy. In 1947, just before the British granted Burma independence, he sent a four-man delegation to present the Karen case to Prime Minister Clement Attlee. He and his daughter Luisa also joined the Karen insurgents and fought militarily against the Burmese. For these activities, Benson was incarcerated by the Burmese Government and served three and a half years in prison (1949–1952), followed by six and a half years under house arrest (1953–1959), both times without being brought to trial. Despite these "inconveniences," Benson was able to establish several businesses between 1945–1960 that brought him considerable wealth, and earned him honorable mention in Marquis' *World Who's Who in Commerce and Industry*, 1961. Like his Koder relatives in Cochin, Saw Benson was apparently a talented entrepreneur: he supplied food to the British Armed Forces; operated a fleet of 140 trucks transporting cargo throughout Burma; imported and exported all manner of goods; and established an ice factory and a soft drink bottling company. This all came to an end when his businesses were nationalized by the Burmese Government. Until he could arrange for departure from Burma to the United States in 1965, he became the Burma representative for United States companies.

But this was not all. Before such contests were banned in Burma, Saw Benson held the franchise for the Miss Universe contest, the Miss International Beauty contest, and the Miss World contest. In 1956, his own daughter Luisa was Burma's first entry into the Miss Universe contest. She was Miss Burma again, and a film star in Burma's nascent movie industry, until 1962, when Ne Win changed the direction of the country.

NOTES

1. Moshe Yegar, "A Rapid and Recent Rise and Fall," *Sephardi World*, July–August 1984, 8. Five hundred is a common estimate of the number of returnees, but emigration lists and other data suggest the lower figure.

2. Central and Lower Burma were two of the areas most ravaged by World War II. Bayly and Harper, 438.

3. Photo archives, Beit Hatefutsot, Tel Aviv.

4. "How the Rangoon Synagogue Was Saved," *Sephardi Bulletin*, 1946, 3.

5. To this day, postal restrictions for items destined for Myanmar include: "All goods manufactured outside Her Majesty's dominions and bearing the British Royal Arms or imitations thereof; or bearing as a mark or label a portrait of any member of the Royal Family of England." United States Postal Service Country Conditions for Mailing—Burma (Myanmar).

6. Smith, 113.

7. Nissim A. Meyer, "The Jewish Community of Rangoon," *Shema*, 1949, Vol. III, No. 8, 15.

8. Letter, Charles Manassah to J. Vainstein, Jewish Agency, May 3, 1949. Jacob Rader Marcus Center, American Jewish Archives, Box H71/10.

9. Letter, Charles R. Manasseh to J. Vainstein, May 3, 1939. American Jewish Archives. Box H71/10. Letter copied to the World Jewish Congress, Tel Aviv.

10. JDC 44/65 File #584 Zionist Association of Rangoon, letter to AJJDV, by S. Abraham, February 11, 1949.

11. Appendices B and C.

12. Letter, Charles R. Manasseh to Kurt R. Grossman, World Jewish Congress, February, 1949. Jacob Rader Marcus Center, American Jewish Archives, Box H71/10.

13. Letter, E. N. Abraham to Kurt R. Grossman, WJC, New York, January 28, 1949. Jacob Rader Marcus Center, American Jewish Archives, Box B38/6.

14. Letter, Dr. I. Schwarzbart, WJC, to R. Solomon, President, Musmeah Yeshua, October 13, 1947. Jacob Rader Marcus Center, American Jewish Archives, Box H71/10.

15. Draft memo, by Dr. I. Schwarzbart, WJC, March 7, 1950. Jacob Rader Marcus Center, American Jewish Archives, Box H71/10.

16. Letter, Charles Manasseh to Kurt R. Grossman, WJC, January 1949. Jacob Rader Marcus Center, American Jewish Archives, Box H71/10.

17. Letter, Arthur C. Schiff to World Jewish Congress, June 10, 1949. Jacob Rader Marcus Center, American Jewish Archives, Box H71/10; Letter, Wolf Blattenberg, WJC, March 24, 1950, to Charles Manasseh, Box F13/33.

18. Letter, Charles Manasseh to I. Schwarzbart, WJC, March 23, 1950. Jacob Rader Marcus Center, American Jewish Archives, Box F13/33.

19. Letter, Charles Manasseh to I. Schwarzbart, World Jewish Congress, February 16, 1950. American Jewish Archives, Box F13/33.

20. Memo by Robert Serebrenik to the World Jewish Congress Israeli Executive, May 26, 1950.

21. According to Jewish law, a ritual circumcision, *brit milah*, is to be held on the eighth day.

22. Annie Sinai, "Once There Was a Burmese Jewry," *Women's League Outlook*, Spring 1969:12, 13, 26, 28.

23. Letter, Isaac David to I. Schwarzbart, World Jewish Congress, December 12, 1956. Jacob Rader Marcus Center, American Jewish Archives, Box H71/11.

24. Letter, Musmeah Yeshua Synagogue Committee to I. Schwarzbart, WJC, May 3, 1955. Jacob Rader Marcus Center, American Jewish Archives.

25. Letter from S. R. Sassoon to trustees of Musmeah Yeshua, April 7, 1952.

26. Letter from E. R. Joseph. Musmeah Yeshua Archives, Rangoon.

27. Letter from Marcus Carr, Clerk of the Court, February 28, 1961. Musmeah Yeshua Archives, Rangoon.

28. The reply seems to indicate that the woman was married to someone not Jewish.

29. Letter, August 10, 1961. Musmeah Yeshua Archives, Rangoon.

30. Letter, from Beth Din, London, February 11, 1963. Archives, Musmeah Yeshua, Rangoon.

31. Letter, August 21, 1961. Musmeah Yeshua Archives, Rangoon.

32. Civil Regular Suit No. 141, High Court of Rangoon. Referred to in Opinion, 26th December, 1952, Basu and Venkatram, Advocates. Archives, Musmeah Yeshua, Rangoon.

33. Opinion, 26th December, 1952, Basu and Venkatram, Advocates. Archives, Musmeah Yeshua, Rangoon.

34. E. S. Meyer to Robert Serebrenik, World Jewish Congress, March 19, 1953. American Jewish Archives, Box H71/11. Synagogue trustees, 1953: President, E. S. Meyer; Secretary, Isaac A. J. A. David; Treasurer; Joseph Samuels; Community members: Solomon Raymond and Isaac Joseph.

35. Archives, Musmeah Yeshua, Rangoon.

36. Letter from Y. Barnea, Attaché, to N. R. Burjorjee, February 26, 1957, Archives, Musmeah Yeshua, Rangoon.

37. Letter, August 21, 1956. Archives, Musmeah Yeshua, Rangoon.

38. High Court of Rangoon, Civil Regular No. 135, March 5, 1958. Archives, Musmeah Yeshua, Rangoon.

39. High Court of Burma, Civil Regular Suit No. 367 of 1959, dated January 22, 1960. Archives, Musmeah Yeshua, Rangoon. In response, the defendants claimed, in highly charged language, that J. S. Meyer had been causing trouble to the community for many years. In a separate opinion, the Court agreed with J. S. Meyer that the language used was inappropriate and uncivil and that the Court, "in aid of the public morals, is bound to interfere to suppress such indecencies, which may stain the reputation and wound the feelings of the parties concerned."

40. High Court of Burma, Criminal Trial No. 380 of 1959, July 21, 1959. Archives, Musmeah Yeshua, Rangoon. The full transcript is lost, and therefore the outcome of the trial is uncertain.

41. High Court of Rangoon, Civil Regular No. 6 of 1961. Archives, Musmeah Yeshua, Rangoon. This amendment was the result of a suit by E. R. Joseph and Moses Jacob vs Trustees Maurice Dawood, President; Solomon Joseph, Treasurer; Isaac David, Secretary; J. S. M. Meyer, Committee Member; and S. E. D. Sassoon, Committee Member.

42. Civil Miscellaneous No. 35 of 1962 arising out of Civil Regular No. 141 of 1937, September 11, 1962, Chief Court of Burma. Archives, Musmeah Yeshua, Rangoon.

43. London Metropolitan Archives, ACC/3400/RG/LM (letter dated March 26, 1998).

44. Letter, December 19, 1962. Archives, Musmeah Yeshua, Rangoon.

Chapter Eight

Burma and Israel

Feeling its way, the new Republic of Burma needed substantial technical and agricultural assistance. The most likely sources for this assistance were off limits: Britain, for obvious reasons, the United States or the Soviet Union. The new Republic, so recently freed from a colonial presence, was reluctant to align itself with any of these great powers. In this context, the new State of Israel seemed an ideal friend, one with a vast supply of experts in Western technology. Israel could provide assistance in housing, medicine, industry, military aviation and agriculture without the heavy hand of the United States or Russia. For Israel, cooperation with Burma was an opportunity to create an ally, as well as to provide employment for the large skilled population that was arriving in the country in the aftermath of World War II.

Because Burma became independent in January, 1948, it had participated in deliberations in the UN about the founding of the State of Israel, including the partition of the land between Israelis and Palestinians. Caught up in their own struggle for independence and their own complex history, few Burmese were acquainted with Jewish history and ideology or with the situation of the Jews in postwar Europe. Seen through the eyes of a state that had only recently freed itself from Western colonialism, Israel was identified as a new colonialist power. Therefore, when in the spring of 1949 the State of Israel applied for membership in the UN, Burma voted no. However, after a period of stability in the Middle East, Burma recognized the State of Israel, in December, 1949, and diplomatic contacts were initiated between the two countries. Furthermore, since Burma and Israel achieved independence from Britain in the same year, they seemed to have similar needs and aspirations.

Perhaps reflecting the Western orientation of their readers, the news about Israel in the English papers was generally favorable during this time. On

October 8, 1948, the *Burmese Review* carried the following article by Simon Wolf:

> (The Palestinians) are today immeasurably better off than 30 years ago. This improvement has been brought about by the Jews and, to some extent, by the British mandate administration. One day the Arab countries will comprehend that having a peaceful, and internally developing, Jewish state in their midst, may be a blessing to them.[1]

Subsequent articles told readers that Britain, Belgium, Holland and others had recognized the new State of Israel,[2] and a major article described the range of music in Israel.[3]

Pro-Zionist activity in Rangoon was open and hidden. Jews proudly wore a button with a Star of David in the middle. Across the bottom, it said in English: The Rangoon Jewish Association. Across the top, in Hebrew letters, it announced: Rangoon Committee for the Recognition of Israel.

As disparate as these two new states were, their early relationship flourished in the context of the warm personal relationship between U Nu and David Ben-Gurion, and a common belief in socialism as the best approach to economic and social vitality. The two leaders shared an interest in the moral teachings and practices of Buddhism. Ben-Gurion studied Buddhism seriously, spent two days in 1961 in conversation with Buddhist monks, and discussed Buddhism with the scholarly and devout U Nu.[4]

The first Israeli diplomatic official appointed to Burma, David Hacohen, was selected because of his extensive experience in building the Histadrut, Israel's Federation of Labor.[5] A Burmese socialist mission visited Israel in 1952, and Burmese-Israeli contacts were reinforced in 1953 when an Israeli delegation headed by Foreign Minister Moshe Sharett participated in the Asian Socialist Congress in Rangoon. In 1953 Israel opened its first diplomatic presence in Rangoon in the former mansion of Charles Joseph on 2 Wingaaba Road. Two years later, a Burmese legation was established in Israel.[6] That same year, Prime Minister U Nu tried unsuccessfully to secure Israel's acceptance into the African-Asian Caucus at the Bandung Conference.

Prime Minister U Nu's state visit to Israel in 1955 inaugurated an era of agricultural innovation in Burma. Vastly impressed with the great strides that young country was making in agriculture and with Israel's social experiments—the *moshavim* and *kibbutzim*—that were enabling this growth, he saw the potential for application of these initiatives in Burma. Of particular interest was the Lachish Project which, in a few years, had developed a semiarid region in the south of Israel into land suitable for resettling thousands of refugees. Farming villages were clustered around a rural center; each cluster was a "satellite" of an urban hub designed to provide regional services and infrastructure. In June, 1954, I. J. Linton, of the Legation of the State of Israel in Tokyo, had been appointed Minister Plenipotentiary to Burma, but the relationship now called for a more formal relationship. On March 5, 1956, Burma and Israel signed a tentative agreement on economic cooperation, which was amended and formalized on June 11, 1957. Israel's Minister to Burma, Y. Shimoni, signed on behalf of Israel, and Deputy Prime Minister and Foreign Minister Sao Hkun Hkio signed on behalf of Burma.[7]

The agreement created a structure for economic cooperation between the countries, including joint agricultural and businesses ventures. Israel was to help in establishing a model agricultural settlement in the northern dry zone of Burma, the Namsang Project,[8] which would result in five to ten *moshav*-type villages in the northern Shan States. With an eye to the future, it is interesting to note that the designation "Shan State" was stricken from the agreement and the words "Union of Burma" substituted. The goal was to bring up to a million acres of waste land under cultivation for crops such as corn, soy beans, and wheat, which would be exported to Israel. Also planned was the production of cotton, tobacco, groundnuts and citrus fruits. Israeli agronomists, water engineers, irrigation experts, sociologists and other specialists were sent to Burma to aid in the effort.[9] Israeli experts comanaged several projects for the new country and, under special contract, exported large quantities of rice to Israel.

Several cooperative projects were initiated: a joint shipping line, the Burma Five Star Line, and a joint construction and contracting firm. Israeli assistance was provided for irrigation projects, for the Burma pharmaceutical industry, for nurses' training, and for the training of an initial group of parachutists for the Burmese Army. Also considered were factories for the production of rubber tires, ceramic glassware, and paint and varnish.

A key part of the agreement was Israel's training of Burmese personnel and the exchange of technical information. A core group of settlers for the Namsang Project was sent to Israel to learn advanced agricultural techniques. This training was part of Israel's overall diplomatic initiative between 1958 and 1969 that brought 13,025 foreign trainees to Israel from Africa, Asia, Latin America and Africa.[10]

During this halcyon period in Burma-Israel relations, legations of both countries were raised to the status of embassies, in 1957.[11] The exchange of visits between the two countries continued: Knesset member Moshe Sharett came to Rangoon in 1956; Moshe Dayan, Shimon Peres, and Israel's President Ben-Zvi visited in 1958; Prime Minister Ben-Gurion in 1961; and Foreign Minister Golda Meir in 1962. In his memoirs, Shimon Peres recalls those optimistic days of Israel-Burma cooperation:

> In 1958, [Moshe Dayan and I] were invited to Burma as the guests of General Ne Win, the army chief of staff and effectively the country's strongman. We were entertained lavishly and graciously. A splendid government guest house, set amid lakes and woodland, was at our disposal in Rangoon; in the countryside, we visited temples and pagodas and made our stately way through Mandalay by river, rowed by oarsmen whose oars were tied to their feet. The scenes seemed so different from the descriptions in Kipling. Wherever we went, we were warmly greeted by ordinary folk and fussed over by officials. Each evening colorful pageants and dances were laid on in our honor. When these were finished, storytellers would take over, terrifying the company—ourselves included—with tales of tigers and poisonous snakes.
>
> Ne Win, a military man to his fingertips, accompanied us throughout our two-week stay. He was an extreme nationalist, determined not just to shore up his country's hard-won independence but in effect to sever Burma—which he increasingly and brutally did in later years—from much of the rest of the world. He said the only country he believed in was Israel. At that time, he seemed to us incorruptible in a country riddled with corruption. Despite his single-mindedness, not to say fanaticism, we built a close personal relationship. Later, Israel helped Burma develop its agriculture. The Burmese sent hundreds of youngsters to Israel for courses. Some of them had never seen mechanized farming until their experiences on our kibbutzim and in our agricultural schools. Some had never even seen a wristwatch before they were flown to Israel.[12]

The visits by Israelis to Burma were front page news. Moshe Sharett's September, 1956, visit to Burma was announced in the *Rangoon Guardian* under the headline: "Boy from Russia Who Grew Up to Lead Israel"[13] and his arrival featured a large photo of U Nu meeting him at the airport.[14] Each of the Israelis who came to Burma also visited the Musmeah Yeshua Synagogue, greatly enhancing not only the traditional ideological commitment of the Baghdadi Jews to the ideal Jerusalem, but also the pragmatic, Zionist view of Israel as a potential haven during these increasingly difficult political and economic times.

Throughout, the Israeli Embassy was a reassuring presence, both for the political protection it offered through the Burma-Israel relationship, and the avenue for emigration it provided. With a diminishing community, Israeli diplomats were very welcome to contribute to a *minyan*, but this seems to have happened mostly on special occasions. Israel Independence Day was celebrated at a special synagogue service on May 5, 1957, and by the Legation of Israel the following day.

While in normal times, the Embassy avoided entanglements with the internal policies of the community, visits by dignitaries offered occasions when the two could come together for mutual benefit. The program for the visit of Dr. and Mrs. Israel Goldstein, from January 30 to February 1, 1959, exemplifies this merging of interests. Dr. Goldstein was on the Executive Board of the World Jewish Congress as well as the World Zionist Organization, and rabbi of a major Jewish congregation in New York City, B'nai Jeshurun. His wife was President of the Pioneer Women of America. The World Jewish Congress had urged full hospitality when he arrived, and the small community responded fully. The Goldsteins were met at the airport by community members and Israeli Embassy personnel. They lunched at the home of Israeli Ambassador Dr. Daniel Lewin; were honored at evening services at Musmeah Yeshua attended by Israeli and American Embassy staff, Israeli experts, and visitors from the United States; and were celebrated at a dinner for eighty hosted by Mr. and Mrs. E. S. Meyer, President of Musmeah Yeshua. The next day they called on Prime Minister U Nu and were hosted at dinner by the Charge d'Affaires of the American Embassy. A large gathering of community members and Ambassador and Mrs. Lewin saw them off on Sunday at Mingladon Airport.[15] On his return to Israel, Dr. Goldstein noted that "neither in Burma nor in any other Far Eastern country has Nasser's propaganda succeeded in disturbing relations with Israel."[16]

This promising period of Burma-Israel cooperation died at the same time as the lingering hopes of the Jews remaining in Burma. In 1962, General Ne Win declared a policy of strict self-reliance, nationalization of industries, and strict neutrality, and disassociated the nation from outside influences, including those of Israel. In so doing, he also deprived his country of an effective source of technical education and economic stimulation. The Israeli Embassy has remained in Rangoon and the Burma/Myanmar Embassy is still in Tel Aviv, but the substantive collaboration of the 1950s and early 1960s has been erased.

NOTES

1. *Israel Today and Tomorrow*, 3.
2. January 31, 1949, 1.
3. August 5, 1957, 7.
4. Rodger Kamenetz, *The Jew in the Lotus*, 165.
5. Mordechai E. Kreinin, *Israel and Africa: The Early Years*, in Curtis and Gitelson, 54.
6. The selling price was LL 350,000 Sterling, according to Yascha Malkhoo, letter, May 29, 1995.
7. "Burma & Israel Sign Formal Economic Co-operation Pact," *Rangoon Gazette*, June 12, 1957. Jacob Rader Marcus Center, American Jewish Archives, Box H71/11.
8. "Burma-Israel Relations," *Encyclopedia Judaica Jerusalem*, 1971, Vol. 4, 1528.

9. Mike Rogoff, "Integrated Development: Beginnings of the Settlement Study Centre," *Shalom Magazine*, 1988, No. 1, 4–5.

10. D. V. Segre, *The Philosophy and Practice of Israel's International Cooperation*, in Curtis and Gitelson, 18.

11. *Encyclopedia Judaica Jerusalem*, 4: 1528.

12. Shimon Peres, *Battling for Peace: A Memoir*, 133.

13. September 16, 1956, 1.

14. September 22, 1956, 1.

15. Letter, Isaac David, Secretary, Musmeah Yeshua, to I. Schwarzbart, WJC, February 10, 1959. American Jewish Archives, Box H71/11.

16. Letter, I. Schwarzbart, WJC, to Isaac David, March 9, 1959. American Jewish Archives, Box H71/11.

Chapter Nine

Embers

Lingering, cautious hope for a restoration of the Jews' former life in beautiful Burma died in 1962. The Burmese Way to Socialism was to steer the nation between the evils of capitalism and communism. Instead, the economy collapsed, and the country further deteriorated. Xenophobia was the order of the day, and few foreigners could penetrate Ne Win's border control. Small businessmen could not operate, and employees of foreign businesses or the state saw no future under the military dictatorship. The synagogue was directly affected in 1964 when the government nationalized its stores along Dalhousie Street, which had been providing income for synagogue maintenance since 1881. And then, in 1967, came the first ever direct attack on the synagogue. Anti-Jewish sentiment was not something Jews had previously encountered in Burma, but times had changed. By 1969, another 116 persons had left the country, according to a census taken by Isaac David. Ten made *aliya* to Israel with assistance from the Israeli Embassy. Many of those still remaining lived on Sandwith Road, while others were scattered throughout the central area, still close to the synagogue.[1]

Musmeah Yeshua's Board of Trustees report of February, 1965, lists J. S. Meyer, Chairman and Treasurer; S. E. Joseph, Secretary; and Isaac Samuels, Committee Member. As the population diminished, there seemed no purpose in keeping the beautiful articles that had enhanced the prewar congregation. On February 28, 1966, it was decided to send to Israel three Torahs, as well as another Torah with torn pages, and many of the synagogue's silver items, including three silver trays, thirty-one *rimonim* (Torah ornaments), and four silver plates, as well as two large brass candle stands and assorted other items. A synagogue record dated August 7, 1967, notes that even on festival days, there was no longer a *minyan*, and that the Israeli Embassy had received permission to export the silverware.

By July, 1968, there were only two trustees of the synagogue, Chairman Solomon Joseph and Treasurer/Secretary Isaac Samuels. And then, a year later, on Solomon Joseph's death, there was only one, Isaac Samuels, and one staff, caretaker David Moses. The last rabbi left in 1969, but since then the Israeli Embassy staff has helped out when needed to read the Hebrew prayers. In 1971, the World Jewish Congress estimated that a hundred Jews remained in Burma, out of a total population of twenty-five million, two hundred thousand. In Rangoon, the WJC counted seven Sephardi[2] families, with about thirty-five persons, and ten Bene Israel families, with another forty members. A few Jews remained in Mandalay and Maymyo.

An American businessman, one of the few foreigners able to enter Burma during the 1970s, suggested an even more diminished picture of the once vibrant Jewish community in Burma:

> With the assistance of a gentleman from the Israeli Embassy, I met Mr. Isaac Samuels and Mr. David Moses. I did not see the synagogue, which is supposed to be very nice and has served a large community before Burmese independence. The present status is very dismal. Let me tell you what I have ascertained.
>
> The total number of Jews living in Burma today consists of about 10/15 families. Of these, one family and 4 to 5 single gentlemen live in Rangoon (including the above two gentlemen). The balance of the families are scattered throughout the country. The family in Rangoon is all Jewish. The families outside Rangoon consist, without exception, of Jewish husbands and native wives.
>
> There is as such no Jewish life whatsoever remaining, except that on the High Holidays a few of them come down to Rangoon. They have a service in the synagogue—but never a *minyan*. . . . Since there is no Jewish life to speak of, the children all grow up without any Jewish education whatsoever. In the past, the Israeli Embassy has supplied them with sufficient prayer books, Talithim, and things like matzos and wine. Therefore, such needs do not exist.
>
> Mr. Samuels is a Burmese citizen and earns a living by hiring out furniture, cutleries, etc. Mr. Moses is a British subject and has no (other) job. The few other single people in Rangoon are mostly without work because in Burma, everything is nationalized and there is no private industry. Adjacent to the synagogue is a building with a series of rooms which was built and is owned by the defunct community. In the past, these rooms were rented to the single people and outsiders, and the proceeds were used to maintain the Synagogue and the grounds. Recently, the government has levied high taxes on this income as a result of which the community is in tax debt to the government. This situation has reached a point whereby the government has threatened and is expected to confiscate this adjacent building, which would mean that the community will be without this income and unable to keep up the synagogue and its grounds. Naturally, the government will not confiscate the Synagogue itself but if the situation is not remedied, there will be no income to keep up the Synagogue. Furthermore, 3 or 4 people who live off this income will probably become destitute.

The total income and upkeep involved amounts to U.S. $200 per month. Messers. Samuels and Moses, therefore, are very much afraid that the last remains of a once prosperous community will be eliminated.

The Israeli Embassy is powerless to intervene because, as a result of this technically being a tax matter, the Israelis cannot intervene in the domestic affairs of the country. It would be very nice if you would be able to induce the Burmese Government not to confiscate this adjacent building and leave the renting of these rooms and the income and upkeep and support a few jobless people remaining . . .

Whatever you do, please do not mention my name because very few foreigners are permitted to enter Burma. I go often because I purchase raw material on behalf of my New York principles and I cannot afford to endanger this position. However, somebody must help and your organization seems to be the most logical first step to start the ball rolling. . . .

P.S. Mr. Samuels and Mr. Moses have no Jewish calendar for next year. Do you have some that can be sent to them? If so, please send them by "registered airmail, printed matter"—otherwise, they will not arrive.[3]

The calendars were sent, and received. The letter was forwarded to the World Jewish Congress, which asked members of the diplomatic community in Rangoon to help with the alleviation of the tax burden. It appears they were successful.

As can be expected, finances were a major concern for the tiny community. The wealthier members of the congregation had long since emigrated, those who remained in Burma had little money to spare, and the loss of the income from the shops on Dalhousie Street was sorely felt. It was within this context that Isaac Samuels's son Jack sought government permission to construct stalls for shops on synagogue land facing 26th Street. It took four years to receive permission, and the shops were finally constructed in 1974. The shops obscure the entrance to the synagogue courtyard, and continue to provide essential funds for the maintenance of the building and the cemetery.

On his death in 1978, Isaac Samuels's sons Jack and Moses continued his stewardship of the synagogue. A Burmese Buddhist friend and former employee of Isaac Samuels, U Aung Kwye, who was skilled in written English, assisted with communication with institutions and individuals abroad. A. K., as he was known, also made beautiful posters for the holidays which were displayed in Musmeah Yeshua.

A receipt, dated Rangoon, 24th July, 1980, documents what must have been a sad though foresighted event for the last trustees of Musmeah Yeshua. Signed by Kalman Anner, Ambassador, the State of Israel, it states:

To Whom It May Concern
I hereby acknowledge receipt of two Community Registration books from Mr. J. Samuels, today, 24th July, 1980.

1. Book registering deaths of Jews in Rangoon.
2. Book registering births of Jews in Rangoon.

The thick brown leather registries transferred to Israel were written in an old Sephardi-Iraqi Hebrew script, similar to the Rashi script, and date from 1893 until the 1970s, with most entries before 1942. In 1954, the writing changed from Hebrew to English. Only 150 of the birth registry's 605 pages were used, the grand future for the community envisioned in 1893 now aborted. The books now reside in the Central Archives of the Jewish People in Jerusalem, their worn brown covers indicating the vibrant life that once existed—the joys of births, the sadness of deaths, the centrality of the synagogue to the daily life of the Jews of Burma. Fortunately, English copies of these registries were also made and remain in Rangoon, and a copy of the birth registry is also in the headquarters of the American Sephardi Federation in New York City and on the web.

Most other Jewish sites are gone. The Jewish school was demolished long ago when the land was sold. From Maha Bandoola Street/Dalhousie Street, once the heart of the Jewish commercial area, one can see the Magen David high up on the side wall of Musmeah Yeshua Synagogue. It was placed there by Moses Samuels after his father's death. Similarly, the Magen David on the Solomon Brothers' American Ice Factory still peers above the bushes. The wrought iron bandstand contributed by the Cohen brothers in Fytche Square Gardens (now Bandoola Square) is gone, as are the Sofaer gates at the Zoo, but the Sofaer Building on the corner of Phayre and Merchant Streets still stands,[4] as do some of the buildings housing former Jewish shops and homes. Even the names of the towns have changed: Rangoon is now Yangon; Moulmein is called Mawlamyine; Bassein is Pathein; Pegu is Bago; and Maymyo is Pyin Oo Lwin.

While many markers of Jewish life in Burma no longer exist, the coordinates of the community remain the same: by wandering by the Sule Pagoda, the synagogue on 26th Street and the community's building on 31st Street, and along Maha Bandoola Street, Tseekai Maung Tauley Street, and Merchant Street, one can stroll through the memories and experience of other days. In 1993 an important ritual had a rare revival in the synagogue when Sammy Samuels, heir to the Baghdadi tradition in Burma, became a bar mitzvah. The ceremony was conducted by Israel's Ambassador to Burma Ori Noy.

Many years have elapsed since the emigration of those who best remember the bright days of Baghdadi life in Burma, as is true of many places of the Jewish diaspora. It is the curiosity of outsiders such as anthropologists and historians, and the efforts of current caretakers of the sites, that bridge the gap in memory between the adventurers, innovators and builders, and their descendants.

CEMETERY

For the time being, the white walled Jewish cemetery of Rangoon lies two kilometers northeast of the synagogue, closed by a tall iron gate (figure 9.1). Line upon line of rounded tombstones, 679 in all, huddle across two levels; 428 are on the low ground, 251 on the high ground. The inscriptions are shadowed by deep frames and by the tall grasses that grow so quickly in the tropical humidity and sunshine. In this climate, it is a daunting task to keep the cemetery clear. Still, Moses Samuels tries to do so—one of his continual obligations to the past and to his father's memory. Also within the cemetery enclosure is an oven for burning the last clothing and a small house for the caretakers and night watchmen.

The earliest tombstone is dated October 3, 1876. The last burial recorded in the Death Registry of Musmeah Yeshua is that of former teacher Rifka Halegwa, who "died on 16th December, 1979. Buried the same day corresponding to 26th day of Kislev (2nd day of Hannuca). Age 73 years." Tombstones along the back of the low ground indicate another part of the Jewish residence in Burma, that of Ashkenazim who came to the country during the British period. Whether colonial administrators, British military or representatives of overseas business interests in Burma, they were buried apart from the Baghdadis, just as they lived apart: in Jewish consecrated ground, but in an area to themselves. Next to each other are the graves of Herman Werndorfer, who died on November 1889 at thirty-seven years; Kaya Muscowich,

Figure 9.1. Jewish Cemetery, Rangoon. *Credit:* **Ruth Fredman Cernea.**

died December 27, 1899; Aron Sponder, December 31, 1905; Saul Daniel, Clerk, Reserve Secretariat, Rangoon, December 10, 1906; Jeremiah Shikolker, March 28, 1910, nineteen years; David Tulker, July 26, 1912; Eckel Leopold, August 6, 1889; and Daniel Samuel, Military Police Battalion, who died January 8, 1905. Another group buried separately are those who died an unnatural death.

How much longer Moses Samuels can continue to care for this precious cemetery is unclear. The government has given notice that the cemetery must be moved and a site has already been selected, but without provision for funds to accomplish the move such relocation is extremely difficult. The adjacent Muslim cemetery has already been moved. In Mandalay, the Muslim and Jewish cemeteries were not relocated, and today they are rubble. Moving graves is not a simple matter: there are ritual prescriptions to be followed and it is extremely expensive, surely beyond the finances of the tiny "community." A few years back the University of Rangoon took rubbings of the tombstones, perhaps in anticipation of their final destruction.

The twenty-three shops surrounding Musmeah Yeshua today are occupied by Muslims, Buddhists and Chinese, and most sell house paint. Rent from these shops—about forty-seven dollars a month (35,200 kyats)[5]—does not fully cover the maintenance costs and municipal bills for the synagogue and cemetery. The current political situation in Myanmar, as Burma is now known, has discouraged tourists, whose contributions once more substantially supplemented the rental income. The difference today is met by Moses Samuels himself, from income from his business. The community still receives some welfare funds from abroad for the more indigent members of the community. However, with the exception of the Samuels family, few Baghdadi Jews still live in Burma, unless one counts the children of a woman who married a Muslim man early in the twentieth century. The son of the prewar Jewish superintendent of the Bassein jail, from the Aaron family, lives on Mt. Popa in central Burma as a *phongyi* in the folk religion of Burma, the Nats.

Burma's Jews are scattered today throughout the world, primarily in London, Los Angeles, Sydney, and Israel. While London was the natural, "promised" destination for Jews from Burma, a surprise awaited them. They thought they were "coming home" but that's not what it seemed, apparently, to the British or the British Jews. In Burma they felt as though they were "British," but once in England it was clear that they were outsiders. Until they arrived in England, they had encountered it through its idealization abroad, but the reality they met was a dash of cold water that dampened their first days and chilled them in the years that followed. In Hendon, Od Yosef Hai Synagogue serves as a center for many who share the Baghdadi tradition of worship, including Jews from Burma, India, and other areas of Southeast Asia, as well as from

Iraq, Iran and Israel. The Hasidic rabbi is Dayan Abraham David, whose father was a coffee merchant in Rangoon, where he was born.

In Sydney and Los Angeles, as in London and Israel, Torahs and *parochets* from Burma provoke memories of Burma and may act, at the same time, as reminders of what has been lost.[6] The three Sifrei Torah from Mandalay were brought to Sydney in 1948 by Ezra Saul, who placed them on the seat of the taxi carrying him from the airport while he sat on the floor. Even then he could not place himself above the holy Torah. These Torahs are still used by the Sephardi Synagogue in Bondi Junction. Ezra Saul's great-grandson Gabriel read from one of the scrolls when he became a bar mitzvah a few years ago.

Across the Pacific, in Santa Monica, California, worshippers read from silver-clad Sifrei Torah from Rangoon in Kahal Joseph Synagogue, a congregation of Jews from Southeast Asia that still prays in the Baghdadi tradition.[7] So too, on Yom Kippur, the *parochets* that once lined the grand pillars of Musmeah Yeshua Synagogue again bring color and memory to the walls of Kahal Joseph.

A few miles from Kahal Joseph is the home of Saw Benson's daughter, Louisa Benson Craig, former Miss Burma, former Burmese film star, former Karen guerilla freedom fighter. This descendent of Jews from Cochin and from Spain, and of Karen tribesmen, is now one of the world's leading spokespersons in the fight to bring attention to human rights abuses in Myanmar. She played a leading role in a lawsuit against Unocol Corporation for abuses in construction of the Yadana gas pipeline and for their collaboration with and payments to the government of Myanmar.

Many other descendents of Jews from Burma have made important contributions to their adopted homelands. Among them was physicist Morris (Moses) Battat, born in Yenangyaung, who worked in Los Alamos on the atomic bomb project; his writings have been translated into thirty-five languages. Ezra Solomon, descendent of the important Solomon family of Rangoon, became a renowned economist. A graduate in economics from the University of Rangoon, after the war Solomon earned a doctorate in economics at the University of Chicago, joined the Chicago faculty, and later became an eminent professor of finance at Stanford University. During the Nixon Administration, Ezra Solomon was appointed to the President's Council of Economic Advisers. He died in Palo Alto in 2002.

Close to the former home of Ezra Solomon in Palo Alto, California, is that of his cousin, Abraham D. Sofaer, grandson of Meyer Sofaer of Rangoon, whose store stood at Tseekai Maung Tauley and Dalhousie Streets in Rangoon. A former U.S. district judge in the Southern District of New York, and Legal Adviser to the Department of State, he is now the George P. Shultz Distinguished Scholar and Senior Fellow at Stanford's Hoover Institution.

Figure 9.2. Abraham Sofaer as King Lear, Shakespeare Memorial Theatre, Stratford-on-Avon, 1943. Courtesy of Ruth Sofaer.

Isaac Sofaer's son Abraham (figure 9.2) achieved fame as an actor on the London stage and continued to star in films after his move to Hollywood. He lived close to his daughter, interior decorator Ruth Sofaer, and died in 1988. Despite the affronts he endured, his English Diocesan School education stayed with him throughout his life, as the following summary of his acting career suggests:

> Burmese actor Abraham Sofaer had the strong semitic features and cultured mannerisms to allow him to play a variety of ethnic types. In various films and TV shows, Sofaer portrayed Jews, Arabs, Armenians, Turks and plenty of East Indians (though he usually shied away from the latter because, in his words, it is so ridiculously easy). Off screen, Sofaer thought of himself as an old-school-tie Englishman. He came to London at age 19 to complete his education, secured a job as stage manager with a Shakespearian company, and went on to a British stage career in 1921—making his BBC radio debut as early as 1936. One of his most famous portrayals on Broadway was as Disraeli in the original Helen Hayes production of Victoria Regina. Ensconced in Hollywood by the '50s, Sofaer continued to live the life of an English gentleman, playing cricket in his spare time. He also was a keen scholar of different cultures, especially Hebrew tribal customs. Among Abraham Sofaer's many films were *Dreyfus* (1931), *Elephant Walk* (1956), *The King of Kings* (1961) and *Head* (1969); certainly Sofaer's most conspicuous film performance was as God Himself in *A Matter of Life and Death* (known in America as *Stairway to Heaven*).[8]

Embers

When, in the late 1930s, this "English gentleman" toured America for three years with Helen Hayes, his contracts stipulated that he could return to England for a few months each year to play his beloved cricket. And when *Bhowani Junction* was shown in Rangoon, the entire school was adjourned for the day so the students could see the film starring the English Diocesan School's very famous alumnus.

After a drift from Judaism in her extended family, Seemah Saul Betz's granddaughter Evelyn Dean is reclaiming her heritage, reintroducing Passover Seders to her family, and studying at Indiana University to be a scholar of Jewish society and culture.

An interesting photograph is owned by Sarah Sassoon Raphaeli, of Israel, who remained in Pegu with her family during the war. It shows her at her wedding, on the way to the *huppah*, the marriage canopy. Across her path is a string, held by her mother, Naw Erra, from Yado Wathawkho Village, Leiktho Township, Toungoo District, who converted to Judaism in Musmeah Yeshua Synagogue. In Burma, a marriage procession might encounter several such strings playfully put up by the villagers, who threaten to cut the cord as a curse if payment by the bridegroom is not received. In Israel, this Burmese tradition "barred" the way to the Jewish wedding. A mixture of customs, a

Figure 9.3. Moses and Sammy Samuels, in Musmeah Yeshua Synagogue, 2006. *Credit:* Sammy Samuels.

mixture of histories. The wedding was performed by Rabbi Yosef Levi, who came from Rangoon to Israel.

Another occasional echo of the days when Burma's Jewish community was numerous and vibrant is the quest by Israeli "second families" to find long-lost half-brothers and sisters, the children of their father's liaisons with Burmese women. Years later, stories emerge about how such hidden families were left behind and forgotten when the men immigrated to Israel. At times, using the valuable synagogue registries, Musmeah Yeshua has helped Burmese who can prove Jewish parentage to return to Judaism. Ironically, many other descendents of Burmese Jews no longer practice Judaism.

Each day, Moses Samuels—U Than Lwin—sits in the silent synagogue, his sanctuary in the midst of teeming Rangoon. He sits quietly in his family's pew, in the afternoon light, thinking how he can keep the building beautiful, in honor and memory of his father and for the community that he hopes, some day, will again fill the pews.[9] This is clearly his place, his home: he has lived all his life in the house, with the *mezuzah* on the doorpost, on 31st Street and the streets between his residential home and his spiritual home. The heir to this tradition, his son Sammy—Aung Soe Lwin—is thousands of miles away, having graduated with high honors from Yeshiva University in New York City (figure 9.3). Moses and Nellie's daughters Kuzna (Me Me Lwin) and Dinah (Gogo) (Tin Wint Wint) remain in Burma. Moses believes that the day will come, in a freer political climate, when Jews will return to Burma and the beautiful carved pews will again be filled with worshippers.

Until then, Moses Samuels stays in Rangoon, anchoring a tangible world that exists for others only in memories. In his lifetime, he has seen the Jewish community of his childhood diminish one by one. But this is his home and his history, since the 1870s or even earlier, when his great-grandparents, Joseph Samuels and Kuzna Jacob, and Joseph Solomon and Azeeza Moses, left Baghdad to start life anew in the dynamic city of Rangoon. During the war, his father Isaac risked his life for the synagogue; today, Moses Samuels devotes his life to the same building, a material structure that captures the past as well as his heart.

His son Sammy is equally optimistic that Jews will once more fill the beautiful building, but this time they will not be Baghdadis but people coming to Myanmar to serve the international business world he envisions in Rangoon. Meanwhile, he is preparing himself to continue his father's role in preserving the Baghdadi Jewish heritage in Burma. He has acquired Jewish knowledge in more depth than the generations before him, has lived for more than a year on a *kibbutz* in Israel, and understands and speaks Hebrew well. And with his computer and technical skills, he is bringing Musmeah Yeshua into the modern age, producing beautiful postcards of the synagogue, facilitating communication by Internet, and creating a museum that will house the story of his heritage (figure 9.4). But the synagogue itself is not a museum. Visitors often come to marvel at the beautiful building, sometimes groups from abroad come to celebrate holidays in the synagogue, and occasionally there is a *minyan* of tourists and Embassy staff. And Moses Samuels is there every day, keeping Musmeah Yeshua open and ready to be used.

No matter where the Jews from Burma and their descendents now live, the Burmese days form the backgrounds of their lives. It was a time of peace and beauty before their world erupted. With nostalgia, Solly Saul writes:

> It was always a desire of mine to return to Burma for a visit. This longing was more than just sentimental—the attachment to the country where one was born is, I am sure, deeply felt by most. Sadly, it is unlikely that I will ever be able to fulfill my dream ... And so I must rest content with reliving in my imagination the most happy memories I possess of the city and country of my birth: the peaceful days, the happy and friendly Burmese, the torrential monsoon rains, the rich vegetation, the tropical fruits, the imposing Shwedagon and Sule Pagodas, the City Hall, my school, teachers, and fellow students, my synagogue and my home.[10]

NOTES

1. Appendix D.
2. "Sephardic" is being used here as an encompassing term in opposition to "Ashkenazic," or Jews of European origin. *The Jewish Communities of the World*, 60.
3. Letter, Harry Z. Bornstein to Nathan Jacobson, Federation of Jewish Communities of Asia and the Far East, Melbourne, Australia, July 20, 1971. Jacob Rader Marcus Center, American Jewish Archives, Box H71/12.
4. The Sofaer Building is now called the Rander Building.
5. Value in 2004.
6. Jonathan Boyarin, *Storm from Paradise*, 5.
7. This synagogue is the only Sephardic congregation in the western United States that follows *Nusakh Baghdad* (Baghdad custom and usage).
8. Hal Erickson, All Movie Guide, *Moviephone Entertainment Guide*, on the Internet.
9. Moses Samuels is currently restoring the synagogue's ritual bath.
10. *Sephardi Bulletin*, 14.

Figure 9.4. Torahs, Musmeah Yeshua Synagogue, 2006. *Credit:* Sammy Samuels.

Appendix A: Proceedings of the High Court of Judicature, Rangoon, 1935–1936

THE HIGH COURT OF JUDICATURE AT RANGOON. CIVIL FIRST APPEAL NO. 78 OF 1935 (MAY 14TH 1935)

E. S. Cohen, residing at No. 325 Tzeekai Maung Taulay Street, Rangoon. Trustee of the Musmeah Yeshua Synagogue, Rangoon. Appellant Versus.

1. J. M. Ezekiel, residing at No. 41, Village Road, Gyogon, Insein.
2. N. S. Ezekiel, residing at No. 201, Rangoon-Insein Road, Gyogon, Insein.
3. S. S. Aaron, residing at No. 110, Lewis Street, Rangoon.
4. C. S. Joseph, residing at No. 61, Barr Street, Rangoon.
5. Trustee of the Musmeah Yeshua Synagogue, Rangoon.
6. A. Benjamin, Trustee of the Musmeah Yeshua Synagogue, Rangoon, Present whereabouts unknown, left Rangoon for good.
7. E. S. E. Mordecai of 31 Prome Road, Trustee of the Musmeah Yeshua Synagogue, Rangoon.

Respondents

Appeal lisc under clause 13 of the letters patent.
The appeal is valued as upon a Declaration for which a
Court Stamp of Rs.10/- is payable.

The appellant(s) being aggrieved and dissatisfied with the judgement and decree of the Original side of this Honourable Court in Civil Regular Suit No. 35 beg to appeal therefore on the following amongst other grounds namely:

1. For that the learned Judge erred in holding that the Bene Israel are eligible for appointment as Trustees of the Synagogue and are entitled to vote at the elections of trustees.

2. For that the learned Judge should have held that the Bene Israel constitute a separate community and that the Bene Israel are not within the expression "the Jewish faith and community."
3. For that the learned Judge should have held that the expression "the Jewish faith and community" used in clauses 3 and 8 of the scheme for the management of the Synagogue is to be strictly construed and that it eliminates members of the Bene Israel community.
4. For that the learned Judge failed to consider that the expression "the Jewish faith and community" have been specifically inserted in the scheme with a view to excluding the possibility of a Bene Israel claiming the rights of the "Jewish community."
5. For that the learned Judge has not taken into consideration the important fact that in India the Bene Israel have been regarded as a Community separate from the Jewish Community and that the Bene Israel have Synagogues of their own distinct from the Synagogues of the Jewish community.
6. For that the learned Judge failed to attach sufficient importance to the fact that since the inception of the Synagogue no Bene Israel had ever claimed or been allowed the right of standing for election to the Trusteeship.
7. For that the learned Judge failed to attach sufficient importance to the fact that no Bene Israel had ever been allowed to be called to the pulpit to read one of the seven prescribed portions of the Holy Thora, such right being the birthright of a male Jew.
8. For that the learned Judge failed to consider that up to 1923 no Bene Israel had been admitted even to the voters' list of the Synagogue, and then too from improper motives.
9. For that the learned Judge should have held that the Bene Israel are not prima facie members of the Jewish community in as much as the history of the Bene Israel Community presupposes a union between a Jew or a Bene Israel and the non-Jewish women of India.
10. For that the learned Judge has failed to apply his mind to the fact that a Jew is unable to contract a valid marriage with a party who is not a Jew or has not been converted to the Jewish faith prior to marriage, with the result that the children of a union between a Jew and a non-Jew are not legitimate and are not Jews by birth.
11. For that the learned Judge should have held that the Bene Israel and the offspring of union between Jews and non-Jewish women are not and cannot be considered to be Jews without formal admission into the Jewish faith and community and the learned Judge should have proceeded to judgement on the basis of the decision of the Rabbis and religious courts to the effect that in order to entitle a Bene Israel to the rights of a member of the Jewish Community the Bene Israel should give an undertaking

Appendix A 141

in writing that they will observe the religious teachings and practices of (a) Issuing a bill of divorcement, (b) Yibboom, (c) Halissa, such a declaration amounting to conversion, the other requisite of circumcision having already been performed.

12. For that the learned Judge failed to observe that in 1924 the Rabbi of Palestine visited Rangoon, on which occasion there was a meeting of the Jewish Community and the Bene Israel Community in the presence of the Trustees of the Synagogue at the Synagogue when the question of the rights of the Bene Israel to be called to the pulpit was considered, and the Rabbi was asked to give his decision; and on such occasion the Rabbi after due consideration and enquiry declared that the Bene Israel Community would be entitled to the rights of the Jewish Community provided that the Bene Israel would give the aforesaid undertaking in the Synagogue.
13. For that the learned Judge failed to consider that it was in accordance with such decision of the Rabbi that one of the sons of the first plaintiff on the 10th of April 1926 did give an undertaking as aforesaid in the Synagogue and was admitted to the rights of a member of the Jewish Community.
14. For that the learned Judge erred in holding that there was a presumption that the Bene Israel were members of the Jewish Community.
15. For that the learned Judge should have held that the Bene Israel were not prima facie members of the Jewish Community and would not become members unless and until they had given the said undertaking.
16. For that the learned Judge should have held that there was a presumption that the Bene-Israel were not members of the Jewish Community and should have cast the burden on them to prove that they were members of the Jewish Community.
17. For that the learned Judge should have held that the question involved was a matter for the religious courts to decide and should have referred the matter to the Jewish religious courts of London or Palestine.
18. For that no costs should have been awarded to the plaintiff in the suit.
19. For that the learned Judge's judgement is otherwise contrary to facts and is bad law.

> WHEREFORE appellant(s) pray that the said judgement and decree may be set aside and the suit dismissed with costs.
>
> Sd. Cowasjee, Anklesaria and Jeejeebhoy,
> APPELLANT(S)' ADVOCATE.

RANGOON,
Dated the 24th May 1935.

Appendix A

IN THE HIGH COURT OF JUDICATURE AT RANGOON CIVIL FIRST APPEAL NO. 78 OF 1935

Against the decree of this Court on the Original Side in Civil Regular No. 85 of a934

| E. S. Cohen & 1 | Vs. | J. M. Ezekiel and Others |
| Appellants | | Respondants |

For Appellant—Mr. Jeejeebhoy

For Respondents 1 & 2—Mr. Lambert

Dated Rangoon, the 8th day of January 1936.

JUDGMENT

The question that falls for the determination in this case is whether a community of persons known as the Bene-Israel are "persons of the Jewish faith and community" within the deed of trust for the management of the Musmeah Yeshua Synagogue at Rangoon. At the trial Leach J. held that they were.

Now, it is contended on the appeal that the Bene-Israel have separated from the Jews, and, whether they profess Judaism or conform to Jewish practices or not, that they have formed and are, a separate and distinct community from the *Yahudis* or the Jewish community. That appears to us to be a question of considerable historical interest, and it must not be assumed by reason of our decision in this appeal that we think that the case for the appellants on this question is not maintainable—indeed, it may be if the matter were fully investigated that it would be answered in favour of the appellants. But having regard to the course adopted by the appellants in the present proceedings, in our opinion, it is not open to the appellants to raise this question for the first time in the appeal. We have perused the record, and we are of opinion that the appellants have only themselves to blame for the position in which they now stand.

> In paragraph 8 of the written statement it is pleaded that "The plaintiffs who are members of the Bene-Israel Community have never observed all the laws and customs of the Holy Thora and in particular those relating to divorce, *halissa* and *yibboom*. . . . . The defendants aver that the plaintiffs are well aware that until they give an undertaking to observe the laws of the Holy Thora and in particular Divorce, *halissa* and *yibboom* the religious Courts of the Jewish faith and community will not allow them to be admitted as members of the Jewish Community."

Appendix A

Similarly on an application presented for an *interim* injunction in the present proceedings and also in the evidence of their witnesses the case for the appellants has always and solely been that the Bene-Israel are not persons of the Jewish faith and community because they do not conform to the practices of the Jews in regard to *get, yibboom* and *halissa*; in other words the appellants' case has been not that they are members of a separate community but they are unorthodox members of the Jewish community.

On the 26th March at the trial, at the close of the case on behalf of the plaintiffs, the learned advocates for the parties came to an agreement before the learned trial Judge as to the issues in controversy between the parties upon which the learned Judge was invited to give his decision, and there is the diary note to the following effect by Leach J.:

> "The learned advocate for the defendants states that it will not be suggested that there are any differences in the practice of the Bene-Israel and the other Jews so far as marriage and burial are concerned. The defendants maintain that the Bene-Israel do not observe the Jewish law of divorce and the laws regarding *halissa* and *yibboom*."

Further, at the outset of his judgement the learned trial Judge stated that:

> " . . . the plaintiffs claim that the Bene-Israel are members of the Jewish faith and community within the meaning of these clauses. (Clauses 3 and 8 of the scheme.) The defendants deny the validity of this claim and say that the Bene-Israel are not of the Jewish faith or community within the meaning of the scheme, because they do not observe the Mosaic Law with regard to divorce, *yibboom* and *halissa*. The plaintiffs on the other hand maintain that the Bene-Israel are orthodox in all respects."

Again, Mr. Charles S. Joseph, who at the time when the trial was held was one of the trustees and President of the Synagogue, in the course of his evidence stated:

> "I do not regard Bene-Israel as gentiles. I regard them as Jews but different from the others. Apart from the fact that they do not observe Sabbath, I have no personal knowledge of there being any difference in the practices. . . . I have approved of Bene-Israels being excluded because of the general opinion prevailing among the community the Bene-Israels do not observe the laws relating to divorce, *halissa* and *yibboom*."

In these circumstances it is not open to the appellants to raise for the first time on appeal what would appear to me to be the real question in dispute, namely, whether or not, for reasons upon which I am not disposed to enter, the Bene-Israel have become a sect or community separate from the Jewish community, such as the Parsees were held to be in *Sir Dinsha Manekji Petit, Bart., and others* V. *Sir Jansetji Jijibhai, Bart, and others* (L.L.R. XXXIII Bombay, 509). If the appellants at the trial had founded their claim upon such a contention it may well be that the course of the trial would have been different to what it was, and that the defendants would have desired to adduce evidence to counter such a contention. As it is manifest, however, that the claim of the plaintiffs was not rested upon such a basis at the trial, in my opinion, it is not open to them on the appeal to raise it for the first time.

As regards the question that was raised at the trial and in the respect of which evidence was led and which was the issue determined by the learned trial Judge, namely, whether the Bene-Israel in Rangoon who frequented the Musmeah Yeshua Synagogue did conform to the Jewish practices of *get, yibboom,* and *halissa*, it would appear that the Mosaic Law in these respects is not so strictly enforced at the present time as it used to be in days long since gone by. Sitting as a Judge of appeal upon this question of fact I am not disposed to hold that the decision arrived at by the learned trial Judge upon the evidence was wrong, and in my opinion it must be confirmed. That being the only question raised, heard and determined at the trial there is no substance in this appeal. Whether and in what circumstances, if any, the question to which I have adverted, namely, whether the Bene-Israel are a community separate from the Jewish community, is one that can be raised hereafter by the present trustees or trustees that may be elected in the future to manage the affairs of the Synagogue I express no opinion, for it is not necessary to determine such a question in the present appeal.

For these reasons, in my opinion, the appeal fails and must be dismissed with costs. The costs of the 1st and 2nd respondents will be paid by the trustees out the Synagogue funds. Advocate's fee 10 gold mohurs each day.

I agree.

Sd/ Mya Bu, Judge   Sd/ Arthur Page, Chief Justice

Appendix B

Detailed List of Families to Be Evacuated from Burma to Israel, 1949

Father's Name and Age	Mother's Name and Age	Children's Name and Age	Dependents	Father's Profession
1. Solomon Narome (58)	Nora Nahome (28)	Abe (stepson, 13), Norman (stepson, 18), Jacob (3) Joseph (1)		Manufacturer of cordials
2. Ezekial Mordecai (58)	Hilda Mordecai			Merchant
3. Father deceased	Flora E. Shamash (54)	Maurice (salesman, 24), Moses (salesman, 19), Seemah (stenographer, 21)	Sima Cohen (mother-in-law) Grandchildren: Raymond (9), Dinah (8)	——
4. Father deceased	Rachel Dawood (stenographer)	——		——
5. Isaac R. Shamash (31)	Rebecca (29)	3 yrs., 5 yrs; 3 yrs & 3 months		Merchant
6. Ezekiel K. Solomon (35)	Rachel (36)	Saul (11), Kelly (1 1/2)		Mechanical engineer
7. Joseph Judah (66)	Mrs. Joseph Judah (58)	Isaac (merchant, 24), Jacob (merchant, 20), Abraham (salesman, 18)		Retired merchant
8. Albert Judah (33)	Mrs. A. Judah	Joseph (5 months)		
9. Father deceased	Mrs. Naima E. Kodar (38)	Shaboo (16), Hannah (15)		——
10. G. Solomon (73)	Mozelle (52)	Abraham (merchant, 22), Reemah (secy/steno. 32), Hilda (secy/steno. 30), Matilda (secy/steno., 20), Freda (student, 15), Charles (student, 11)	Mrs. H. Cohen (mother-in-law)	Hazan (priest)
11. Ezra Sopher (27)	Sarah (23)	Veronica (4)		Engineer
12. M. E. M. Cohen (57)	Georgina (46)	Elias (telegraph operator, 22)		Retired clerk

#	Name (age)	Spouse	Household members	Occupation
13.	J. J. Shamash (54)	Tobah (34)	Seemah (wireless operator, 17), Reuben (17), Jacob (wireless operator, 19), Ramah (6)	Merchant
14.	Sion A. Shamash (75)	Flora (65)	Kitty (saleswoman, 38), David (student, 19)	Retired caretaker of synagogue
15.	Father deceased	Sally Samuel (54)	Ezekiel (storekeeper, 24), Flora (19), Moses (17, apprentice engineer)	—
16.	Solomon Jacob (43)	Sally (36)	Flora (student, 17), Myer (8)	Merchant
17.	J. K. David (40)	(Widower)	Harry (5), Hannah (4), Khalaif (1)	Merchant
18.	Solomon Joseph (54)	Flossie (32)	K. D. Solomon (father-in-law)	Authority on timber
19.	Howard D. Samuels (33)	Ramah (typist/clerk, 26)	—	Merchant
20.	S. N. M. Saleh (56)	Ramah (48)	Ezra (clerk/typist, 31), Elias (clerk, 25), Lily (dressmaker, 27), Esther (dressmaker, 22), Maurice (clerk, 19), Helen (student, 16), Shalom (student, 11), Mozelle (5)	Retired conservancy supervisor
			Jacob J. Cohen (father-in-law, merchant)	
			Mrs. L. E. Sopher (Mother-in-law, 64), Matooka (Sister-in-law, 44), Maurice Saleh (nephew, stenographer-acct., 49)	
21.	Husband deceased	Mrs. K. E. M. Joseph (54)	E. K. Joseph (Clerk, 34), M. E. Joseph (Merchant, 30), Miss M. M. Joseph (17)	—
22.	A. E. Joseph (37)	Florence (17)	Sally (10 months)	Merchant
23.	S. R. Sassoon (53)	Rachel (49)	Isaac (optician, 20), Abraham (student, 18), Jacob (student, 16), Sarah (student, 14)	Optician
24.	Sassoon S. Sopher (33)	Ruby (33)	Florence (12), Sally (5)	—
25.	Joseph H. Nehemiah (20)	Sippora (45)	Mariam (student, 14), Rachel (student, 15), Isaac (student, 17), Hannah (student, 18), Nehemiah (motor mechanic, 20)	Accountant

Detailed List of Families to Be Evacuated from Burma to Israel, 1949

Father's Name and Age	Mother's Name and Age	Children's Name and Age	Dependents	Father's Profession
26. E. A. Solomon (46)	—	—	—	Motor driver
27. Joseph Solomon (24)	—	—	—	Trader
28. Joseph H. Joseph (31)	—	—	—	Merchant
29. Solomon Elias (50)	—	—	—	Trader
30. —	Mrs. Ruby Elias (45)	—	—	Destitute
31. —	Mrs. Moselle Samuel (68)	—	—	Destitute
32. —	Miss Lilly Cohen (53)	—	—	Destitute
33. Salah S. Solomon (52)	—	—	—	Trader
34. Benjamin Aaron (45)	—	—	—	Broker
35. Ben. Jacob (27)	—	—	—	Newspaper reporter
36. Jacob E. Samuel (38)	—	—	—	English tutor
37. Eliyahoo Cohen (70)	—	—	—	Trader
38. Abraham S. Isaac (40)	—	—	—	Merchant
39. Elias Jacob (20)	—	—	—	Wireless operator
40. J. M. Jacob (54)	Flora (45)	Aziza (18), Simha (16), Dinah (13), Ezra (8), Eliahoo (7), Ezekiel (6)	—	Merchant
41. Ezekiel Solomon (61)	Flora (47)	Lily (15), Myer (10), Elias (12), Hertzel (13)	Mrs. Leah Mordecai (mother-in-law, 75)	Merchant
42. —	—	Rebecca (46), David (45), Mrs. Hannah K. David (62), Rachel (42), Sullha (38), Eleazer (38), Rahamin (40)		

Appendix C

Additional List of Potential Emigrants to Israel, 1949

No.	Head of Family	Male	Female	Children	Total
1	Solomon D. Solomon	—	1	1	3
2	S. H. Samuel	2	3	6	11
3	E. N. Abraham	1	1	—	3
4	R. A. Raphael	3	4	—	8
5	I. R. Shamash	—	1	3	5
6	D. S. Gubbay	2	1	—	4
7	Joseph Solomon	2	2	1	6
8	S. E. Moses	—	1	—	2
9	Kelly Moses	1	1	—	3
10	Albert Meyer	—	—	—	1
11	Mrs. Seemah Zaccai	—	—	1	2
12	Albert E. Manasseh	—	1	—	2
13	J. E. E. Manasseh	2	1	—	4
14	Charles Manasseh	—	2	3	6
15	I. Frederick	—	1	4	6
16	A. M. Jacob	—	3	2	6
17	S. M. Raymond	—	1	2	4
18	J. M. Jacob	—	4	3	8
19	Eric Moses	—	1	—	2
20	Jack I. Cohen	—	—	—	1
21	Ezekiel Meyer	1	3	—	5
22	Jack Cohen	—	1	—	2
23	Morris Solomon	—	1	2	4
24	Solomon R. Sassoon	—	1	1	3
25	M. J. Elisa	—	1	—	2
26	J. F. David	—	1	1	3
27	J. S. Meyer	—	3	—	4
28	Mrs. Seemah Dawood	3	3	—	7

Appendix C

No.	Head of Family	Male	Female	Children	Total
29	David K. David	2	4	—	7
30	J. R. Saul	3	1	—	5
31	Isaac Joseph	3	4	—	8
32	D. H. Abraham	2	2	1	6
33	Jack Jacob	1	2	—	4
34	J. G. Solomon	—	—	—	1
35	E. G. Solomon	—	—	—	1
36	Aron Moses	5	3	—	9
37	D. R. Eleazear	3	—	2	6
38	A. E. Sassoon	—	1	—	2
39	Maurice Saleh	—	—	—	1
40	S. E. Meyer	—	1	—	2
41	E. S. Sassoon	3	3	1	8
42	D. H. Moses	—	2	2	5
43	E. R. Joseph	8	5	6	20
44	E. S. Aaron	—	1	—	2
45	Miss Clara Solomon	—	—	—	1
46	Aaron J. A. David	1	6	—	8
47	E. E. Sassoon	—	1	2	4
48	E. J. A. David	1	2	5	9
49	E. S. S. Levoon	1	1	—	3
					Total: 230

Appendix D

Jewish Community of Burma, 1959

No.	Population, 1959*	Address	Emigrated by 1968/69*	Remarks (after 1970)
1	Mr. Isaac Samuels	68, 31st St.	—	Died 1978; buried, Jewish cemetery, Rangoon
2	Mr. Jack Samuels (M)**	"	—	Still in Burma (trustee)
3	Mr. Moses Samuels (M)	"	—	Still in Burma (trustee)
4	Mr. J. S. Meyer	268, Phayre St.	Mr. J. S. Meyer	——
5	Miss R. Meyer	"	Miss R. Meyer	——
6	Miss R. Meyer	"	Miss R. Meyer	——
7	Mr. E. S. Meyer	198, Phayre St.	Mr. E. S. Meyer	——
8	Mrs. K. E. S. Meyer	"	Mrs. R. E. S. Meyer	——
9	Mr. David Moses	210, Lewis St.	—	Died 1979; buried, Jewish cemetery, Rangoon
10	Mr. Ezekiel Solomon	76, Sparks St.	Mr. E. Solomon	——
11	Mrs. Ezekiel Solomon	"	Mrs. E. Solomon	——
12	Miss Lily Solomon	"	Miss Lily Solomon	——
13	Miss Liana Solomon	"	Miss Liana Solomon	——
14	Mr. C. Moses	British Embassy	Mr. C. Moses	——
15	Rachael Isaac (M)	123, 40th St.	Rachael Isaac	——
16	Solomon Isaac (M)	"	Solomon Isaac	——
17	Shirley Isaac (M)	"	Shirley Isaac	——
18	Ezekiel Isaac (M)	"	Ezekiel Isaac	——
19	Rosie Isaac (M)	"	Rosie Isaac	——
20	Mr. D. S. Isaac	"	Mr. D. S. Isaac	——
21	Mrs. D. S. Isaac	"	Mrs. D. S. Isaac	——
22	Mr. Maurice Solomon	42nd St.	Maurice Solomon	——
23	Mrs. M. Solomon	"	Mrs. M. Solomon	——
24	Rachael Solomon	"	Rachael Solomon	——
25	Solomon Solomon	"	Solomon Solomon	——
26	Haskel Solomon	"	Haskel Solomon	——
27	Mrs. Dinah Raeburn	49, 46th St.	Mrs. D. Raeburn	——
28	Mr. William Ezekiel	208, Judah Ezekiel St.	Mr. William Ezekiel	——

29	Mrs. William Ezekiel	"	Mrs. William Ezekiel	
30	Miss Ezekiel (M)	"	Miss Ezekiel	
31	Master Ezekiel (M)	"	Master Ezekiel	
32	Miss Reme Saul	49th St.	Miss Reme Saul	
33	Mr. H. M. Menahem	39, 50th St.	Mr. H. M. Menahem	
34	Mr. Menash Daniels	30, 53rd St.	Menash Daniels	
35	Mrs. M. Daniels	"	Mrs. M. Daniels	
36	E. Daniels (M)	"	E. Daniels	
37	Miss S. Daniels (M)	"	Miss S. Daniels	
38	Master Daniels (M)	"	Master Daniels	
39	Mr. J. S. Reuben	"	Mr. J. S. Reuben	
40	Mr. I. R. Shemash	148, Judah Ezekiel St.	Mr. I. R. Shemash	
41	Mrs. I. R. Shemash	"	Mrs. I. R. Shemash	
42	Flora Shemash (M)	"	Flora Shemash	
43	Ellis Shemash (M)	"	Ellis Shemash	
44	Leah Shemash (M)	"	Leah Shemash	
45	Albert Shemash	"	Albert Shemash	
46	Mr. Noah David	Tamwe Rd.	Mr. Noah David	
47	Mrs. Noah David	"	Mrs. Noah David	
48	Mr. Jack Noah	Burma Corp., Namtu	Mr. Jack Noah	
49	Mrs. Jack Noah	"	Mrs. J. Noah	
50	Mrs. E. S. E. Aaron	Fraser St.	Mrs. E. S. E. Aaron	
51	Mr. Ezekiel S. E. Aaron	"	Mr. Ezekiel S. E. Aaron	
52	Isaac Meyer	Godwin Rd.	Isaac Meyer	
53	Jack J. Cohen	53, Newlyn Rd.	Jack J. Cohen	
54	Mr. Asher David	Kamayut	———	Died; buried, Jewish cemetery, Rangoon Survived by one son
55	Miss Sarah Albert	"	Sarah Albert	
56	Mr. Reuben Albert	"	———	Died 1982; buried, Jewish cemetery, Rangoon
57	Mrs. Molly Albert	"	———	Died 1980, buried, Jewish cemetery, Rangoon

Jewish Community of Burma, 1959

No.	Population, 1959i	Address	Emigrated by 1968/69ii	Remarks (after 1970)
58	Solly Albert (M)	"	—	Solly Albert and Polly Albert made aliya. Jolly Albert still in Burma
59	Mr. Daniel Daniels	"	Mr. Daniel Daniels	
60	Mrs. Daniel Daniels	"	Mrs. Daniel Daniels	
61	Samson Daniels	"	Samson Daniels	
62	David Daniels	"	David Daniels	
63	Master Samson Daniels	"	Master S. Daniels	
64	Esther Daniels	"	Esther Daniels	
65	Mr. J. Joseph	19, York Rd.	Mr. J. Joseph	
66	Mrs. J. Joseph	"	Mrs. J. Joseph	
67	Florence Joseph (M)	"	Florence Joseph	
68	Fortune Joseph (M)	"	Fortune Joseph	
69	Sarah Raphael	45, York Rd.	—	Died 1970; buried, Jewish cemetery, Rangoon
70	Mr. I. F. David	"	Mr. I. R. David	
71	Mrs. M. R. David	"	Mrs. M. R. David	
72	John David (M)	"	John David	
73	Sharon David (M)	"	Sharon David	
74	Sardia Elias	22, Sandwith Rd.	—	Died 1971; buried, Jewish cemetery, Rangoon
75	Mr. Solomon Joseph	"	—	Died 1969; buried, Jewish cemetery, Rangoon
76	Mrs. Solomon Joseph	"	Mrs. Solomon Joseph	
77	Mrs. Rachel Solomon	"	Mrs. Rachel Solomon	
78	Mr. Allan Solomon	"	Allan Solomon	
79	Mr. D. Moses	"	Mr. D. Moses	
80	Mr. Nahoum Solomon	"	Nahoum Solomon	
81	Mrs. N. Solomon	"	Mrs. N. Solomon	
82	Abe N. Solomon	"	Abe N. Solomon	
83	Norman Solomon	"	Norman Solomon	
84	Joseph Solomon (M)	"	Joseph Solomon	

85	Saul Solomon (M)	"	Saul Solomon	—	
86	Baby Solomon (M)	"	Baby Solomon	—	
87	Lily Solomon (M)	"	Lily Solomon	—	
88	Mr. Saleh Solomon	"	Mr. Saleh Solomon	Died 1970; buried, Jewish cemetery, Rangoon
89	Mrs. Sally Solomon	"	Mrs. Sally Solomon	—	
90	Regina Solomon	"	Regina Solomon	—	
91	Mr. M. H. Solomon	"	Mr. M. H. Solomon	—	
92	Mr. E. J. A. David	26, Sandwith Rd.	Mr. E. J. A. David	—	
93	Mrs. E. J. A. David	"	Mrs. E. J. A. David	—	
94	Liby David (M)	"	Liby David	—	
95	Mr. Jackie David	"	Mr. Jackie David	—	
96	Queenie David (M)	"	Queenie David	—	
97	Haskel David (M)	"	Haskel David	—	
98	Allan David (M)	"	Allan David	—	
99	David David (M)	"	David David	—	
100	Azeeza David (M)	"	Azeeza David	—	
101	Mathu David	"	Mathu David	—	
102	Mrs. K. E. M. Joseph	48, Sandwith Rd.	Mrs. K. E. M. Joseph	—	
103	Mr. E. K. E. M. Joseph	"	Mr. E. K. E. M. Joseph	—	
104	Sally Joseph (M)	"	Sally Joseph	—	
105	Seema Joseph (M)	"	Seema Joseph	—	
106	Dinah Joseph (M)	"	Dinah Joseph	—	
107	Isaac Joseph	34, Sandwith Rd.	Isaac Joseph	—	
108	Mrs. I. Joseph	"	Mrs. I. Joseph	—	
109	Ezekiel Joseph	"	Ezekiel Joseph	—	
110	Violet Joseph	"	Violet Joseph	—	
111	Mr. E. R. Joseph	55/A, Sandwith Rd.	E. R. Joseph	—	
112	Mr. M. E. Joseph	"	Mr. M. E. Joseph	—	
113	Mrs. M. E. Joseph	"	Mrs. M. E. Joseph	—	
114	Haskel Joseph (M)	"	Haskel Joseph	—	
115	Allan Joseph (M)	"	Allan Joseph	—	

Jewish Community of Burma, 1959

No.	Population, 1959i	Address	Emigrated by 1968/69ii	Remarks (after 1970)
116	Mr. S. E. Joseph		Mr. S. E. Joseph	—
117	Mrs. S. E. Joseph	"	Mrs. S. E. Joseph	—
118	Haskel Joseph (M)	"	Haskel Joseph	—
119	Raymond Joseph (M)	"	Raymond Joseph	—
120	Benjamin Joseph (M)	"	Benjamin Joseph	—
121	Silvia Joseph	"	Silvia Joseph	
122	Mr. M. Dawood	87, Sandwith Rd.	M. Dawood	
123	Mrs. M. Dawood	"	Mrs. M. Dawood	
124	Albert Dawood	"	Albert Dawood	
125	Florence Dawood	"	Florence Dawood	
126	Esther Dawood	"	Esther Dawood	
127	Bubbles Dawood	"	Bubbles Dawood	
128	Mr. S. E. D. Sassoon	"	S. E. D. Sassoon	—
129	Mrs. S. E. D. Sassoon	"	Mrs. S. E. D. Sassoon	—
130	Miss Rachael Halegwa	"	—	Died 1985; buried, Jewish cemetery, Rangoon
131	Miss Ruby Halegwa	"	—	Died 1979; buried, Jewish cemetery, Rangoon
132	Mr. R. A. Raphael	9 Merchant St., Bassein	—	
133	Mr. Abe Raphael	"	—	
134	Mr. A. F. J. Raphael	"	—	
135	Mrs. A. F. J. Raphael	"	—	
136	Jacob Raphael (M)	"	—	
137	Edwin Raphael (M)	"	—	
138	Ingrid Raphael (M)	"	—	
139	Mrs. M. Aaron	30, 53rd St.	—	Made aliya
140	Ruby Aaron	"	—	Made aliya
141	Eugene Aaron	"	—	Made aliya
142	Dennis Aaron	"	—	Made aliya
143	Robin Aaron	"	—	Made aliya

144	Shully Aharon	Goodliffe	—
145	Ramaba Aharon	Goodliffe	Made aliya
146	Dinah Aharon	Goodliffe	Made aliya
147	Aster Aharon	Goodliffe	Made aliya
148	Saul Aharon	Goodliffe	—
149	Lilian Aharon	Goodliffe	—
150	Meeda Albert and four children	120th St.	Still in Burma. Married to a Muslim man

*By 1969, a total 116 persons (men, women, and children) left Burma.
**"M" indicates minor

Ten persons made aliya (assisted by Israel Embassy and Musmeah Yeshua during the period of trusteeship by Jack and Moses Samuels)
Since 1979, a total of ten persons died and were buried in the Jewish cemetery. Burial rituals were performed for three persons by Israel Ambassador Kalman Anner.

Appendix E

Jewish People and Their Descendants in Burma, circa 1986

Name	Father's Name	Place of Birth	Remarks
1 Mr. Jack Samuels	Mr. I. Samuels	Rangoon Burma	
2 Mr. Moses Samuels	"	"	
3 Mrs. M. Samuels	"	"	
4 Diana	Mr. Moses Samuels	"	
5 Khazna	"	"	
6 Sammy	"	"	
7 Mrs. D. Aaron	Mr. S. Daniels	"	Widow
8 Mrs. Ruby Aaron	Mr. D. Aaron	"	Widow
9 Corrinna Arron	Mr. M. Aaron	"	
10 Ducan Aaron	"	"	
11 Eugen Aaron	"	"	
12 Robin Aaron	"	"	
13 Mr. S. Daniels	Mr. M. Daniels	Calcutta India	Left Burma
14 Mr. Jolly Albert	Mr. R. S. Albert	Rangoon Burma	
15 Mrs. Meeda Albert	Mr. S. R. Albert	"	Widow
16 U Shwe Tha (a) Mr. Isaac Asher Abraham David	Mr. Asher Abraham	Rangoon Burma	Both lines represent alternate name
17 Mrs. Hannah Abraham David (a) Daw Ni Ni David	Mr. Asher Abraham	"	Alternate name
18 Mr. B. Samuels (a) U Myo Nwai	Unknown	Unknown	Alternate name
19 Mrs. A. Raphael	"	"	Lives in Bassei
20 Mr. Isaac Moses	"	"	Lives in Mandalay

Bibliography

ARCHIVES

American Jewish Archives, Jacob Rader Marcus Center, Cincinnati Campus, Hebrew Union College/Jewish Institute of Religion
American Jewish Joint Distribution Committee, New York City
Beit Hatefutsot, Museum of the Diaspora, Photo Archives, Tel Aviv, Israel
British Library, Oriental Division, London
Central Archives of the Jewish People, Jerusalem
Library of Congress, Washington, D.C.
London Beth Din, London Metropolitan Library
Musmeah Yeshua Synagogue, Yangon, Myanmar

BOOKS AND ARTICLES

Andrus, J. Russell. 1949. *Burmese Economic Life*. Stanford: Stanford University Press.
Banks, E. Pendleton. 1971. The Tragic Paradox: Burmese Attitudes Toward India and Indians, *Asian Studies II*. Bombay.
Bayly, Christopher, and Tim Harper. 2005. *Forgotten Armies: The Fall of British Asia, 1941–1945*. Cambridge, MA: Harvard University Press.
Bird, George W. 1897. *Wanderings in Burma*. London: Simpkin, Marshall, Hamilton, Kent.
Birnbaum, Philip. 1975. *A Book of Jewish Concepts*. New York: Hebrew Publishing Company.
Boyarin, Jonathan. 1992. *Storm from Paradise: The Politics of Jewish Memory*. Minneapolis: University of Minneapolis Press.
Burma During the Japanese Occupation. 1943. Burma Intelligence Bureau, Vol. I, October 1, 21–23.

Cannadine, David. 2001. *Ornamentalism: How the British Saw Their Empire*. Oxford: Oxford University Press.

Cernea, Ruth Fredman. 1995. *The Passover Seder: An Anthropological Perspective on Jewish Culture*. Lanham, MD: University Press of America.

Christian, John Leroy. 1942. *Modern Burma: A Survey of Political and Economic Development*. Berkeley: University of California Press.

Cohen, Israel. 1925. *The Journal of a Jewish Traveller*. New York: Dodd, Mead and Company.

Collis, Maurice. 1966. *Last and First in Burma (1941–1948)*. London: Faber and Faber.

Coulter, Gay. 1991. *Flowers in the Blood*. New York: New American Library/Signet.

Cowan, Ida G. 1971. *Jews in Remote Corners of the World*. Englewood Cliffs, NJ: Prentice Hall.

Crossette, Barbara. 1998. *The Great Hill Stations of Burma*. Boulder, Co: Westview Press.

Cuming, E. D. 1897. *In the Shadow of the Pagoda: Sketches of Burmese Life and Character*. London: W. H. Allen and Co., Ltd.

Curtis, Michael, and Susan Aurelia Gitelson, ed. 1976. *Israel in the Third World*. New Brunswick, NJ: Transaction Books.

David, Kenneth. 1977. *The New Wind: Changing Identities in South Asia*. The Hague: Mouton.

De Lange, Nicholas. 1984. *Atlas of the Jewish World*. Oxford: Phaedon Press.

Draper, Alfred. 1987. *Dawns Like Thunder: The Retreat from Burma 1942*. London: Arrow.

Elkins, Dov Peretz, ed. 1992. *Moments of Transcendence*. Northvale, NJ: Jason Aronson.

Encyclopedia Judaica Jerusalem. nd. Jerusalem: Keter Publishing House.

Farwell, Byron. 1989. *Armies of the Raj*. New York and London: W.W. Norton and Co.

Ferguson, Niall. 2003. *Empire: How Britain Made the Modern World*. London: Penguin Books.

Forbes, Charles James. 1878. *British Burma and Its People: Being Sketches of Native Manners, Customs, and Religion*. London: John Murray.

Franks, Suzanne. 1987. The Lost Tribes of Manipur, *The Jerusalem Quarterly*, London: 3: 32–35.

Friedman, Ina. 2003. By the Rivers of Babylon, *Jerusalem Report*, May 19, 14–19.

Grant, Colesworthy. 1853. *Rough Pencillings of a Rough Trip to Rangoon, 1846*. Calcutta: Thacker, Spink and Co.

Halbwachs, Maurice. 1992. *On Collective Memory*, ed. Lewis A. Coser. Chicago: University of Chicago Press.

Halkin, Hillel. 2002. *Across the Sabbath River*. Boston and New York: Houghton Mifflin Co.

Harvey, G. E. 1942. *British Rule in Burma 1824–1942*. London: Faber and Faber.

Herzog, Chaim. 1996. *Living History*. New York: Pantheon.

How the Rangoon Synagogue Was Saved, *Sephardi Bulletin*. Sydney: The New South Wales Association of Sephardim, 1945.

Howard, Malcolm. 1850. *Travels in Southeastern Asia.* Philadelphia: American Baptist Publication Society.
Hyman, Mavis. 1995. *Jews of the Raj.* London: Hyman Publishers.
Jackson, Stanley. 1968. *The Sassoons.* New York: E. P. Sutton & Co., Inc.
James, Lawrence. 1997. *Raj: The Making and Unmaking of British India.* New York: St. Martin's Press.
The Jewish Communities of the World, ed. Roberta Cohen. 1971. Institute of Jewish Affairs/World Jewish Congress. New York: Crown Publishers.
Kamenetz, Rodger. 1994. *The Jew in the Lotus.* HarperSanFrancisco.
Kamm, Henry. 1980. Burma's Last Few Jews Living on Proud Memories, *New York Times*, August 10: 6.
Katz, Nathan. 2000. *Who Are the Jews of India?* Berkeley: University of California Press.
———. ed., 1995. *Studies of Indian Jewish Identity.* New Delhi: Manohar.
Katz, Nathan, and Ellen S. Goldberg. 1988. The Last Jews in India and Burma, *Jerusalem Letter*, 101: April 15, 1–8.
———. 1989. The Mysterious Chin-kuki Tribal Jews of the Indo-Burmese Border Region, *Journal of the American Association of Rabbis*, V:1, 14.
———. 1993. *The Last Jews of Cochin: Jewish Identity in Hindu India.* Columbia: University of South Carolina Press.
Khoo Thwe, Pascal. 2002. *From the Land of Green Ghosts.* London: HarperCollins.
Klein, Wilhelm. 1992. *Myanmar.* Hong Kong: APA Publications.
Kreinin, Mordechai E. 1976. Israel and Africa: The Early Years. In, *Israel in the Third World*, ed., Michael Curtis and Susan Aurelia Gitelson, 54–55.
MacMillan, Margaret. 1988. *Women of the Raj.* New York: Thames and Hudson.
Malka, J. S. 2003. *Sephardic Genealogy.* Avotaynu.
Marshall, Andrew. 2002. *The Trouser People: A Story of Burma in the Shadow of the Empire.* Washington, D.C.: Counterpoint.
Mason, Philip. 1985. *The Men Who Ruled India.* New York and London: W. W. Norton and Company.
Memmi, Albert. 1962. *Portrait of a Jew.* New York: Orion Press.
———. 1975. *Jews and Arabs.* Chicago: J. Philip O'Hara.
Meyer, Nissim A. 1969. The Jewish Community of Rangoon, *Shema*, Vol. 3, No: 7, 15.
Mills, Megan Stuart. 1999. Burma, 1942, and the Anglo-Indian and Anglo-Burmese Community. www.alphalink.com.au.
Morris, Jan, and Simon Winchester. 1983. *Stones of Empire: The Buildings of the Raj.* Oxford: Oxford University Press.
Musleah, Ezekiel N. 1974. India's Jewish Communities and Their Ties to Israel. *Philadelphia Jewish Exponent*, April 26.
———. 1975. *On the Banks of the Ganga: The Sojourn of Jews in Calcutta.* North Quincy, MA: The Christopher Publishing Company.
Musleah, Rahel. 1997. Calcutta, *Hadassah Magazine*, November, 28–31.
Nash, Manning. 1965. *The Golden Road to Modernity: Village Life in Contemporary Burma.* New York: John Wiley & Sons.

Orwell, George. 1934. *Burmese Days*. New York and London: Harcourt Brace Jovanovich.

———. 1966. *Homage to Catalonia*. Boston: Beacon Press.

P-B., E. M. 1911. *A Year on the Irrawaddy*. Rangoon: Miles Standish.

Parasuam, T. V. 1982. *India's Jewish Heritage*. New Delhi: Satar Publications.

Peres, Shimon. 1995. *Battling for Peace: A Memoir*. New York: Random House.

Rabin, Keith W. 1982. In Burma, Getting a Minyan Together, Even on Yom Kippur, Is Not Easy, *The Jewish Week-American Examiner*, July 11, 29–30.

Rai, Manahadu. 1992. Godkhali Ayo! Gurkha Soldiers in the Battle for Imphal 1944, *Command* 16: May–June 1992.

Rejwan, Nissim. 1986. *The Jews of Iraq: 3000 Years of History and Culture*. Boulder, CO: Westview Press.

Richards, C. J. 1945. *The Burman: An Appreciation*. Published for the Burma Research Society. London: Longmans, Green & Co., Ltd.

Rogoff, Mike. 1998. Integrated Development: Beginnings of the Settlement Study Center, *Shalom Magazine*, No.1, 4–5.

Roland, Joan G. 1998. *The Jewish Communities of India: Identity in a Colonial Era*. New Brunswick and London: Transaction Publishers.

Samuels, Jacob. 1980. *Appeal to Jewish Brethren Far and Near*. Rangoon: Musmeah Yeshua Synagogue. October 14.

Samuels, Moses and U Aung Kywe. 1990. *Musmeah Yeshua Synagogue and Jewish Community in Burma*. Rangoon: Musmeah Yeshua Synagogue.

Saul, Geoffrey. 2004. *The Road to Mandalay: A History of the Sassoon, Solomon and Saul Families—Jewish Pioneers in Colonial Burma*. Unpublished.

Saul, Solly. 1995. Memories of Burma. *Sephardi Bulletin*. Sydney: The New South Wales Association of Sephardim. March.

Schendel, Jorg. Trade, Identity and Imperialism in Upper Burma, paper presented to the International Burma Studies Conference, October 23, 2004.

Segre, D. V. 1976. The Philosophy and Practice of Israel's International Cooperation, in *Israel in the Third World*, ed., Michael Curtis and Susan Aurelia Gitelson, 7–25.

Selth, Andrew, 1986. Race and Resistance in Burma, 1942–1945, *Modern Asian Studies*, 20, c, 483–507.

Silliman, Jael. 2001. *Jewish Portraits, Indian Frames*. Hanover and London: Brandeis University Press.

Sinai, Annie. 1969. Once There Was a Burmese Jewry, *Women's League Outlook*, Spring, 12–13, 26, 28.

Smith, Donald Eugene. 1965. *Religion and Politics in Burma*. Princeton: Princeton University Press.

Sofaer, Abraham, ed. 1919. *The Fleur de Lys: The Magazine of the Diocesan Schools, 1916–1919*. Rangoon: Hanthawaddy Printing Works.

Sofaer, Ellis. 1987. *Gaya, His Childhood*. Unpublished memoir.

Stark, Gilbert Little. 1908. *Letters of Gilbert Little Stark, July 23, 1907–March 12, 1908*. Cambridge, England: Riverside Press.

Strizower, Schifra. 1962. *Exotic Jewish Communities*. London: Yoseloff.

Thomas Cook, Ltd. 1909. *India, Burma, Ceylon and South Africa*. London: Thomas Cook.

Toledano, Dayan Dr. Pinchas. nd. *The Bene Israel of India*. London: Society of Heshaim, Spanish and Portuguese Jews' Congregation.

Toueg, Rachel. 2005. The Jewish Community in Shanghai, *Points East*. Sino-Judaic Institute, March 20:1.

Trager, Helen. 1966. *Burma Through Alien Eyes: Missionary Views of the Burmese in the Nineteenth Century*. New York: Frederick A. Stokes.

Trachtenberg, Joshua. 1974. *Jewish Magic and Superstition: A Study in Folk Religion*. New York: Atheneum.

Trench Gascoigne, Gwendolen. 1896. *Among Pagodas and Fair Ladies: An Account of a Tour Through Burma*. London: A. D. Innes and Co.

The Universal Jewish Encyclopedia. 1911, 1940.

Uphill, Muriel Sue DeGaa. 1999. *An American in Burma 1930–1942*. Tempe: Arizona State University Press.

Vincent, Frank. 1873. *The Land of the White Elephant: Sights and Scenes in Southeastern Asia*. London: Sampson Low, Marston, Low and Searle.

Webster, Donovan. 2003. *The Burma Road: The Epic Story of the China-Burma-India Theater in World War II*. New York: Farrar, Straus and Giroux.

Winston, W. R. 1892. *Four Years in Upper Burma*. London: C. H. Kelly.

Wright, Arnold, ed. 1910. *Twentieth Century Impressions of Burma: Its History, People, Commerce, Industry and Resources*. London: Lloyd's Greater British Publishing Company.

Yeger, Moshe. 1984. A Rapid and Recent Rise and Fall, *Sephardi World*, July–August.

Index

Aaron, Aaron Jacob Elias Aaron, 5
Aaron, Arnold, 74
Aaron, David Hai, 5, 53
Aaron, David and Sophie, *58*
Aaron, Ramah (Rose), 53
Aaron, Saul, 12, 30
Aaron, Scott, *58*
Aaron, Simon, 68n4
Aaron, S. S., 77
Abraham, E. H. 102
Abraham, Helen, 88
Abraham, Joseph, 82
Agasee, Ramah, 84
Agasie, Hardon, 30
Akyab (Sittwe), xvi, 4–5, 12, 30, 49n23, 83
American Jewish Joint Distribution Committee (AJJDC), 95–96
American Sephardi Federation, 130
Anner, Ambassador Kalman, 129
anti-Semitism, 68, 106. *See also* British in India/Burma: attitudes toward Jews, class system
Arakan Yoma Mountains, 5, 83
Armenians, 8
Ashkenazic Jews in Burma, 10, 28, 61, 72, 131. *See also* Polish Jews in Burma
Assam, 84–85

Aung Kywe, U, 129
Aung San, General, 80, 96n5
Aung San Suu Kyi, 80
Australia, 88. *See also* Sydney

Babylonia, xvii
Badin-Powell, Lord, 38
Baghdad, xvii–xv, xx, 8
Baghdadi Jews: class distinctions, 41, 49n21, 53, 72–74; concepts of community, 41, 51–52, 55, 56, 57–65; conceptual world, xv, xvii, xxiii, 4, 10, 21, 22, 37, 39–48, 49n21, 51, 54, 89, 132; dress, xxiii, 23, 33, 52; economic activities and occupations, xviii– xxv, 4, 7, 11, 13–14, 29–35, 100, 106–7, 127; education, xxiii, 15, 41, 42–46, *44, 45,* 49n19, 107, 128; emissaries, 26, 35n8, 65; food, 33, 45, 49n12, 54, 59, 63–64, 69nn21–24; history and definition, xvii–xviii, xx; homes, 9, 21, 24–26, 32–33; intermarriage with Jewish groups, 10, 53, 72; intermarriage with non-Jewish populations, xix, xxiv, 53–54, 75, 109, 114, 128, 136; in Israel, 93; languages, xxiii, xix, 10, 39–40, 45–46, 74, 89; marriage practices,

xxiv, 31, 52, 53, 58, 63, 74–76; naming practices, 16, 103; philanthropy, xxi–xxii, 7, 22, 26–28, 45, 53, 55; population estimates, xv, xxvn1, 10, 114, 128; postwar economic and religious problems, 99–117; relations with other populations, 21–22, 34, 67–68, 108; religious identity, 37, 40, 45–46, 51, 54–57, 63–64, 87, 93; religious practices, 45–46, 51–52, 54–68, 87, 97n26; servants, 21, 24–25, 32–33; in Southeast Asia, xx–xvi, xix–xxv. *See also* Bene Israel: court case, relations with Baghdadis; customs; emigration from Burma; David Sassoon; specific holidays; weddings; World War II
Bandung Conference, 122
bar mitzvah, 56, 61, 130
Barrie, James, xvii
Basra, xvii
Bassein (Pathein), xvi, 12, 16, 30, 42, 114, 130, 132. *See also* Raphael family; World War II
Battat, Ezekiel Zion, 30
Battat, Morris, 133
Bayly, Christopher, 82
Ben-Gurion, David, 122
Ben Yehuda, Avraham, 18n11
Ben-Zvi, Yitzhak, 123
Bene Israel, xv, xxiv, xxvn1, 3, 114; in Bombay, 73, 77; court case against Baghdadis, 75–78, appendix A; differences from Baghdadis, 71; language, 71, 72, 74; occupations, 4; relations with Baghdadis, 71–77, 78nn9–11, 114; religious practices, 74, 78n9; population estimates (in Burma), 74, 78n11. *See also* Baghdadi Jews: intermarriage
Bene Menase, 68n4
Benjamin, Aslan, 22, 61, 75, 77
Benson, Saw (Moses Ben-Zion Koder), 94, 117–18, 133
Beth Din, London, 76, 110–14

Beth El Synagogue, 74–75
Betz, Seemah Saul, 45–46, 85–87, *91*
Birth registries. *See* Musmeah Yeshua Synagogue: registries
Bombay, xv, xx, xxiv, 12, 46, 105; Bene Israel in, 73, 77; philanthropy, xx; synagogues, xxi. *See also* David Sassoon
Bombay Jewish Advocate, 73
brit milah, 57, 60–61, 107
British East India Company, 2, 8, 16
British in India/Burma, 34; annexation of Burma, 2–3, 23; attitudes toward Burmese, 9, 48n6; attitudes toward Jews, 38, 42, 46–47, 49n13; citizenship, 43–44, 57, 103–5; class system, xxiii, 9–10, 47, 72–73; clubs, 9–10, 49n23, 79; economic goals in Burma, 3; hill stations, xix, 37–39; military, 38; schools, xxiii, 9, 31, 49n13; sports, 2, 17n2; world view, 8–10. *See also* Baghdadi Jews: education; Bene Israel: court case; Christians in Burma; George Orwell; Gymkhana Club; minority populations; Musmeah Yeshua: administration; World War II
Buddhism, 2, 100
Burma, Kingdom of, 2–3, 5–6
Burma, State of: Burma Independence Army, 80, 94; Burmese Way to Socialism, 127; citizenship, 100–103; Constitution, 101; first Jewish settlers in Burma, 3–8, 18n11; independence, 46–47, 57, 100–102, 121; relations with Jews, 105–6. *See also* Israel: Japanese; U Nu; World War II Burma Refugee Organization, 86
Bushire, 5

Calcutta, xv–xvi, xxii, xxvn1, 58, 60, 68n7, 71–72, 81–82, 83, 105; assistance to refugees from Burma, 82, 88–90; bombing of, 88; Ezra family in, xx, xxii; Jewish Refugee

Index

Relief Association, 88; philanthropy, xx, 68n7; schools, 89; synagogues, xxii, 15, 71. *See also* Musleah, Rabbi Ezekiel; World War II
Candacraig Hotel, 38, 48n5
Cannadine, David, xxiii
Central Archives of the Jewish People, 130
cemeteries, Jewish: Akyab, 5; Bassein, 30; Bombay, 71; Calcutta, 71; Mandalay, 31, 36n27, 132; Moulmein, 108; Rangoon, 8, 71–72, 131–32; Thayetmyo, 30.
China. *See* Elias Sassoon; Hong Kong; opium trade; Shanghai
Chindits, 94
Chindwin River, 85–86. *See also* World War II: trek to India
Chinese in Burma, xv, 8, 10, 11, 23, 42, 45, 54, 80, 91, 105, 132
Chittagong, 12, 82–83
Christians in Burma, 8, 9, 13, 31, 42, 45, 49n13, 53, 67–68, 105; missionary societies, 9, 30. *See also* Baghdadi Jews: education
Cochin, 3, 105, 133
Cochini Jews, xv, xxiv, 4, 21, 71–72, 94
Cohen, A. J., 22, 26
Cohen, Abraham and Ramah, 25
Cohen, Abraham ben Aharon, and family, Moulmein, 7
Cohen, Azeeza, 87
Cohen, E. I., 22
Cohen, E. S., 77
Cohen, Jacob Isaac, 10
Cohen, Jacob Moses, 10
Cohen, Israel, 26–28
Cohen, Mordecai Hayim Isaac, 22
collective memory, xvi–xviii
community, concepts of, xvi–xviii
Craig, Luisa Benson, 118, 133
customs: Elijah's chair, 60–61; evil eye, 60; *get*, 74, 75; *halitzah*, 74, 75–76; henna, 59; *kappara*, 59, 66, 68n11; *ketubah*, 58–59; nights before *brit*, 60; *pidyon haben*, 61, 69n18, 107; search for the leaven, 64; *shaloch manot*, 62. *See also* Bene Israel: court case; *brit milah*; Passover; Purim; weddings

Dacca, xv
Dangoor, Rabbi Ezra, 15
Darjeeling. See British in India/Burma: hill stations
Daud Pasha, xix. *See also* David Sassoon
David, Dayan Abraham, 133
David, Isaac, 114, 127
Dawood, Maurice, 115
Dayan, Moshe, 123–24
Dean, Evelyn, 135
de Glanville, Sir Oscar, 75–76
Death, 57, 61, 111
Dehra Dun, 90
Dorman-Smith, Sir Reginald, 79
Draper, Alfred, 79, 86, 97n31

education. *See* Baghdadi Jews: education; English Diocesan School; Jewish English School
Elisha, Rabbi Shaul Yitzhak Meir Yaakov, 15
emigration from Burma, 102–6, 108, 124, 127, 145–148, 149–150
emissaries. *See* Baghdadi Jews: emissaries
English Diocesan School, 42–43, 47, 34. *See also* Baghdadi Jews: education
European populations in Burma, 10, 11, 42, 45, 81–87
Ezekiel, E. M., 75, 77
Ezekiel, J. M., 75
Ezekiel, Judah, 5, 16–17
Ezekiel, N. S., 77
Ezekiel family, 86

Ferguson, Niall, 3, 39

Gabirol, Solomon, 3
Gaster, Rabbi Moses, 76
George, King, 35n24, 44
Georgey, Percy S., xxvn3
Glicksohn, Margaret Raphael, 30–31, 67, 93. *See also* Raphael family, Bassein
Goldstein, Israel, 125
Gurkhas, 32, 85, 94
Gymkhana Club, 9, 47. *See also* British in India/Burma: clubs

Habonim. *See* Zionism: in Calcutta
Hacohen, Ambassador and Mrs. David, 107, 122
Hanukkah, 67–68
Halegwa, Rifka, 131
halitzah. *See* Bene Israel: court case; customs
Hardoon, Silas, xxi
Harper, Tim, 82
Hayeem family, 94
health, 11, 53, 83, 85–88
Hebrew Immigrant Aid Society (HIAS), 95
Hertz, Rabbi J. H., 76, 79
Hindus. *See* Indians in Burma
Hkio, Foreign Minister Sao Hkun, 123
Hong Kong, xv, xx, 29–30, 46, 92
Hukong Valley, 88
Hyman, Mavis, 87, 96n20

India. *See* British in India/Burma; Bombay; Calcutta; David Sassoon; minority populations; opium trade; World War II
Indians in Burma, xv, 8, 10, 11, 18n26, 21, 67–68, 80, 91. *See also* Baghdadi Jews: servants; World War II
Imphal, 86. *See also* World War II, trek to India
Irrawaddy Flotilla Company, 12
Isaac, Asher and Darhood, 29
Israel: agricultural relations with Burma (Lachish Project), 122–23; Bandung Conference, 122; diplomatic relations with Burma, 122–25; Embassy in Burma, 123–25, 127, 129; Iraqi Jews in, xxvn3; Legation of, 108, 113–14; Namsang Project, 123; State visits by Burmese to Israel, 122; State visits to Burma, 122–24; technical support to Burma, 121–23, 125. *See also* Musmeah Yeshua Synagogue: transfer of synagogue items

Jacob, Abraham, 84, 88
Jacob, E. S., 113
Jacob, Eriz, 90
Jacobs, Flora Judah, 28
Jaffe, Rabbi Morris, 99
Japanese: attitude of Burmese toward, 79–80; attitude toward Jews, 90–94; invasion of Burma, 80–88; preparations for war, 80. *See also* World War II
Jerusalem, xv, 26, 130
Jewish Chronicle of London, 73
Jewish English School, 44, *44*, 45, *45*; teachers, 45, 49n19; postwar, 107. *See also* Baghdadi Jews: education
Joseph, A. V., 14
Joseph, Charles, 22, 75, 77, 122
Joseph, I., 114
Joseph, Hazan, 75
Joseph, Solomon, 112, 113, 127, 128
Joshua, J. E., 75, 76
Judah, Abraham Shalom, 25, 52, 54, 83
Judah, Albert, 85, 86, 87, 104
Judah Ezekiel Street, 16, 80, 101, 104

Kadoori family, xx, xxii
Kalaw, xix, 39
Kaleva, 87
Kalimpong. *See* British in India/Burma: hill stations
Karachi, xv
Karen, 94, 117, 133. *See also* Saw Benson; Isaac Sassoon

Katz, Nathan, x
Keiji, Colonel Suzuki, 80
Kobe, 95
Kohina, 87

Lachish Project. *See* Israel: agricultural relations with Burma
Languages in Burma. *See* Baghdadi Jews: languages; minority populations
Lazin, Rachel, xxvn3
Leach, Justice, 75–76
Lewin, Ambassador Daniel, 125
Levi, Rabbi Yosef, 136
Linton, I. J., Minister Plenipotentiary to Burma, 123
London: Baghdadi Jews in, xiv; 132; Od Yosef Hai Synagogue, Hendon, 132. *See also* Beth Din
London *Jewish Chronicle*, 73
Los Angeles, xvi, 56, 132–133; Kahal Joseph Congregation, 133, 137n7

Madhupur. *See* British in India/Burma: hill stations
Magwe, 88
Malays, xv
Malkhoo, Yascha, 75, 76, 78n12
Manasseh, Charles, xxiv, 102
Mandalay, xvi, 26, 37, 42, 82, 85, 114, 128, 132; as Burmese capital, 5–7; early Jewish settlement in 5–7, 18n14; name, 5, 18n13. *See also* cemeteries; minority populations; Saul family; World War II
Manila, 4
Mawbin, 94
Maymyo (Pyin Oo Lwin), xix, 14, 30, 37–39, 48n5, 114, 128, 130
Macartney, Sir George, 39
Meir, Golda, 124
Memmi, Albert, 43
Mergui-Tavoy, 30
Meshed, xix
Meyer, E. S., 113, 114, 125

Meyer, J. S., 110, 114, 115, 117, 119–20, 127
Meyer, Meyer, 26
Meyer, Nissim, 18n11, 101, 102
Meyer, Sir Manasseh, xx, xxiv
Meyer family, Rangoon, 22
Mindon, King, 5, 48n7
minority populations: 1–2, 18n26; in British India, xv, xix; in Mandalay, 6–7, 13; in Moulmein, 7; in Rangoon, 10, 12, 21, 22
Mordecai, E. S. E., 77
Moses family, 22
Moulmein (Maylamyine), xvi, 7, 14, 108, 130
Mount Popa, 132
Musleah, Rabbi Ezekiel, xxii, xxvn1, 59, 72
Muslims in Burma, 8, 11, 21, 127, 68, 78n12, 100, 132; anti-Israel riots, 108; cemeteries, 132; social relations with Jews, 21–22, 34, 132
Musmeah Yeshua Synagogue, 1, 55–56, 58, 60–64, 66; administration (Scheme), 8, 112–15, 127–29; allocation of site by British, 8; British Court cases, 71–77, 112–15, 139–144; community list, 1959, 151–157; community list, 1986, 159; current status, 133–36; during World War II, 92; finances, 8, 15, 116, 127–29, 132; first building, 8, 15; founders, 16; members eligible to vote, 1962, 115–16; *mikveh* (ritual bath), 15, 56, 137n9; new building (1896), 15, 55; *parochets*, 55–56, 107, 112, 133; potential sale of, 116; postwar, 99, 107–17, 127–28, 136–37; registries, xvii, 16, 53, 57, 72, 108–9, 129–30, 134; religious leadership, 15, 74, 109; Torah scrolls, 8, 15, 32, 55, 58, 92, 109–11, 133; transfer of ritual items to Israel, abroad, 103, 107, 109, 111, 112, 127, 129–30, 132–33

Mussoorie. *See* British in India/Burma: hill stations
Myitkyina, 84, 88

Nagasaki, xxi
Nahoum, David, xxvn1
Nash, Manning, 34–35
Nats, 11, 34, 132
Ne Win, General, 124–26
Noy, Ambassador Ori, 130
Nu, U, Prime Minister, 122, 124, 125

oil in Burma, 12, 83
opium trade, xxi, xxvn4, 4
Orwell, George, 37, 48n3, 48n6
Ottoman Empire, xvii–xix, 4

Padaung, 48n9
Page, Chief Justice Arthur, 77
Pa-o, 34
Passover, 45, 46, 55, 63–65; during World War II, 87, 93–94, 97n26; matzah, 63–64, 111; preparations for, 63–64, 69nn21–24
Pegu (Bago), xvi, 135. *See also* Sarah Sassoon Raphaeli
Penang, xv, 26
Peres, Shimon, 123–24
Polish Jews in Burma, 95–96
Poona, xix, xxi, 37
Population estimates, 74, 125, 128
Purim, 62–63

Rangoon (Yangon), xv, xix, 3, 130; British character of, 8, 11, 22; cosmopolitan atmosphere, 7–8, 10, 12, 21, 28, 104, 130; development of, 7–14; economic activity, 5, 100–102; Jewish residential areas, 11, 21, 25–26, 101, 127; land allocations by British, 8; minorities in, 8, 10, 12; population estimates, 10; Municipal Council, 11; travelers' impressions, 11, 26–28; wartime destruction, 80–82, 99. *See also* Japanese; minority populations; World War II
Rangoon Burmese Review, 104
Rangoon Gazette, 8, 11
Raphael, Mayor R. A., 30
Raphael family, Bassein, 30, 93–94, 107
Raphaeli, Sarah Sassoon, 92, 134
Redding, Lord, 32, 36n28
Reinman, Solomon, 3–4
Roland, Joan, 12, 78n6
Rosh Hashanah, 32, 56, 65–66

Sabbath. *See* Shabbat
Sapir, Rabbi Yaakov, 26
Samuel, Azariah, and family, Akyab, 4–5
Samuels, Isaac, 92, 127–29
Samuels, Jack, 129
Samuels, Moses, 129–32, 135–36
Samuels, Sammy, 130, *135*, 136
Sassoon, Albert (Abdullah), xxii
Sassoon, David, xx–xxiii, 71
Sassoon, Elias, xxi
Sassoon, Isaac, 92
Sassoon, Judah, 46–47
Sassoon, Sir Jacob, 73
Sassoon family, Bombay. *See* David Sassoon
Saul, Charles, 85, 87, *91*
Saul, David G., 33
Saul, Ezra, 16, 31–34, 133
Saul, Geoff, 31
Saul, Mordecai, 5, 6, 16, 31
Saul, Saul Ezra, 6, 32, 34, 38, 94. *See also* Saul family, Mandalay
Saul, Simon, 85, 87, *91*
Saul, Solly, *44*, 81, 85, 87, 89, 90, *91*, 137
Saul family, Mandalay, 5, 6, 13, 31–34, 39, 85, 133. *See also* Mandalay; World War II
Shabbat, 52, 60, 61, 62
Shamash, E. E., 114
Shamash, Elias, 92

Shamash, Maurice, 56
Shan States, 39, 123
Shavuot, 65, 99
Shanghai, xv, xix, xxi, 4, 41–42, 95
Sharett, Moshe, 122, 123
Shimoni, Ambassador Yitzhak I., 113
Shwebo, 82
Simchat Torah, 55, 56, 66
Simla, 32, 37
Singapore, xv, xix–xx, 12, 46; fall of, 81–82; synagogues in, xxiv. *See also* Sir Manasseh Meyer
Smith, Donald, 8, 100
Sofaer, Abraham (actor), 23, 42–43, 47, 134–35, *134*
Sofaer, Abraham D., 133
Sofaer, Anna, *29*
Sofaer, Ellis, xiii, xvii, 4, 21, 22–24, 40, 42, 45, 46–47, 49n13, 55, 67, 73
Sofaer, Isaac A., 13, 23, *24*, 31, 134
Sofaer, Meyer Abraham, 13, 16, 22, *24*
Sofaer, Ruth, 29, 134
Sofaer family, *24, 25*, 130
Solomon, Alan, 54
Solomon, E., and Sons, 12, 74
Solomon, Esther Moses, 22, *45*
Solomon, Ezra, 38, 47, 94, 133
Solomon, Gabriel, 74
Solomon, Haskel and Ephraim, 30
Solomon, Kelly (Kadoori), 13
Solomon, Sassoon, 13, 25, 28, 47
Solomon family, Rangoon, 8, 13, 22–25, 53, 74
Strand Hotel, 1, 12, 19n35
Succot, 66–67
Surabaya, xv
Swift, Dawn, 25
Sydney, xvi, 132–33; Sephardi Synagogue, Bondi Junction, 133
synagogues and prayer halls: Bassein, 31–32; London, 132; Los Angeles, 133; Mandalay, 31–32; Sydney, 133. *See also* Beth El Synagogue; Musmeah Yeshua Synagogue

Tamu Pass, 84, 86, 87
Taungup Pass, 83, 84
Thayetmyo, 30
Thibaw, King, 6, 18n16, 22, 23
Tisha b'Av, 56
Toueg, Rebecca, 41
Toungoo, xvi, 30
tribal Jews. *See* Bene Menase

Ullman, Yoma, 88
United Jewish Appeal, 108

weddings, 57–60, *58*
Wingate, General Orde, 94
Wolfson Museum, Sir Isaac and Lady, 18n14
World Jewish Congress (WJC), xxvn1, 103, 105–6, 108, 125, 128
World War II, 79–97; aftermath in Rangoon, 99; Bassein, 85, 93–94; British army, 79, 81–83, 85–86, 97n31; disease, 83, 85; flight from Burma, 81–88, 96n20; Japanese advance into Burma, 80–82, 84, 85; Jewish population during, 87–96; Mandalay, 82, 84, 87; Mawbin, 94; Pegu, 92; Rangoon, 80–81, 85, 99; retreat north, 82–83; trek to India, 84–88. *See also* Calcutta: assistance to refugees from Burma; Japanese: attitude toward Jews; Polish Jews in Burma
World Zionist Organization, 125

Yandon, 30
Yenangyaung, xvi, 12, 30, 133
Yokahama, xv
Yom Kippur, 32, 51, 55–56, 59, 65–66
Yusaif, Rabbi, 74–75

Zaccai family, 82
Zionism: in Burma, 122, 124; in Calcutta, 89
Zohar, 61

About the Author

Anthropologist **Ruth Fredman Cernea** has been researching the history of the Baghdadi Jewish communities of Southeast Asia since her first visit to Burma in 1987. Her book *The Passover Seder: Afikoman in Exile*, an anthropological perspective on Jewish culture, has been published in several editions. She is the editor of the collection *The Great Latke-Hamantash Debate* (2006), and has authored several studies of immigrant Sephardic communities in the United States, including *Cosmopolitans at Home: The Sephardic Jews of Washington, D.C.* She served as Director of Research and Publications for the Hillel Foundations, and as editor of *The Hillel Guide to Jewish Life on Campus*. She resides in Bethesda, Maryland.

Made in the USA
San Bernardino, CA
21 July 2019